THE
SCIENCE OF PEACE

THE SCIENCE OF PEACE.

AN ATTEMPT AT AN EXPOSITION OF THE FIRST PRINCIPLES OF THE SCIENCE OF THE SELF

Adhyatma-Vidya

BY

BHAGAVAN DAS

GYAN

Published by

GYAN

Gyan Publishing House
5, Ansari Road
Daryaganj, New Delhi-110002
Phone: 011-47034999, 9811692060
E-mail: books@gyanbooks.com

Distribution Network
gyanbooks.com
India, USA, Canada, UK, Australia

ISBN: 978-93-6208-262-6 (HB)
First Published, 1904

2nd Impression 2024

Printed at: Gyan Press, Delhi.

THE SCIENCE OF PEACE
Author: BHAGAVAN DAS

THE SCIENCE OF PEACE

THE
SCIENCE OF PEACE

AN ATTEMPT AT AN
EXPOSITION OF THE FIRST PRINCIPLES OF
THE SCIENCE OF THE SELF

Adhyâtma-Vidyâ

BY

BHAGAVÂN DÂS

Author of "The Science of the Emotions"

Theosophical Publishing Society
London and Benares
1904

گر ز سر معرفت اگه شوي
لفظ بگزاري سوي معني روي

" Wouldst thou enclasp the beauty of the True?
Let pass the word, the thought, the thought pursue!"
Maulânâ Rûm.

"Live neither in the present, nor the future, but in the Eternal, ... because nothing that is embodied, nothing that is conscious of separation, nothing that is out of the Eternal, can aid you; . . . . within you is the light of the world; . . . . Read the larger word of life."
Light on the Path.

"There is a peace that passeth and yet passeth not the pure understanding. It abides everlastingly in the hearts of those that live in the Eternal."

यस्तु सर्वाणि भूतानि आत्मन्येवाऽनुपश्यति ।
सर्वभूतेषु चात्मानं ततो न विचिकित्सति ॥

यस्मिन् सर्वाणि भूतानि आत्मैवाभूद्विजानतः ।
तत्र को मोहः कः शोक एकत्वमनुपश्यतः ॥

—*Îsha-Upanishat.* 6, 7.

"He that seeth all things in the Self, and the Self in all things, he thenceforth doubteth no more."

"Where is faintness, where is sorrow, there, in the consciousness wherein all things have become the Self, of the knower that beholdeth the oneness."

यदा भूतपृथग्भावमेकस्थमनुपश्यति ।
तत एव च विस्तारं ब्रह्म संपद्यते तदा ॥

—*Bhagavad-Gîtâ.* xiii. 27.

"When he seeth the separateness of all things centred in the One, and also the manyness arising from that One, then he becometh Brahman."

CONTENTS.

PREFACE.

The scheme of metaphysic outlined in this book began definitely to be thought out in 1887 in Benares. Some unshaped sketches of it were published as articles in the *Theosophist* in 1894, and subsequent years, and one portion of the scheme was written out, in some little detail, in 1899, and, mainly because of encouragement in that behalf received from Mrs. Annie Besant, published in 1900, as *The Science of the Emotions.* The portion published herewith, as well as another, forming a continuation of this, were jotted down in rough notes in the summer and rains of 1900, partly at the seaside town of Vizagapatam, in the province of Madras, whither I had gone in search of health. It was faired out in 1901 in Shrînagar, Kâshmir. In 1903 a hundred proof copies of it were printed, and circulated in the early part of 1904, amongst persons interested in the subject, members of the Theosophical Society, professors of philosophy, and metaphysicians of note, in the east and the west, with the following letter:

"My only excuse for claiming a little of your time and attention for this booklet, of which I am now sending you an interleaved proof-copy, is that I have therein endeavoured earnestly to be of service to all those earnest seekers after a final solution of the ultimate problems of life, who are not content with the solutions now extant. I believe that such an endeavour deserves sympathy; I believe that it will be more successful if I have the help and co-operation of sympathetic friends than if it were left to my own unaided resources; and I believe that you can and will give such help effectively. This help from you is the more needed as the many distractions of a life, which past karma has thrown along the lines of office and the business of the householder, rather than those of literary pursuits and the studious leisure of the scholar, have prevented me from making this work anything more than the merest outlines of the all-embracing subject of metaphysic, well defined as 'completely unified knowledge,' treated therein—and those outlines too, full of immaturity of thought, possible extravagance of expression, and certain lack of the finish of scholarship.

"I therefore pray that you will look through this little book and, unless you think it wholly useless for the purpose mentioned, will send it back to me after having noted on the blank pages all obscure or doubtful and debatable or positively inaccurate and inconsistent statements of fact, falseness or exaggeration of sentiment, and confusion or illogic of argument and marshalling of ideas, that you may notice."

Suggestions for improvement were received in chronological order from: Pt. Gaṇgânâth Jhâ, Professor of Saṃskṛit, Muir Central College, Allahabad. Bâbu Govinda Dâs, of Benares (my elder brother). Dr. Hübbe-Schleiden, of Döhren bei Hannover, Germany. Dr. J. H. Stirling, of Edinburgh. Prof. J. E. McTaggart, of Trinity College, Cambridge. Pt. M. S. Tripathi, author of *A Sketch of Vedânta Philosophy*, of Nadiad. P. T. Shrînivâsa Iyengar, Esq., M.A., Principal Narsingh Row College, Vizagapatam. J. Scott, Esq., M.A., Principal, Bahâuddin College, Junâgadh. Ayodhya Dâs, Esq., B.A., Barrister-at-Law, Gorakhpur. Pt. Sakhârâm G. Pandit, Branch Inspector, Theosophical Society, Benares. Pt. Bhavânî Shañkar, Branch Inspector, Theosophical Society, Benares. M. André Chevrillon, of Paris. B. Keightley, Esq., M.A., Barrister-at-Law, of London.

I gratefully record the names of these friends, personally known or not known, but most truly friends in the spirit and helpers in a common cause.

But far more than to all these friends are this book and I under obligations to Mrs. Annie

Besant, who first saw the rough draft of the work in manuscript, encouraged me to persevere with it, then carefully went over every line of the printed proof-copy, suggested innumerable improvements, and finally saw it through the press.

BHAGAVÂN DÂS.

Do Thou mend, O Master, with Thy perfectness, Thy servant's imperfection, lest any earnest seeker after Truth be led astray by error of his. Subtile is that utter Truth, though all so simple, very difficult to set on high so it shall shine out strong and clear and steady, and very feeble for such purpose is the hand that would now do so. Guide Thou that hand aright.

CHAPTER I.

THE GREAT QUESTIONING.

येयम् प्रेते विचिकित्सा मनुष्ये
अस्तीत्येके नायमस्तीति चान्ये ।
एतद् विद्याम् ऽनुशिष्टस्त्वयाऽहम्
वराणामेष वरस्तृतीयः ॥

Katha-Upanishat. I. i.

"The doubt that seizeth the beholders when a man passeth away, so that one sayeth, 'He still is,' and another, 'No, he is no more'—I would know the truth of this, taught by thee, O Death! This is the third of the (three) boons (thou gavest)!"

This is the boon that Nachiketâ asked of Yama. And Yama shrank from the great task imposed on him and answered: "Even the Gods have suffered from this doubt, and very subtle is the science that resolveth it. Ask thou another boon! Besiege me not with this. Take all the pleasures that the earth can give; take undivided sovereignty of it!" But Nachiketâ: "Where shall all these pleasures be when the end comes! The pleasures are no pleasures, poisoned by the constant fear of Thee! The Gods too suffer from the doubt, for they are only longer-lived and not eternal; and that they suffer is but reason why I would not be as they. I crave my boon alone. Nachiketâ asks not for another."

"If all this earth with all its gems and jewels were mine without dispute, should I become immortal?" So Maitreyî questioned Yâjñavalkya when he offered wealth to her at parting. And Yâjñavalkya answered: "No, thou couldst only live as the wealthy live and die as they. Wealth brings not immortality!" Then Maitreyî: "What shall I do with that which makes me not immortal? Tell me what thou knowest brings assurance of eternity."[1]

So Râma also asks Vasiṣhṭha: "The books that say that Brahmâ, Viṣhṇu and Mahesha are the three highest Gods that rule our solar system, say also that They die. Brahmâ, the highest-seated, falls; the unborn Hari dis-

[1] *Bṛihad-Âraṇyaka-Upaniṣhat.* II. iv.

appears; and Bhava, source of the existence of this world, Himself goes into non-existence! How then may feeble souls like mine find peace and rest from fear of death and change and ending?"[1]

"To be dependent on another, (to be at the mercy of another, to be subject to the relentlessness of death)—this is misery. To be self-dependent—this, this is happiness."[2]

Thus, instinctively in the beginning, consciously and deliberately at the stage when self-consciousness and intelligence are developed, the Jîva[3] feels the terror of annihilation and struggles to escape from it into the refuge of some faith or other, low or high. And in such struggles only, and always, begin religion and philosophy, each shade of these according, step by step, with the stage and grade of evolution and intelligence of the Jîva concerned.

But when this fear of death of soul and body, this fear of loss and change and ending, pervades the intelligent and self-conscious Jîva;

---

[1] *Yoga-Vâsiṣhṭha.* Vairâgya Prakaraṇa. xxvi. 29.

[2] *Manu.* iv. 160.

[3] Jîva means a separate self, a spirit or soul, an individual unit and centre of latent or evolved consciousness, a single part, so to say, of the universal Self, developing from the mineral through the vegetable and animal into the human and superhuman kingdoms; here of course a human soul or spirit.

when it destroys his joy in the things that pass, makes him withdraw from all the old accustomed objects of enjoyment, and fills him for that time with sadness and disgust and loathing for all the possible means of pleasure that ever hide within their lying hearts the means of pain ; when it leaves him naked and alone, intensely conscious of his solitude and sorrow, shrinking violently from the false and fleeting show of the world, desolate with his own misery and the misery of others, longing, yearning, pining, for the Permanent, the Eternal, the Restful, for a lasting explanation of the use and purpose, origin and end, of this vast slaughter-house, as the whole world then seems to him to be—then is that searching Jîva passing through the fires of burning thought, reflection, and discrimination between the transient and the permanent, of passionate rejection of all personal and selfish pleasures and attachments in himself as well as others, of the self-suppression, the intense quiescence and compassionate sadness of utter renunciation, and of a consuming, ever-present craving and travailing for the means of liberation from that seeming slaughter-house for himself and for all others ; then is he passing through the fires that shall purify him and make him worthy of Vedânta, of that final knowledge which he craves, and which alone can bring him peace and fit him for the work that lies before him. Then is his consciousness, his individuality, his personal self, focussed into an infinitesimal point and, thus oppressed with the feeling of its own extreme littleness, is it ready for the supreme reaction, ready to lose itself and merge into and realise the all-consciousness of the infinite and universal Self.

Why and at what stage of his evolution this most fearful and most fruitful mood comes necessarily on every Jîva will appear of itself when, later on, the mystery of the world-process has been grasped.

NOTE.—The first six chapters of this work constitute, in a way, the psychological autobiography of the writer. They describe the stages of thought through which he passed to the finding embodied in the seventh chapter. And they have been written down only as a possible guide-book to travellers along the same path. All the opinions and beliefs criticised in them and, for the time, left behind, in order to pass further on, have served as staging-places to the writer himself, have been held by him closely for a longer or a shorter time, and then, failing to bring lasting satisfaction of the particular kind that he was seeking, have been passed by. But this does not mean that the staging-places and the rest-houses have been abolished, or are of no use. They continue to exist, and will always exist, and will always be of use to future travellers. No depreciation of any opinion whatsoever is ever seriously intended by the writer. Indeed, it is a necessary corollary of the view embodied in the seventh and subsequent chapters of the work that every opinion, every darshana, *i.e.*, view-point, catches and embodies one part of truth; and he himself now holds each and every one and all of the opinions that appear to be refuted in these preliminary six chapters—but he holds them *in a transmuted form.* Each form of faith, each rite of religion, each way of worship has its own justification. And if the writer has unwittingly used, in the passion of his own struggle onwards, any words that are harsh and offend, he earnestly begs the forgiveness of every reader really interested in the subject, and assures him that if he does think it worth while to read this book through systematically, he will realise that it verily endeavours not to depreciate any but to appreciate all thoughts, and put each into its proper place in the whole world-scheme.

CHAPTER II.

THE FIRST AND SECOND ANSWERS.

Thus we find that the Jîva doubts and asks for immortality alone, and in the doubting and the asking he ever instinctively feels that the answer lies in a basic 'unity' of some sort or other, and that peace can never be found in an unreconciled and conflicting 'many.' This feeling conditions his search throughout for reasons inherent in the world-process, as will appear later.

The first answer that the Jîva shapes for himself to the great question, the first tentative solution of this overpowering doubt, is embodied in the view which is called the आरम्भवाद, ârambha-vâda, the theory of a beginning, an origination, a creation of the world by an agency external to the questioner. From so-called fetish-worship to highest deism and theism, all may be grouped under this first class of answer.

Instinctively or intelligently, the Jîva sees that effects do not arise without causes; that what is not effected by himself must be caused by another; that he himself (as he then regards himself) is an effect and that his cause must be another; that whatever is the more permanent, the older, is the cause of the temporary, the younger; and he finally infers and believes that his well-being, permanence, immortality, lies in, is dependent on, his cause, his creator. From such working of the mind arise the multifarious forms of faith, beginning with belief in and worship of stone and plant and animal, and ending in belief in and worship of a personal First Cause. The general form of worship is the same throughout, *i.e.*, prayer for some benefit or grace. The accompanying condition of worship is the same also, *viz.*, giving assurance of humility in order to evoke benevolence in the object of worship, by prostration and obeisance and sacrifice of objects held most dear, to prove (sometimes, alas! with cruellest heartrending, though at others with a most beautiful and most noble self-surrender) that they are not held dearer than that worshipped object.

This first answer is a religion as well as a philosophy, but the Jîva finds not rest for long therein.

The concrete material idols fail again and again; and so does the mental idol. The incompatibility of evil and suffering with a being who is at once omnipotent, omniscient, and all-good; the unsatisfied need for an explanation why a personal being who is perfect should create a world at all, and how he can create it out of nothing—as he must, if it is not to be coexistent with and so at least to some extent independent of him—these distressing doubts, insoluble on 'the theory of a beginning,' that have always shaken faith first in the power and goodness of the creator and then in his very existence, inevitably, earlier or later, wrench the earnestly-enquiring Jîva away from his anchorage in that theory, and set him adrift again, again asearching.

The truth that underlies this first answer, in all its forms, he will discern again when he has obtained what he now wants so urgently.

His next haven of rest, the second answer, is the परिणामवाद, pariṇâma-vâda, the theory of change, transformation, evolution and dissolution, by the interaction of two factors. By a great generalisation he reduces all the phenomena of the universe to two permanent elements, present always, universally, under all circumstances, throughout all the changes that he sees and feels.

The materialism and agnosticism which

believe in 'Matter and Force,' and declare all else unknown; the ordinary Sâñkhya doctrine of 'Purușha and Prakṛiti,' 'Ego and non-Ego,' 'Self and not-Self,' 'Spirit and Matter'—all fall under this second category. Most of the philosophies of the world are here; the variations as to detail are endless, but the view that the universe is due to two finals is common to them all.

At this stage, if the duality be made the basis of a religion at all, the believer proclaims the factor of good as superior to the factor of evil, and assigns to it a final triumph, regarding God as prevailing over Satan, Hormuzd over Ahriman, Purușha over Prakṛiti, Spirit over Matter, in a vague undefined way, sacrificing strict logic to the instinctive need for unity, which, as said before, conditions the search throughout. But where the two are seen as equal, as in the Sâñkhya, religion vanishes, no practice corresponds to the theory. Thus a current Saṃskṛit verse belonging to the Sâñkhya system describes Purușha as 'lame,' and Prakṛiti as 'blind.' The struggle between the two weakens both; each factor neutralises the other. There is no worship in the absence of a one supreme to worship. Only philosophy remains, a belief wavering and satisfactionless; for an explanation by two eternals, a plurality of infinites, each unlimited and yet not interfering with the unlimitedness of the other though existing *out of* and independently of it—such an explanation is no explanation at all. It is a contradiction in terms; it is mere arbitrariness; there is no order, no certainty, no law, no reason in it. However correct it may be as a generalised statement of indubitable facts, *viz.*, an endlessness of spirit and an endlessness of matter, those facts themselves remain unexplained, unreconciled, impossible to understand.

The truth that underlies this belief also will appear when the final answer is found.

CHAPTER III.

UNCERTAINTIES.

Tentative, temporary, full of uncertainty and full of question is this stage. Baffled in his efforts to understand the world-process completely, barred out from a perfect religion-philosophy, a system of knowledge which would consistently and directly unify and guide his thought, desire, and action, in the present life as well as in all possible lives to come, unable to rest peacefully in a mere incomplete knowledge, in a mere belief which remains outside of his daily life and is often coming into conflict with it, the Jîva goes back again and again to that earlier answer, which, if only belief, only incomplete knowledge, is yet a religion also, a religion-philosophy, however imperfect. But each such going back is only the preliminary to a still stronger going forward. The Jîva is now in the grasp of an indefeasible reflectiveness, of a craving of the intellect that may not be repressed.[1] He has attained his majority and must now stand on his own feet; his parents may not fondle him in their lap any longer. And so he progresses onwards through and from the second stage, full of doubts and full of questions. For though of course the main object of his quest is but this: "How shall I make sure of my eternity?" "How shall I be freed from the fear of death?" yet in the searching he has trodden many paths which have allured him with promise of profit, have sometimes made him forget for the time being the goal of his enquiry, and have even, now and then, led him to a short-lived peace and confidence in agnosticism, in a declaration of the impossibility of final knowledge and the futility of all search. And all these paths he has discovered again and again to be blind alleys, each only leading to a new question and a new wall of difficulty—all the questions awaiting solution by means of the one solution only, the whole labyrinthine maze clearly leading him back again and again to the same starting-point, the whole to be mastered and traversed by means of only a single clue.

---

[1] विवेक, viveka, ever-present discrimination between the transient and the permanent; and विचार, vichâra, ever-present reflection on the why and wherefore of things.

The many doubts and questions which the Jîva gathers under the one great question are mainly these :—

What am I ? what is Spirit, the Self, the Ego, the Subject ? what are these other selves, Jîvas, like and unlike myself ? what is Matter, the World, the Not-Self, the non-Ego, the Object ? what is life ? what is death ? what is motion ? what are space and time ? what are being and non-being ? what is consciousness ? what is unconsciousness ? what is pleasure ? what is pain ? what is mind ?

What are knowledge, knower, known ? What is sensation ? what are the senses ? what are the objects sensed, the various elements of matter ? what is the meaning, use, and necessity of *media* of sensation ? what is an idea ? what are perception, conception, memory, imagination, expectation, design, judgment, reason, intuition ? What are dreams, wakings, and sleepings ? what are abstract and concrete ? what are archetype, genus, and species ? what are universals, particulars, and singulars ? what is truth ? what are illusion and error ?

What is desire ? what are the subjects and the objects of desire ? what are attraction and repulsion, harmony, and discord ? what is an emotion ? what are love and hate, pity and scorn, humility and fear ? what is will ?

What are action, acted on, and actor? what are organs? what an organism? what is the meaning of stimulus and response, action and reaction? what is the real meaning and significance of power, might, ability, force or energy? what is change, creation, transformation? what are cause and effect, accident and chance, necessity and destiny, law and breach of law, possible and impossible?

What is a thing? what are noumena and phenomena? what are essence, substance, attribute, quality, quantity, number? what are one and many, some and all, identity and difference?

What are speech and language, command and request and narration, social life and organisation? what is art? what is the relation between things and Jîvas?

What is good and what is evil? what are right and wrong? what is a law? what are compulsion and destiny? what is a right? what is a duty? what is conscience? what is liberty? what are order and evolution and the world-process? are Jîvas bound and helpless, or are they free, and if not free, मुक्त, mukta, 'liberated,' how may they become so?

Such are the harassing questions concerning every moment and aspect of his life, that follow on the heels of the searcher. Small blame to him if he despair of mastering them! Well may he give up the task again and again as hopeless, and try to climb out of their way with the help of the weakling plants that rise up here and there before him, growths of temporary belief and uncertain knowledge, naturally belonging only to the first stage of his journey. But the branches which he clings to fail him at the last, after having served their purpose of giving him rest and strength for a greater effort, and he is shaken down from them by his pursuers and compelled to press forward again.

Let him not despair. The intensity and stress of his vairâgya[1] will soon break up the shell of selfishness that limits consciousness in him into a personal - self - consciousness and transform it into the all-Self-consciousness, when that inmost mystery of the universe that is now hidden from his sight shall stand revealed; the energy of that vairâgya will transform his hurrying feet into wings on which he will rise high above the labyrinth of doubts and questions; and from that height he will be able

---

[1] वैराग्य, vairâgya, the passionate revolt from all limitation of the Self, from all selfishness, all selfish and personal attachments in himself as well as others, which constitutes the indispensable pre-requisite to a true, earnest and fruitful enquiry into the origin and end of things.

to master all the foes that harassed and pursued him so relentlessly.[1]

It should be noted here that each of the first two answers to the great question carries with it its own corresponding set of answers to all these questions. But, like those two, these also are unsatisfactory, external and superficial. The earnest enquirer must search deeper. How to answer them in terms of consciousness, of the Self, which is the nearest to him and therefore after all the most intelligible? He must interpret all things in their deepest connection with and origin from the Self; otherwise doubt will remain and satisfaction not be gained. For as the answer to the one great question is to disclose the answer to all these, so in turn the good answering of these will be the test that that one answer itself is good.

---

[1] The expression employed here may appear a little too emotional. This has been done purposely to show that metaphysic deals, not only with the single, cold and sober department of intellectual life, but with the whole of it as manifesting in cognition, desire, and action, and has to show forth the travail of a thought that would encompass all these. The whole life of the true and earnest enquirer is put into such search, hence the mixture of science and emotion.

CHAPTER IV.

The Preliminaries of the Third and Last Answer—the Self and the Not-Self.

The second answer remains, as said before, wavering and satisfactionless. Explanation of the world, which is the sole purpose of philosophy, by means of two factors can only be a tentative, and not a final solution. It is a great advance to have reduced the multifariousness of the world to a duality. But what the searcher wants is a unity, and in this respect indeed the first answer was even better than the second, for it reduced all things to a unity, the will of an omnipotent being. That unity was, however, a false unity. It had no elements of permanence in it. The will of an individual by itself carries within it no true and satisfactory explanation of the contradictions that make up the world; it embodies no reason and no safeguard against caprice. Tenure of immortality at the will of another is a mockery and a contradiction in terms, and therefore the Jîva, however reluctantly, however painfully, has to give up that first unity and search for a higher one. In this search his next step leads him, by means of a close examination of the multiplicity which presses on him from all sides, to a duality which seems to him, and indeed is, at the time, the nearest approach to that higher unity that he is seeking.

The forms of this duality, wherein he is centred for the time being, beginning with rough general conceptions of spirit or force and matter, end in the subtlest and most refined ideas of Self and Not-Self.

These, the Self and the Not-Self, are the last two irreducible facts of all consciousness. They cannot be analysed any further. All concrete life, in cognition, desire, and action, begins and ends with these. They are the two simplest constituents of the last result of all philosophical research.

None doubts "am I or am I not."[1] This has been said over and over again by thinkers of all ages and of all countries. The *existence* of the Self is certain and indubitable.

The next question about it is: *What* is it? Is it black? is it white? is it flesh and blood and bone, or nerve and brain, or rocks and

---

[1] नहि कश्चित् संदिग्धे ऽहं वा नाहं वेति । *Bhâmati.* P. 2. (Bib. Ind.)

rivers, mountains, heavenly orbs, or light or heat or force invisible, or time or space? is it identical with or coextensive with the living body, or is it centred in one limb, organ or point thereof? The single answer to all this questioning is that because "what varies not nor changes in the midst of things that vary and change is different from them,"[1] therefore the I-consciousness which persists unchanged and one throughout all the changes of the material body and of all its surroundings is different from them all. 'I' who played and leaped and slept as an infant in my parent's lap so many years ago have now infants in mine. What unchanged and persistent particle of matter continues throughout these years in my physical organism? What identity is there between that infantine and this adult bodies of mine? But the 'I' has not changed. It is the same. Talking of myself I always name myself 'I,' and nothing more nor less. The sheaths in which I am always enwrapping the 'I'—thus: I am happy, I am miserable, I am rich, I am poor, I am sick, I am strong, I am young, I am old, I am black, I am white—these are accidents and incidents in the continuity of the 'I.' They are ever passing and varying. The

---

[1] व्यावर्तमानेषु यदनुवर्तते तत्तेभ्यो भिन्नं । *Ibid.*

'I' remains the same. Conditions change, but they always surround the same 'I,' the unchanging amid the changing; and anything that changes is at first instinctively, and later deliberately, rejected from the 'I,' as no part of itself. And as it remains unchanged through the changes of one organism, so it remains unchanged through the changes and multiplicity of all organisms. Ask anyone and everyone in the dark, behind a screen, through closed doorleaves: "Who is it?" The first impulsive answer is: "It is I." Thus potent is the stamped impress, the unchecked outrush, the irresistible manifestation of the common 'I' in all beings. The special naming and description: "I am so and so," follows only afterwards, on second thought. So real is the 'I' to the 'I' that it expects others to recognise it as surely as it recognises itself. Again, what is true of the 'I' with regard to the body is also true of it with regard to all other things. The house, the town, the country, the earth, the solar system, which 'I' live in and identify and connect with myself are all changing momentarily; but 'I' feel myself persisting unchanged through all their changes. 'I' am never and can never be conscious of myself having ever been born or of dying, of experiencing a beginning or an end. "In all the endless months, years, and small and great cycles, past and to come, this Self-luminous consciousness alone neither arises nor ever sets."[1] But as regards all the things other than 'I,' that 'I' am conscious of, 'I' am or can become conscious also of their beginnings and endings, their changes. "Never has the cessation of consciousness been *experienced*, been witnessed directly; or if it has been, then the witness, the experiencer, himself still remains behind as the continued embodiment of that same consciousness."[2] Thus may we determine what the 'I' is. "Omnis determinatio est negatio." "All determination is negation" is a well-known and well-established law. We determine, define, delimit, recognise by change, by contrast, by means of opposites; so much so that even a physical sensation disappears entirely if endeavoured to be continued too long without change; thus we cease to feel the touch of the clothes we put on after a few minutes. And scrutinising closely, the enquirer will find that everything particular, limited,

---

[1] *Panchadaṣhi.* i. 7.

मासाब्दयुगकल्पेषु गतागम्येष्वनेकधा ।
नोदेति नास्तमेत्येका संविदेषा स्वयंप्रभा ॥

[2] *Devî-Bhâgavata.* III. xxxii. 15—16.

संविदो व्यभिचारस्तु नानुभूतोऽस्ति कर्हिचित् ॥
यदि तस्याप्यनुभवस्तर्ह्ययं येन साक्षिणा ।
अनुभूतः स एवात्र शिष्टः संविद्वपुः स्वयम् ॥

changing, must be negated of the 'I'; and yet the 'I,' as proved by the direct cognition of all, cannot at all be denied altogether. It is indeed the very foundation of all existence. 'Existence,' 'being' (using the two words roughly as synonymous at this stage), means nothing more than 'presence in our consciousness,' 'presence within the cognition of the I, of the Self, of me.' What a thing is, or may be, or must be, entirely apart from us, from the consciousness which is 'I,' of this we simply cannot speak. It may not be within our consciousness in detail and with its specifications, but generally, in some sort or other, it must be so within consciousness, if we are to speak of it at all.

The third step, the immortality of the 'I,' necessarily follows from, is part of, the very nature of the 'I.' What does not change, what is not anything limited, of which we know neither beginning nor end, that is necessarily immortal.

Let us dwell upon these considerations; let us pause on them till it is perfectly clear to us that our consciousness is the one witness to, the sole evidence and the only possible support and substratum of, all that we regard as real, of all our world. Let us make sure, further, that by eliminating the common factor 'our' from both sides of the equation, the proposition stands, and stands confidently, that "consciousness is the only basis and support of the world." For how can we distinguish between 'our' consciousness and 'another's' consciousness, between 'our' world and 'another's' world? That another has a consciousness, that another has a world, that there is another at all, is still only 'our' consciousness. And as this holds true for every one, at every point, does it not follow that all these 'every ones' are only *one*, that all these 'our' consciousnesses are only one universal consciousness, which makes all this *appearance* of *mutual* intelligence and converse possible? for it is *really* only the *one* talking to itself in different guises. More may be said, later on, in dealing with consciousness from the standpoint of the final explanation of the world-process. In the meanwhile we need not be disturbed by any random statements that "thought (or the 'I'-consciousness) is the product of the brain as much as the bile is the product of the liver." If any earnest-minded student feel himself disturbed by any such, then let him ask himself and the maker of the statement, by what laws of deductive or inductive logic is such statement justified? If there are many points in common between the liver and the brain, what similarity is there between bile and thought to justify an inference as to the similarity of their causes? And, again, how do we know that such things as liver and bile and brain *are?* Because we see and feel them! But how are we sure that we see and feel? Do we see our eyes that see, and touch our hands that touch? Is it not that we are sure of our seeings and feelings, of our having the senses wherewith we do so, of our existence at all, only becanse we are *conscious* of such things? It is far easier to walk on the head comfortably without the aid of arms or legs, than to live and breathe and move and speak without the incessant *pre*supposition that consciousness is behind and beyond and around everything. Argue as we may, we are always driven back, again and again, inexorably, to the position that consciousness is verily our all in all, the one thing of which we are absolutely sure, which cannot be explained away, and that the pure and universal Self, the one common 'I' of all creatures, is our last and only refuge.

Perhaps, in our long-practised love of the concrete, we like to tell ourselves that the 'I' is only a series of separate experiences, separate acts of consciousness. We have then only explained the more intelligible by the less intelligible. The separate experiences, the separate acts of consciousness, are intelligible only by presupposing a one continuous consciousness, a self. The acts or modifications are of and belong to the self, not the self to the former. Wherever we see unity, continuity, similarity, there we see the impress of the Self, the One. The concrete is held together only by the abstract. "The Self-born pierced the senses outwards, hence the Jîva seeth the outward (the concrete 'many' and), not the inner Self. One thinker, here and there, turneth his gaze inwards, desirous of immortality, and beholdeth the Pratyag-âtmâ (the abstract Self)."[1]

We feel impatient, we exclaim: "What is this 'I' that is neither this nor that?" Let us define it, if we can, by any particular 'this' or 'that.' The whole of the world-process has been now endeavouring so to define it, for the whole past half of all time and by the whole half of all countless possible 'this's'; and it has not succeeded. It will go on similarly endeavouring to define it in the whole future half of all time and by the remaining half of endless possible ways; and it will not succeed.[2] It

---

[1] *Kaṭha*. iv. 1.

[2] The full significance of this statement will appear later, when the distinction between eternity and time, true infinity and the mere boundlessness of space, totality and countlessness, कूटस्थसत्ता, kûṭastha-sattâ, 'rock-seated being,' and अनादिप्रवाहसत्ता, anâdi-pravâha-sattâ, 'endless-flow existence' is understood.

has not succeeded and will not succeed because the very being of the 'I' is the negation, the opposite, of all 'not-I's,' all that is object, all that can be cognised by 'I' as a knowable object, all that is particular, limited, defined, all that can be pointed to as a 'this.' Do we think that we will evade this inevitable conclusion by denying the 'I' altogether? We cannot do that, as already said. We will only stultify ourselves. 'I' is not nothing, but it is not any-one-thing. Let us ponder deeply on this for days and days and weeks and months and years if necessary, till we see the pure, unique, universal, and abstract being of the 'I.' We will do so if we are in earnest with our search; and when we have done so more than half the battle is won. We have attained to the Pratyag-âtmâ, the abstract and universal Ego, and are now in sight of the Param-âtmâ, the supreme, the Absolute Self (which is truly the full significance and nature of the Self and is named after it for special reasons), the Brahman which is the final goal and the final place of peace.

Or perhaps we feel another difficulty. Perhaps we feel a sudden revulsion at this stage and cry: "This commonplace 'I' that everyone is glibly talking about and relishing acutely every moment of his life, from babbling baby to garrulous old man in dotage—is this the mysterious, marvellous and mystic vision of beatitude and perfection that we hoped for? I that am so small, so weak, how can I be the unreachable, all-glorious Supreme!" Let us be patient if we would understand. Let us go back to our question; reformulate it to ourselves. Have we been, at the bottom of our heart, seeking so long for *immortality*, or only for a 'glorious vision' of something which is *graded on* to our present experiences, for an enlargement of our powers and our worldly possessions transformed into subtler *material* but the same in *kind?* If we have longed for such then let us seek for them by all means; but the way is different; and the result is limited and poor by comparison. Nachiketâ refused such glorious states. He wanted *immortality*. If the emmet were to sigh for sovereignty of a world-wide human empire, it would be a glorious consummation indeed, as compared with its present condition, when it attained thereto, as it surely would if it desired persistently and ardently enough. But would that glorious consummation be a final consummation? Do we wish for only such a one? What if one were ruler of a solar system, omniscient and omnipotent—but omniscient and omnipotent within the poor limits of a solar system only! One solar system may be, nay, must be, to another solar system—circumscribed by a sufficiently greater breadth of space and length of time—even as a small molecule is to the whole earth-globe; and such comparative smallness and greatness are endless. The ruler of a solar system, of a hundred, of a thousand, of a million solar systems rolled into one, must die, *as such ruler*. His life, as such ruler, had a beginning and must have an end. This fact is almost plain to the physical senses, to say nothing of logical inferences. Physical science *sees* stars and systems beginning and ending. Whatever tenure of true immortality such a ruler has, he has it because of the identity of his self with the Pratyag-âtmâ, the universal Self, even as much as, and no more and no less than, the meanest worm whose form exists within his system. We do not at present seek for anything that is only comparative and circumscribed and limited by death at both ends. We want an immortality that is unlimited and uncomparative. Such can be found only in the pure 'I.' Thoughtlessness says: "This thing is commonplace and unimportant," only because it is familiar. Serious thought on the other hand perceives, in that same ever-present and everywhere-present nearness and pervasion of all life and all consciousness and all universal processes, the conclusive evidence of unlimitedness and true immortality and everlastingness. This Pratyag-âtmâ declares its utter purity and transparency and transcendence of all limitations whatever, gross and glorious, through the mouth of Kṛiṣhṇa: "The 'I' is the origin and the end of all the worlds. There is nothing higher than the 'I,' O winner of (the) wealth (of wisdom)! All this (world) is strung together on the 'I' even as jewels on a thread."[1]

We may think again, with lurking doubt as to the value of our finding: "I knew this 'I' indeed before I started on my quest!" That we did so is no detraction from the value of our finding now. We knew it then, it is true, but how vaguely, how doubtingly, bandying it about between a hundred different and conflicting hypotheses; compare that knowledge with the utter all-embracing fulness of the knowledge of the nature of the 'I' that we have now attained to. Indeed it is the law of all enquiry about anything and everything that we begin with a partial knowledge and end with a fuller one. None can turn attention to that of which he knows nothing at all; none needs to enquire about that of which he knows all already. To start on the quest of the north pole we must have at least the know-

---

[1] *Bhagavad-Gîtâ.* vii. 6, 7.

ledge that it possibly exists and in a certain direction. This knowledge is very different in fulness from the knowledge we would acquire if we actually stood on the north pole; still it is partial knowledge of it. The reconciliation of the antitheses involved in the paradox that we cannot talk about what we do not know, and need not talk about what we do know, will be seen later on to lie in this: As everything in the universe is connected with everything else therein, so every piece of knowledge is connected with every other; and therefore every Jîva possessing any piece of knowledge is potentially in possession of all knowledge; and enquiry and finding, in the individual life, mean only the passing from the less full to the fuller, from the potential to the actual, knowledge. In other words, the *unfolding* of the knowledge existing, but concealed, within the Jîva, appears as *enquiry and finding*. Thus then we *can* talk about all things because we know a *little* of them all, and *need* to talk about them because we wish to know *more*. Look we not then with slight upon this simple 'I.' "The heedless ones contemn the 'I' embodied in the human frame, unwitting of the supreme status of that 'I,' as the Great Lord of all that hath come forth."[1]

[1] *Ibid.* ix. 11.

There is one point here which should be borne in mind. The full knowledge obtained by the traveller when he has attained his goal may be set down by him exhaustively in a book, reading which another may acquire that knowledge; and yet there will be a difference of degree, the difference between direct and indirect, between the knowledge of the two. And such difference will always hold good as regards things material, whether gross or subtle (even those loosely but not accurately called spiritual). But as regards abstract principles, the universal 'I' and the abstract laws and lower principles that flow from that 'I' direct, and are imposed by its being as laws on the world-process—in their case knowledge and finding are one; there is no distinction between direct and indirect knowledge, intellectual cognition and realisation. In this respect metaphysic is on the same level as arithmetic and geometry. What the true significance is of the distinction currently made between the so-called 'mere intellectual cognition' of Brahman and the 'realisation' thereof, परोक्ष, parokṣha, beyond sight, and अपरोक्ष, aparokṣha, not beyond sight, knowledge, will appear later.[1]

Having thus necessarily abstracted and sepa-

---

[1] See the last page.

rated out from the world-process the true, universal, and unlimited One, out of which all so-called universals borrow their pseudo-universality, we equally necessarily find left behind a mass of particulars. And just as it is not possible to define the 'I' any further than by naming it the 'I,' so is it not possible to define this mass of particulars otherwise than by naming it the 'Not-I,' the 'Not-Self,' the 'Non-Ego,' Mûla-prakṛiti. Take it at any point of space and time, it is always a particular *something* which can be cognised as *object* in contrast with the cognising subject. As the characteristic of the 'I' is universality and abstractness, so is the characteristic of the 'Not-I' particularity and concreteness. It is always a 'this,' a 'that,' a something that is always, in ultimate analysis, limited and definable in terms of the senses. Its special name is the Many, as that of the Self is the One. That it is generalised under the word 'Not-Self' is only a pseudo-generalisation by reflection of the universality of the 'I.' The word pseudo is used to distinguish the universality of the one from that of the other. It does not mean false in the sense of 'non-existent,' but only in the sense of 'apparent,' 'not real,' 'borrowed,' 'reflected.' The physical fact of the continuance and indestructibility of matter illustrates this fact. Because the 'I' and the 'Not-I' always imply each other and can never be actually separated, they are always imposing on each other one another's attributes. The 'I' is always becoming particularised into individuals, and the 'Not-I' always becoming generalised into the elements and classes and kinds of matter, because of this juxtaposition of the two, because of their immanence within each other.

Further treatment of this point belongs to a later stage of the discussion. It is enough to show here that the searcher necessarily comes at the last stage but one to these two, the Self and the Not-Self.

It should be added that at this stage, having traced his ego into the universal Ego, the Jîva finds a partial satisfaction and peace. Seeing that the universal Ego is unlimited by space and time, he feels sure of his immortality, and does not yet feel any great care and anxiety precisely to define the nature of that immortality. He is for the time being content to take it as a universal immortality in which all egos are merged into one without any clear distinction and specialisation, for he feels that such specialisation is part of the limited and perishing, and so incapable of such immortality as belongs to the Pratyag-âtmâ. Later on he will begin to ask whether there is any such thing as personal immortality also; he will find that in the constitution of the material sheaths which make of him an individual ego out of the universal Ego, there is a craving for such personal immortality,[1] for a continuance of existence as separate; and he will also find that such is possible, nay certain, in its own special sense and manner. Just now, there is but one last remaining doubt that makes him find but a partial peace and satisfaction in the finding of the universal Ego.

---

[1] See Stirling's *Secret of Hegel.* 2nd Ed. Pp. 213, 214, and his *Schwegler.* Pp. 435,436.

CHAPTER V.

THE MUTUAL RELATION OF THE SELF AND THE NOT-SELF.

Seeing the unvarying continuity of the universal Ego, the Pratyag-âtmâ, through and amidst the endless flux of particulars, of not-selves, we have separated it out and identified ourselves with it, and so derived a certain sense of absence of limitation, of immortality. But the separation now begins to seem to us to be merely 'mental' and not 'real.' For while we see, without doubt, that the 'I' continues unchanged through changing things, we also see that it continues to do so only *in* these things and never apart from them; and if it must do so, is it not after all limited by some inherent want and defect, so that it is dependent for its manifestation, its existence in fact, upon these things, just as much as these things may depend upon it? And so we come back to the old difficulties of two eternals and two infinites. We must reconcile these two infinites, indeed we must derive the one from the other, maintaining all the while their coevalness, their simultaneity, for it is not in our power to deny the beginninglessness and endlessness of either. How to perform this most impossible task, to combine all the statements of the first and the second answers, and also obviate all the possible objections to them? How relate the Self and the Not-Self so that the Self—myself—shall no longer feel bound, feel small, feel dependent, feel helpless and at the mercy of the Not-Self?

We do not want to know how and why and whence the Self. When we come to a true eternal infinite One, further search for causes ceases. To ask for a cause of that which is unlimited and changeless is meaningless. None really and sincerely does or can do so. All enquiry starts with a certain standard; when we have found such and such a one, we shall toil and seek no further and no longer; and un-causedness, self-existence, is, on the very face of it, part of the standard of the enquiry after the unlimited. We do not want to engage in an endless pastime of asking 'why' after every answer, without considering whether the answer is, or is not, complete and final. What we want is to derive all and every thing from one true unchanging and unlimited something, which something shall be ourself. But we must do this and nothing less. We must prove conclusively to ourselves that our Self is the true eternal and unlimited, that it is not based in any way on the Not-Self, but that from it is derived the Not-Self and a countless, boundless, endless series too of not-selves. We have to create everything, all things, out of the 'I,' and not only every thing and all things but an endless series of such. We have to create in a rational and intelligible manner not only something but an infinite something, *viz.*, the second of two co-infinites, and create it out of nothing, or, which is the same thing, out of the first co-infinite without changing this first infinite in the very minutest, in the very least, degree, for otherwise its unlimitedness is lost and it is no longer infinite but subject to finiteness, to change, to beginning and end.[1] Impossible, truly, to all appearance! And yet until this so impossible task is done there is no final peace, no final satisfaction. Amass worldly wealth and powers, amass endless particulars upon particulars of science, amass occult knowledge and powers of high and low degree, for a thousand

---

[1] The words infinite and eternal have been used, so far, from the standpoint of the enquirer who has not yet made the technical and profoundly significant distinction between the true eternal and infinite, on the one hand, and the merely endless, on the other, which will appear later on.

years, for a thousand thousand years, and do not this, set not at rest this doubt—and there will be no peace for you. Secure this and all else will follow in its proper time, serenely, certainly, and peacefully. The Gods have suffered from this doubt, as Yama said. Indra, the king of the Gods, found no pleasure in his heavenly kingdom and, forsaking it, studied the science of this peace, Adhyâtma-vidyâ, the science of the Self, for a hundred years and one in all humility at the feet of Prajâpati.[1] Even Vișhņu had to master it before he could become the ruler of a system.[2] Let us then set our hearts on mastering it.

The first result of this last effort is a return to the first answer on a higher level. The universal Self, the One without a second, by its own inherent power of desire, creates the Not-Self, at the same dividing itself into many selves, assuming names and forms by combination with the Not-Self. "It willed: May I become many, may I be born forth."[3] "Having created (all this) it entered thereinto itself."[4] Such are the first of the scripture-texts which seek to sum up the world-process in one single

---

[1] *Chhândogya-Upanișhat.* VIII.
[2] *Devî-Bhâgavata.* I. xv.
[3] *Chhândogya-Upanișhat.* VI. ii.
[4] *Taittirîya-Upanișhat.* II. vi.

act of consciousness, and bring it all within the Self.[1]

This first result, corresponding to the Dvaita or dualistic form of the Vedânta, is only the theory of creation on a higher level, with a new added and important significance. Instead of a personal, extra-cosmical, separate God, the universal Self immanent in the universe has been reached. Instead of craftsman and knick-knacks, potter and pots, builder and houses, we have ensouling life and organisms. The world is, though vaguely, included in the being of the One; the sense of unity is greater and that of irreconcilable difference and opposition less. As to what is the exact relation between that universal Self and the individual selves and living material organisms and so-called dead inanimate matter[2] there is as yet no really

---

[1] Cf. Karl Pearson, *Grammar of Science* (1st edn.): "There is an insatiable desire in the human breast to resume in some short formula, some brief statement, the facts of human experience." (P. 44). If he had added, "in such a manner as to derive these all from the Self," he would have explained the why of the insatiable desire at the same time.

[2] The five kinds of separateness and relationship referred to in the Dvaita-Vedânta, are:

जीवजीवभेद, जीव-ईश्वरभेद, जीवजगद्भेद, जगद्-ईश्वरभेद, जड़जड़भेद. *i.e.*, the difference between Jîva and Jîva, between Jîva and Îshvara, between Jîva and the world (or inanimate matter), between the world and Îshvara, and between inanimate matter and inanimate matter.

satisfactory idea. It appears in a general way, at this stage, that the three—God, individual spirits, and 'nature'—are all eternal and ever distinct from each other, but yet that the latter two are entirely subordinate to the first, and that the relation between God and Jîva is that of an indivisible conjunction, the individual Jîva being unable to exist without the energising support of the universal Spirit, as the tree cannot live and subsist without its sap.

But this transmuted form of the theory of creation fails and falls short of final satisfaction for reasons the same as those that demolish that theory. It explains the beginning of the world-process as being dependent on, and the result of, the desire, the will, of the Self. It thus explains motion, change; but it does this by means of a mysterious power which itself requires rational explanation. There is also no reason assigned for the exercise of such power, and, finally, it does not explain and contain changelessness. The Perfect, the Supreme, must be changeless. What changes, desires, feels want, is imperfect, is limited, is less than the Supreme. Our final search is for that which shall be changeless and yet shall explain and contain all the multiplicity of endless change within itself.

The next step, the second result of the last

effort, is the Vishiṣhṭâdvaita form of the Vedânta: One substance, eternal, restful, changeless, Îshvara, has two aspects, is animate and inanimate, chit and achit, conscious and unconscious, Self and Not-Self; and by its power, माया, Mâyâ, शक्ति, Shakti, causes an interplay of the two, for its own high pleasure which there is none other to question, without any compulsion from without. "It has two natures, the one formless, and the other form."[1] "It became husband and wife."[2] "It is being and nothing."[3] Such is the second series of scripture-texts that correspond to this stage.

This second result, it is clear, is again only the second answer, the theory of transformation, on a higher level. Two factors are recognised, but subordinated to, made parts and aspects of, a third, which is not a third however; and the two are thus rather forcibly reduced to a pseudo-unity. Instead of the complete separateness of seer and seen, instead of the ordinary Sâñkhya doctrine of Puruṣha and Prakṛiti, Subject and Object, we have a complete pantheism of ensouling life and organism. The two are not only seer and seen, subject and object, desiror and desired, actor and acted on, but also soul and

---

[1] *Bṛihad-Âraṇyaka-Upaniṣhat.* II. iii. 1.

[2] *Ibid.* I. iv. 3. [3] *Prashna-Upaniṣhat.* ii. 5.

body, cause and instrument, desire and means of desire, actor and means of action. But the objections to the original form of the transformation-theory hold good, with only the slightest modifications, against this subtler form of it also. Why the need for, the want of, amusement and manifestation and interplay? Why so much evil and misery instead of happiness in the course of the manifestation? And what after all is the duality? Are there two, or are there not two? If two, and there must be two if there is interplay, as there self-evidently is, nothing has really been explained. Prove that one of the two is naught, is nothing, and then you will have said something! What is this mysterious mâyâ, shakti, power, which brings about the interplay? What is this unexplained power? How am I, the individual enquirer, to feel the satisfaction of being the owner, the master, and not the slave, of that power? How does this explanation assure me of my own freedom? Where is the law, the regular method, the reliable process, in all this manifestation and interplay and unrestrained power, which may assure me of orderliness and sequence, assure me against caprice, and be in accord with what I see in the world around? I, as an individual, do not feel my assonance with this explanation. It does not yet lead me to the heart of the world-process. It does not explain my life, in reference to and in connection with the world around me, systematically, satisfactorily. The laws of karma and compensation, the law of re-birth, do not fit into it quite plainly. To say that I am (*i.e.*, the 'I' is) feeling happy in a million forms and also feeling miserable in another million does not assimilate readily with the constitution of my being. I feel the statement as something external to me. In order to be satisfied I must see the identity of the countless individual 'I's,' not only in essence but in every detail and particular.

Such are the doubts and difficulties that vitiate the second result and render it of no avail.

CHAPTER VI.

THE MUTUAL RELATION OF THE SELF AND THE NOT-SELF *(Continued).*

It may perhaps be useful to the reader, especially the western reader, if a rapid sketch of modern European thought on the subject is given here, showing how its developments stand at the same level, though necessarily with very great differences of method and details, as the second form of Vedânta above given in essence, and the third form current thereof also, *viz.*, the Advaita or non-dualistic. The nature of the Advaita view will also appear in the course of this sketch.

Indian thought—in all departments of research in which we possess tangible results of it in the shape of Saṃskṛit and Prâkṛit works—has seldom lost sight of the fact that the end and aim of knowledge is, directly or indirectly, the alleviation of pain and the promotion of happiness; the end and aim of the supreme knowledge being the alleviation of the supreme pain of the fear of annihilation, and the promotion of the supreme pleasure of the assurance of immortality and self-dependence. The dominant motive of that thought therefore is ethico-religious. Even works on grammar and mathematics do not forget to state at the outset that they subserve the attainment of mukti, liberation, salvation, in some way or other.

Modern western thought, on the other hand, has, for various reasons, historical and evolutionary, become disconnected with religion—which in its perfection and completeness is the one science of all sciences, *knowledge* pre-eminently, the Veda as it is named in Saṃskṛit. The mainspring of this western knowledge is mainly intellectual, knowledge for the sake of knowledge—at least as that mainspring is described by some of those in whose hands it has made progress, especially in science. This fallacy, as it is, despite its brilliant results in science and philosophy, has its own good reasons for coming into existence, as may be understood later. That it is a fallacy may be inferred, in passing, even from the one single and simple fact that public common sense and public instinct and public need have declined to rest content with a mere subjective and poetical admiration of the scientific discoveries recorded and registered in bulky tomes and journals, but have assiduously applied them, and continue to apply them, with an ever-increasing eagerness and demand, to the purposes of daily life, for the amelioration of its pains and the enhancement of its pleasures; and this, with a success in the mechanical arts and appliances of peace and war, conquest and commerce, which makes the western races the rulers of the surface of this earth at the present day.

In the meanwhile, that western thought has approached metaphysic proper from the side of psychology or rather epistemology, the theory of knowledge, almost exclusively. It examines the nature of the Self and the Not-Self in their relation to each other as cogniser and cognised, subject and object, knower and known, rather than in their other relations to each other of desiror and desired, and actor and acted on. In other words, it at first confined itself mainly to the relation of jñâna, cognition, and did not take much more than incidental account of ichchhâ, *i.e.*, desire, and kriyâ, *i.e.*, action. These, in their metaphysical bearing, it left for long entirely to theology, though, of course, the later thinkers have not been able to avoid a survey of the whole field of life from the standpoint they ultimately reached.

Thus it has happened that Berkeley, enquiring into the relation of the knower and known under the names of mind and matter, came to the conclusion that the very being of matter is its perceptibility by a mind. Its *esse* is its *percipi*. What matter is apart from its cognisability by the mind, we cannot say; indeed, we may well say, it is nothing apart from the mind. Thus that which we have regarded so long as out of us, apart from us, independent of us, is in reality dependent on us, is within us; "*without* is *within*."[1]

Hume came after Berkeley and he may be said to have shown with equal cogency that, if the being of matter is perceptibility, the being of mind is percipience; that if we do not know matter except as it is known—almost an Irishism (Bishop Berkeley was an Irish Bishop!), but with a special fulness of significance—we also do not know mind except as it knows, and apart from what it knows. What is mind but something cognising something? Vacant mind, empty of all cognition, we know nothing about; therefore *within* is *without*.

Thus then between Berkeley and Hume the *status quo* of the problem was restored, and the shopkeeper in his shop and the ploughman

[1] J. H. Stirling's English Translation of Schwegler's *History of Philosophy*. P. 419 (annotations).

at his plough might well feel delighted to think that these two philosophers in combination were no wiser than they, though each taken separately might have appeared something very fearfully profound; that the net product of these mountains in labour was that mind was that which knew matter, and that matter was that which was known by mind. And yet to the careful scrutiny it was apparent that the fact of a very close and intimate tie, an unbreakable nexus, of mutual and complete interdependence between these opposites, mind and matter, had been made apparent, as it was not before apparent, to all who had not travelled along the paths of enquiry trodden by these two, either in their company, or in those of their elders and predecessors in the race of thinkers, or, it may be, by themselves and alone. The problem was therefore the richer for the labours of Berkeley and Hume, and had now a newer and deeper significance.

Kant took it up at this stage. What is the nature, what are the laws, of this unbreakable bond between mind and matter? What are they? How do they affect each other? Within is without and without is within is all right enough: but this mutual absorption shows independence as well as interdependence. Two men may appear to be standing on each other's shoulders by twisting themselves double; but even this can be only appearance; each must have at least a secret fulcrum, a solid standing-ground. After many years' hard thinking he came to the conclusion that each man did have such a separate standing-ground. Behind mind was a thing-in-itself,[1] and behind matter was a thing-in-itself; and from these two noumena there irradiated and corruscated, spontaneously and by inherent nature, phenomena which entangled themselves with each other and produced what we know as mind and matter. But, Kant added, the phenomena that issued from the mental thing-in-itself were few in number and took the shape of laws and 'forms,' into which the phenomena that streamed from the material thing-in-itself as 'sensations'—the 'matter' of knowledge, as opposed to its 'form,' in technical language—fitted in exactly and helplessly, and so an organic whole of systematised knowledge was produced.

But this was worse and worse. The shop-keeper and the ploughman might be excused for staring aghast. We had two difficulties to deal with before, *viz.*, mind and matter;

---

[1] Compare the स्वलक्षण, sva-lakṣhaṇa, 'own-mark,' of the Bauddhas.

now we have four, *viz.*, two things-in-themselves and two (or rather an endless number) of things-in-other-than-themselves! What are these things-in-themselves? Some ran away with the idea that they were the unknowable ultimates of the universe; and whenever that which it most concerns us to know, that which is most necessary for us to know, that which is a matter of life or of death for us to be intimate with or strangers to—whenever that comes up before us, then, these people declared, we must shut our eyes and turn away and say: "We cannot know you, the limits of human knowledge have been already reached and circumscribed." Others, impressed by the stately technical harness and trappings of the philosophy, but not caring to examine beneath those externals, took to themselves the belief that these things-in-themselves were knowable in some mystic state, unmindful that the very definition of "thing-in-itself" excluded any such possibility of cognition, that as soon as anything is cognised it ceases by that very fact to be a thing-in-itself, and that the thing-in-itself retires inwards, beneath and behind that which has been cognised, and which forthwith becomes an attribute and a phenomenon veiling the now deeper thing-in-itself. Thus many theories and schools arose on the basis of the labours of Kant and under the shadow of his 'critical philosophy,' as it was called. But the plain and patent objection to the conclusions of Kant was that instead of an explanation he had given us only an increase of confusion. As Stirling has pointed out in his annotations to Schwegler's *History of Philosophy* and his *Text-book to Kant*, and as Schelling also seems to have hinted,[1] there was no superior law provided by Kant, as was most imperatively needed, to regulate and govern the fitting of sense-phenomena (the matter) into the so-called laws (the forms) of mind, the mind-phenomena. If there was something inherent in the sense-phenomena which guided them instinctively to close with the right laws, then that same instinct might well enable them to marshal themselves out into systematic knowledge without the help of any of these mental laws either. On the other hand, if the mind-phenomena had something in them which would enable them to select the right sense-phenomena for operation, then they might also very well have in themselves the power to create such phenomena without the aid of any material thing-in-itself. Kant himself seems to have

[1] Ueberweg. *History of Philosophy* (English translation). II., 216. (Art. 'Schelling.')

felt these difficulties in his later days, and to have begun to see that the mental thing-in-itself was nothing else than the pure Ego, and that this Ego was the law and the source of all laws. Perhaps he had also begun to see that the pure Ego was not only thing-in-itself to mind, but also, in some way or other, thing-in-itself to matter too. But it was not given to him to work out and attain those last results in that life of his; and Fichte took up and onward the work left unfinished by Kant.

Fichte clearly saw the necessity, in the interests of mental satisfaction, true internal liberty and respite from restless doubt, of deducing the whole mass and detail of the universe from a single principle with which the human Jîva could find the inviolable refuge of identity; and he also saw therefore that this principle must be the Ego. Fichte is the western thinker who, of all known western thinkers, ancient as well as modern, appears to have come nearest the final truth, attained closest to the ultimate explanation of the universe. He divides with Schelling and Hegel, in current public judgment, the high honour of leading a large mass of humanity, in the west, away from the deadly pits of blind belief on the one hand and blind scepticism on the other, towards the lifeful and magnificent mountain heights of a reasoned knowledge of the boundlessness and unsurpassable dignity of the Jîva's life. Some are inclined to place Hegel's work higher than Fichte's, especially Stirling, who has spent a lifetime on the study of German thinkers, and whose opinion on any matter connected with them is therefore entitled to the highest respect. Yet it may be said that, though Hegel's work was fuller in detail and more encyclopædic in its comprehension of the sciences than Fichte's, Fichte's enunciation of the basic principle of the world-process is more centre-reaching, more luminous — one would almost say wholly luminous, were it not for a last remaining unexplained difficulty — than Hegel's. And therefore it may also be said that Fichte has gone a step further than Hegel. The man's noble and transparent personal life deserved too that he should see more closely and clearly the nobility and transparence of the truth. Hegel's life was also free from blame, and yet it does not seem to have been so selfless as Fichte's, and therefore he probably saw the truth under a slightly thicker veil. It may be that if Fichte had lived longer he would have explained the last difficulty that remains behind at the end of his work; he would then have applied a master-key to all the problems and the sciences that Hegel has dealt with, and opened up their hearts with a surer touch. It may also be that if Hegel had lived longer he might have completed his system, which also suffers from a single last want, by means of Fichte's single principle, and so have done the same work that might have been done by Fichte. In the combination of the two lies great promise of satisfaction. On the whole, then, because of the view that Fichte has gone further than Hegel, what has to be said here about Hegel will be said first and Fichte taken up afterwards.

But before taking up Hegel, a word should be given to Schelling, who has very much in common with Hegel. The two were contemporaries and associates of each other and partly of Fichte's also, both being greatly influenced by Fichte. But Schelling failed to make such a lasting impression on European philosophy as did Hegel, because of a certain lack of consistency and of stringency and rigour of thought and genetic construction such as those which Hegel carried into effect. The net addition made by Schelling to the stock of western philosophy may be said to be a deeper and fuller view of the law of relativity, *viz.*, the law that two opposites imply each other. The point which Hegel emphasised so much does not seem to have occurred to him, that such opposites further inhere in a third something, which is not exclusively and wholly either the one or the other, but somehow includes and contains both, and is itself the aggregate of the two. What Hamilton and Mansel of England derived from Schelling, and Herbert Spencer from them, is that as everything implies its opposite so the whole of the world, the whole mass of relatives, of opposites, being taken together as one term—which may be called the Relative—this whole would necessarily imply its opposite, the Absolute. Hamilton and Mansel vaguely called this Absolute, God; Herbert Spencer called it the Unknowable. In one sense this conclusion is true; in another it is only a verbal quibble, so that critics have not been wanting to point out that the absolute and the relative make a new relation, a new pair of opposites which also requires an opposite in a higher absolute and so on endlessly.[1]

Hegel put a stop to this unfruitful and fatuous endlessness of higher and higher absolutes, which really explains nothing and is a contradiction in terms, by showing that when all opposites had been once heaped together under

[1] For various criticisms of Spencer's view on this subject, see Caird, *Introduction to the Philosophy of Religion*, ch. i.; and also Spencer's own *Replies to Criticisms*, published in his collected Essays.

the Relative, no further opposite could be left outside of this mass in the shape of an absolute; that if such a train of reasoning was to be followed at all, the logical conclusion should be that the Absolute was immanent in the mass of the Relative; that every thing contained its opposite within itself, and that the true Absolute would be complete when opposites had been resolved into each other, so that no further search for a higher absolute was left to make. Hegel's most important contribution to metaphysic accordingly seems to be a full development and application of the law that two opposites, two extremes, always find their reconciliation in a third something, a mean, which, as said before, is neither the one nor the other exclusively but both taken together. Applying this principle to the world-process in the mass, he first analyses it into two pure opposites, pure Being and pure Nothing, and then proceeds to state that the collapse of these two into each other is 'becoming,' is the world-process. The fact that 'becoming' is the conjunction of Being and Nothing, and that every particular combines and reconciles within itself two opposites; and the consequent law that the reconciliation of two extremes should be always sought for in the mean, and that extremes should always be regarded as a violent and unnatural disruption of the mean—this fact and this law are profoundly significant and very helpful to bear in mind in all departments of life. But yet the mere statement of them, which is practically all that Hegel has done, leaves behind a sense of dissatisfaction. The why and the how are not explained; and the why and the how necessarily come up when we begin with two and not with one. If we begin with one and can maintain it changeless, then none may ask why and how. Merely to say that every change implies a falling of Being into Nothing and of Nothing into Being is perfectly true; but is true only as breaking down some old preconceived notions obstructive to further progress, true as a stimulus to further enquiry; it is not quite immediately satisfactory in itself or helpful towards the solution of the final doubt. It was declared long before Hegel, and declared a thousand times, that the world of things is Being, सत्, sat, as well as Non-Being, असत्, asat; that it is both and that it is neither; but the statement remains dark, unlighted. Where is the lamp to light it up and to make all clear at once?

Then this speaking in the third person, Being and Nothing, instead of in the first and second person, Self and Not-Self, ('I' and 'you,')[1] rein-

---

[1] Shañkara. *Shârîraka-Bhâshya*, the very first paragraph.

vests the whole problem with the old strangeness, which we were at so much pains to transform into the home-feeling that goes with the words Self and Not-Self. Being means Self to us; and Nothing is nothing else than Not-Self (in the sense of a denial of the Self), if it is anything at all. To talk of Being and Nothing after Fichte has talked of Ego and Non-Ego is to take a regressive rather than a progressive step. Indeed, this may be said, in a sense, to be the greatest defect of Hegel's system. To speak in terms of 'pure universal notions,' of Being and Nothing, &c., instead of Self and Not-Self and their derivatives, to imply that 'spirit' (in the sense of Self) is subsequent to 'pure immaterial thought,' is to walk on the head and hands instead of the feet. There may be a little progress made even in that way. But the tumbles are frequent, and the whole process is invested with an immense and most unnatural strain. Of course, it is clear that if we would deal with psychology and metaphysic we must introspect, we must look inwards, more or less, we must turn our eyes in a direction opposite to that in which we usually employ them in ordinary life. But Hegel insists that while we should so turn our head and eyes, we must keep our chests in the old position! This involves a twisting-round of the neck which is well-nigh impossible. Hence Hegel's preternatural difficulty.

Moreover while pure Being and pure Nothing might well be allowed to combine into *pure* becoming, whence comes this endless multiplicity of *particular* becomings, or rather 'becomes,' *i.e.*, of special things that have become? Hegel does not seem to have explained this; although it seems necessary and even quite easy to do so from the standpoint of a true definition of the Absolute. A single word explains it. Has Hegel said that word? It does not appear that he has. If he has, then there is nothing more to be said against him on this score. Yet the story goes that Krug once asked Hegel to deduce his particular writing quill from the general principle that Being and Nothing make becoming, and that Hegel could reply with a smile only. Stirling talks of Krug's 'ridiculous expectation'; it seems to others that Krug's request was perfectly fair and legitimate. The *arbitrariness* of Krug's particular quill does require to be explained away.

Again, Hegel's fundamental proposition, the very base and foundation of his system—*viz.*, that Being and Nothing are the same and yet opposite, and that their mutual mergence makes becoming, which indeed is the true Absolute—is full of dissatisfaction. It may be true, nay, it is true, in a certain sense, that Being and Nothing are the same and yet opposed; but it is not Hegel who tells us what that certain sense is. It may be true, nay, it is true, in a certain sense, that becoming is the Absolute; but it is not Hegel who tells us what that sense is. On the contrary, the general impression is that Hegel began with a violent *petitio principii* when he assumed that Being and Nothing though opposite are the same, and so took for granted the very reconciliation of opposites which it was his business to prove. After assuming that the two most opposed of all opposites are identical with each other, it is truly easy to reconcile all other opposites that may come up for treatment later.

Then, what is meant by saying or implying that becoming is the Absolute? If the word becoming is taken to mean the totality of the world-process from the beginning to the end of beginningless and endless time, then of course an absolute may be meant, but such an absolute remains absolutely unilluminative and useless. Hegel says (as summarised by Schwegler): "the absolute is, firstly, pure immaterial thought; secondly, heterisation of pure thought, disruption of thought into the infinite atomism of time and space—nature; thirdly, it returns out of this its self-externalisation and self-alienation back into its own self, it resolves the heterisation of nature, and only in this way becomes at last actual, self-cognisant thought, spirit." Perhaps, then, he means not the totality of the world-process, but a growing, maturing, absolute. But the absoluteness of an evolving changing thing or thought is a very doubtful thing and thought. Indeed there should be no distinction of thing and thought in the Absolute; and this it is one of the very hardest and subtlest tasks of metaphysic to explain away. The general impression left by Hegel is that the Absolute is an idea which finds its gradual expression and manifestation and realisation in the things, the becomings, of the world-process; and that consequently there is a difference of nature between the idea and the things. But if there is any such difference, then the things fall outside of the idea and have to be explained, and the whole task begins again. But even apart from this difficulty, which constitutes a separate doubt by itself, is the main difficulty of a changing absolute. The elementary Veda-texts, which helped as temporary guides at an earlier stage of the journey, and which said that the Self multiplied itself into many, had to be abandoned (for the time being at least) for want of sufficient reason and justification for the changing moods of a Supreme. We have been pining all along for changelessness, for rest and peace amidst this fearful turmoil. Hegel gives us an endlessness of change. He says the Absolute realises itself through nature in and into the individual; otherwise, the already supreme and perfect God developes into and finds himself in perfected man. A doctrine unsatisfactory enough in the mouth of any one and much more so in the mouth of Hegel—who knows nothing, or at least indicates nothing of the knowledge, of the vast evolution and involution of worlds upon worlds, material elements and Jîvas, of the incessant descent of spirit into matter and its reascent into itself. What does Hegel say as to where and when the Absolute began its evolution and when it will complete and end it? Has he anywhere entered into the question whether this actual self-cognisant spirit, this perfected individual, this perfected man who has achieved that combination of reason with desire or will which makes the true freedom, the true internal liberty, moksha—whether such an individual is completed in and arises at a definite point of time, or is only an infinitely receding possibility of the endless future? There were millions of individualised human Jîvas upon earth in the time of Hegel. Had the Absolute finished evolution in them or any of them, and if not, as it clearly had not, then why not? Such are the legitimate questions that may in all fairness be put to Hegel. He does not seem to have answered them. And yet each and everyone of them should and can be answered from the standpoint of a complete metaphysic.

It is not probable that Hegel in this birth, and in the life and surroundings of the period he lived and worked in, *viz.*, the last quarter of the eighteenth and the first quarter of the nineteenth century of the Christian era, knew all the even general details about the kosmic evolution of combined spirit and matter, which have since then become accessible to the human race. He ridicules the doctrine of rebirth,[1] showing thereby that he did not realise the full significance and extensive application of some of the metaphysical laws which he himself, or Fichte and Schelling before him, stated. Yet these details, as ascertained by the masters of yoga and embodied to a certain extent in the extant Purâṇas and other Saṃskṛit and Prâkṛit writings, are alone capable of providing a basis for a true and

---

[1] Hegel. *History of Philosophy.* English Translation. I. Art. "Pythagoras."

comprehensive metaphysic; for they, in the very act of pointing out the way to the final goal, explain how they themselves are inseparately connected with and derived from that goal. And if Hegel was not acquainted with such details, it is no wonder that his metaphysic remains incomplete. It is, indeed, a wonder, on the contrary, that it is so full as it is. It may, on the other hand, be that it was given to a man who saw so much and so deeply to see more also, and that he did not say all he knew for special internal or external reasons. This is the view that Stirling takes, in pointing out Hegel's shortcomings, especially in his work entitled, *What is Thought?* Stirling probably had not in mind, when stating such a view, anything about information derivable by means of a higher development of human faculties through yoga. What most concerns us here to know is that such a lifelong student of Hegel as Stirling declares, with all the weight and authority of such study, that there is a radical defect in the system, and that a key is wanted which perhaps Hegel *might* have given if he had lived longer, that is to say assuming that he himself had it.

We see thus that, while Schelling and Hegel made a very close approach to the final explanation, they do not seem to have quite grasped it. Let us now examine what appears to have been in some respects an even closer approach than theirs.

Fichte, as said before, realised and stated that the Ego was the only true universal, perfectly unconditioned in matter as well as in form (in the technical language of German thinkers), about the certainty of which there was not possible any doubt. And from this universal, he endeavoured to deduce the whole of the world-process. His deduction is usually summed up in three steps: Ego = Ego; Non-Ego is not = Ego; Ego in part = Non-Ego, and Non-Ego in part = Ego. There is first the thesis, the position of identity: 'I' is 'I'; secondly, there is the antithesis, the op-position of contradiction: 'I' is not 'Not-I'; lastly, there is the synthesis, the com-position of a reconciliation of the opposites by mutual limitation, mutual yielding, a compromise in which the 'I' becomes, *i.e.*, takes on the characteristics of, the 'Not-I,' and the 'Not-I' of the 'I.' And this is entirely and irrefutably in accordance with the facts of the world-process as they are there under our very eyes. No known western thinker has improved upon this summary of the essential nature of the world-process; and it is difficult to understand how Stirling has failed to give due meed to this great work. In his annotation to *Schwegler* he says with regard to Fichte: "What is said about the universal Ego . . . is not satisfactory. Let us generalise as much as we please, we still know no Ego but the empirical Ego and can refer to none other."[1] Now, with the respect one has for Stirling's metaphysical acumen, one can only say that this statement of his is very difficult to understand. For it is exactly equivalent to the entire denial of the possibility of an 'abstract,' simply because we can never definitely cognise anything but a concrete with our physical senses. As said before, in dealing with the process by which the nature of the universal Self is established, the mere fact of a diversity, of the many, of concretes and particulars, necessarily requires for its existence, for its being brought into relief, the support and background of a continuity, a unity, an abstract and universal. The two, abstract and concrete, universal and particular, are just as inseparable as back and front. But looking for a highest universal and a lowest particular we find that the extremes meet. The highest universal, pure Being, सत्तासामान्य, sattâ-sâmânya, is also the most irreducible point. The universal Ego is also the individual ego (the so-called empirical ego); the

---

[1] Stirling's *Schwegler*. P. 428.

universal Being and the aṇû, atom, of the Vaisheṣhika system of philosophy, correspond to the Pratyag-âtmâ and the atom which, enshrining a self, is the Jîv-âtmâ. Between these two limits, which are not two but one, the all-comprehending substratum of all the world-process, there fall and flow all other pseudo-universals and pseudo-particulars; pseudo, because each falls as a particular under a higher universal (or general) and at the same time covers some lower particulars (specials). The universal Ego is thus the only true, absolutely certain and final universal. "Hegel, in opposition to Fichte, . . . held that it is . . . not the Ego that is the prius of all reality, but, on the contrary, something universal, a universal which comprehends within it every individual."[1] This is where the deviation from the straight path began. It began with Hegel. And the results were: (1) that dissatisfaction with Hegel which Stirling confesses to again and again; and (2) a tacit reversion, by Stirling himself, to that impregnable position of Fichte (as shown throughout Stirling's last work, *What is Thought?* in which he endeavours to make out that the double subject-object, 'I-me,' is the true Absolute). For if "we know no ego

---

[1] *Ibid.* P. 315.

but the empirical ego," how much more do we know no being but empirical and particular beings, no nothing but empirical and particular non-commencements or destructions. Ego and Non-Ego we understand; they are directly and primarily in our constitution; nay, they are the whole of our constitution, essence and accidence, core and crust, inside and outside, the very whole of it. But Being and Nothing we understand only *through* Ego and Non-Ego; otherwise they are entirely strange and unfamiliar. Being is nothing else than position, positing, affirmation by consciousness, by the 'I'; Non-Being is nothing else than opposition, contra-position, denial by that same 'I.' Stirling practically admits as much in *What is Thought?* Fichte's approach, then, is the closer and not Hegel's, and Stirling's opinion that "the historical value of the method of Fichte will shrink, in the end, to its influence on Hegel"[1] is annulled by his own latest research and finding. The probability indeed, on the contrary, is that Hegel's work will come to take its proper place in the appreciation of true students as only an attempt at a filling and completion of the outlines traced out by the earnest,

---

[1] *Ibid.* P. 427.

intense, noble and therefore truth-seeing spirit of Fichte.[1]

By sheer force of intense gaze after the truth Fichte has reached, even amidst the storm and stress of a life cast in times when empires were rising and falling around him, conclusions which were generally reached in India only with the help of a yoga-vision developed by long practice amidst the contemplative calm of forest-solitudes and mountain-heights.[2] Page

---

[1] Dr. J. H. Stirling, in a very kind letter, writes as below, on this point: "Dr. Hutchinson Stirling would beg to remark only that he is not sure that Mr. Bhagavân Dâs has quite correctly followed the distinction between Fichte's and Hegel's use of the Ego in deduction of the categories—the distinction at least that is proper to *Stirling's interpretation* of both: Stirling holding, namely, that Fichte, while without provision for an external world as an external world, has only an external motive or movement in his Dialectic, and is withal in his deduction itself incomplete; whereas Hegel, *with* provision for externality, is *inside* of his principle, and in his deduction infinitely deeper, fuller, and at least completer." I give this extract from Dr. Stirling's letter with the view that it may help readers to check and correct any errors made in this chapter, in the comparative appreciation of Hegel and Fichte.

Professor J. E. McTaggart, of Trinity College, Cambridge, also writes: ". . . I still maintain that Hegel has got nearer the truth than Fichte."

[2] Fichte's lecture on *The Dignity of Man* (pp. 331—336 of the *Science of Knowledge*, translated by A. Kroeger) is full of statements, which might be read as meaning, on Fichte's part, a belief in the evolution of the Jîv-âtmâ of the kind described in vedântic and theosophical literature, in direct contrast to Hegel's statements.

after page of his work reads like translations from Vedânta works. Schwegler, apparently unmindful of their value and even disagreeing with them, sums up the conclusions of Fichte in words which simply reproduce the conclusions of the Advaita-Vedânta as now current in India. Fichte's statement, quoted above, as to the transference of their characteristics to each other by the Ego and the Non-Ego, is the language of Shañkara at the very commencement of his commentary, the *Shârîraka-Bhâshya*, on the *Brahma-Sûtra*. His distinction between the absolute Ego and the individual or empirical ego is the distinction between the higher Âtmâ and the Jîva. The words 'higher Âtmâ' are used here because one of the last defects and difficulties of the current Advaita-Vedânta turns exactly, as it does in Fichte, on the confusion between Pratyag-âtmâ and Param-âtmâ, the universal Ego and the true Absolute. Again, Fichte's view is thus stated by Schwegler: "The business of the theoretical part was to conciliate Ego and Non-Ego. To this end middle term after middle term was intercalated without success. Then came reason with the absolute decision: 'Inasmuch as the Non-Ego is incapable of union with the Ego, Non-Ego there shall be none.'" This is to all appearance exactly the Vedânta method, whereby predicate after predicate is superimposed upon the Supreme, and predicate after predicate refuted and struck away as inappropriate, till the naked Ego remains as the unlimited which is the negation of all that is not-unlimited, and the searcher exclaims, "I am Brahman,"[1] and "the Many is not at all,"[2] as the two most famous Veda-texts, great sentences (in the Saṃskṛit phrase, mahâ-vâkyas) or logia, the foundation of the Advaita-Vedânta, describe it. The opposition between the (undistinguished) Brahman or Âtmâ or Ego, on the one hand, and the Non-Ego, on the other, is stated correctly by the vedântîs thus: (The Âtmâ is) that of which âkâsha (ether), air, fire, water and earth are the vivartas, opposites, perversions.[3] The relation between them is indicated by Madhusûdana Sarasvatî in a manner which comes home to the reader even more closely than Fichte's: "Brahman dreams all this universe, and its waking is the reduction of it all to illusion."[4]

Thus we see that some of the most important conclusions of the current Advaita-Vedânta

---

[1] *Bṛihad-Âraṇyaka.* I. iv. 10.

[2] *Ibid.* IV. iv. 19.

[3] *Bhâmati.* P. 1.

[4] *Sañkṣhepa-Shârîraka-Tîka.* iii. 240.

have been independently reached by this truly great German thinker. And in seeing this, we have ourselves taken a step further than we had done when we left the Vishiṣhṭâdvaita system as the second result of the last endeavour to solve the supreme question of questions. We have seen that the current Advaita-Vedânta is an advance upon the Vishiṣhṭâdvaita. We have also seen that Fichte and Hegel are supplementary to each other. For, while Fichte's dialectic is the more internal, starting with the Ego, and therefore the truer and less artificial, it follows out the world-process up to the end of two stages only, as it were, those of origination and preservation, *i.e.*, the present existing order of things, a commingling of the Ego and the Non-Ego; whereas Hegel's dialectic—though external, starting with Being, returning however to thought afterwards, and therefore the more artificial—in a way completes the circuit of the world-process to the last stage, that of destruction, dissolution, or return to the original condition. (The words 'in a way' have been used for want of the certainty that the full significance of this cyclic law and triple succession of origin, preservation and dissolution of the kosmic systems which make up the world-process, and which law is reiterated over and over again in all Saṃskṛit literature, was present to the minds of Fichte and Hegel). We feel now that Hegel, Fichte and current Advaita-Vedânta have come quite close to the very heart of the secret; we feel that it cannot now be very far off; we are not only face to face with the lock that closes the whole treasure-house of explanations of all possible mysteries and secrets and confusions, but also hold in our hands the key which we feel is the only key to the lock; and not only do we hold the key, but in our struggles with the key and the lock we have, in the good company of the Indian vedântîs and the German idealists, broken through panes of the door-leaves and almost moved the door away from its hinges, and obtained many a glimpse and even plain view of many of those treasures and secrets. Yet the key will not quite turn in the lock. Some rust-stain somewhere, some defect of construction, prevents this.

The defect, some features of which have been already pointed out in treating of Hegel, is that we cannot deny altogether this Non-Ego. We cannot quite convince ourselves that it is pure Non-being, अत्यंतासत्, atyantâsat. It seems both existent and non-existent, सदसत्, sadasat.

Whence this appearance of existence in it? The last unexplained crux of the current Advaita-Vedânta is the connection between Brahman, the Absolute, and Mâyâ, the illusion of the world-process. As with Fichte's Non-Ego, so with the vedântî's Mâyâ, there remains behind an appearance of artificiality, of a *deus ex machinâ*, a lack of organic connection—a lack of the working of the whole world-process into and out of it, in the arrangement between it, on the one hand, and the Ego, or Brahman, on the other. Why should Brahman dream? A hundred different ways of enunciation and illustration are tried by the ordinary vedântî. None is satisfactory. And therefore the *current* Advaita does not reach to the final stage of a *true* Advaita. When pressed, it, like Fichte, falls back upon the position that Mâyâ (Non-Ego, with Fichte) is wholly Non-being, instead of both existent and non-existent, and this we cannot quite bring home to ourselves. Besides this difficulty there is the *process of change*: the 'I' opposes to itself the 'Not-I' and reverts again to an original condition. Why? Our Absolute must be above change. Again, there seems to be an artificiality and arbitrariness about the 'Not-I' in another way. Why any one particular 'Not-I'? Fichte's deduction of the world-process is effected in a syllogism of three steps, three propositions, and even then it does not quite complete the process but leaves it half-finished. It ought to be complete in one proposition, one single act of consciousness, otherwise the difficulty of *change* in the Absolute remains unsolved.

There are expressions and indications that to the mind of Fichte and other German thinkers, as to the mind of the vedântî, there is present the distinction between eternity or rather timelessness, कालातीतता, kâlâtîtatâ, on the one hand, and time, काल, kâla, on the other. In this distinction lies the clue to much of the secret, and yet it does not seem to have been utilised. It is not properly utilised in the extant books on Advaita-Vedânta, although the fact of Brahman being beyond space and time is reiterated incessantly. Nor does it seem to have been put to much distinct and effective use by Fichte or any other western thinker, though it has been recognised by even such a non-metaphysical but extremely acute reasoner as J. S. Mill, in his *Examination of Sir William Hamilton's Philosophy*, as the distinction between the true and the false infinite. One hesitates to say positively that Fichte has left this last work unperformed; but from the accounts and translations of his writings available in English, this seems to be the case. And yet the secret is there all the time among the ideas expressed in his writings, as much as in the better works of current Advaita-Vedânta. Just the one rust-stain has to be removed from the key, and it will turn and finally unclose the lock and lay open before us what we want.

We want, as said before, that which combines within itself change as well as changelessness. An infinity of change even though it be a change of progress—a progress that has no self-contained and consistent meaning, that is without a definite *final* goal *towards which* it is a progress; an increasing progress which, there is reason to believe, may also be alternating with an ever-increasing regress; a progress in a convolved spiral which, if it turns upwards to ever greater glories of higher and subtler life, may also, by necessary correspondence, in accordance with the law of balance, of compensation, of action and reaction, pass downwards too through ever-increasing miseries of lower and grosser densities of matter—such ceaseless, aimless, process, or progress even, means not satisfaction, brings not happiness, but rather a desolate weariness. Fichte has said (to quote again the words of Schwegler):

"It is our duty at once, and an impossibility to reach the infinite; nevertheless just this striving united to this impossibility is the stamp of our eternity."[1] Schelling has said the same thing.[2] And to the principle of this metaphysical deduction corresponds the actual fact ascertained by yoga and occult science and stated in the Purâṇas and other theosophical and yoga literature, that there is an endless evolution of the Jîva through body after body and world after world. But this fact is not the whole of truth; it does not stand by itself. If it did, then such a mere infinity of change, without a constant and permanent basis of changelessness and peace, would only add the horrors of Sisyphus to the agonies of Tantalus. No soul, however patiently it now accepts—as many do—the doctrine of an endless progress will long feel peace in it by itself. The longing, yearning, all-resistless and unquenchable craving for changelessness and peace and rest will come upon it sooner or later.

Besides this emotional difficulty, this surfeit of unrest, which is now upon us, there is the intellectual difficulty, the impossibility of *understanding* the very fact of *change*. The instinct

---

[1] Schwegler's *History of Philosophy*. P. 270.

[2] J. H. Stirling. *What is Thought?* Pp. 397-398.

of the intellect cries out as the very first words of all logic, as the primary laws of all thought, that A is A and that it is not not-A, that Being is Being only and never Nothing. "The non-existent cannot be, and the existent cannot not be."[1] And yet every mortal moment of our lives, all around and above and below us, these much-vaunted laws of logic are being violated incessantly. Every infinitesimal instant, something, some *existent* thing, is becoming *non-existent*, and some *non-existent* thing is coming into being, is becoming *existent*. We may say that it is only the form that behaves like this. But what is the good of saying so? All that the world really means to us, sounds and sights, tastes, touches, and scents, all is included in the 'form' that changes. Even weight, it is being attempted to prove by mathematical computations, will change, with change of position, from planet to planet. And finally, those mathematical laws themselves, on which such computations are based, can no longer boast permanence. They too are being changed by mathematicians, and it is endeavoured to be shown that parallel lines can meet and two things occupy the same space. That we have an indestructible faith

---

[1] *Bhagavad-Gîtâ*. ii. 16.

that matter is indestructible is, to tell the truth, not due to any limited facts we know, for limited data can never justify limitless inferences, but is only the unavoidable assignment by us, by the 'I,' of a conjugal share in our own indefeasible eternity, to our undivorceable partner in life, the 'Not-I,' matter. Such being the case, it does not help us in any way to say that only the form changes. The form is practically everything; and even if it were not so, even then it is something, it is an existent something at one moment. And what is existent *once*, should be existent *ever*. How, why, does it pass into non-existence? We *do not* understand change. We *do not* understand the world-process. If you would have us understand it, you must show that this world-process is not a *process* at all, but a rock-like fixity. Then only shall we be able to bring it into accord with the primary laws of thought. Such is the difficulty of the exaggerated and yet legitimate demand of the reason, on the one hand.

On the other hand stands the difficulty of what may be called the demand of the senses. A doctrine of mere changelessness is incomplete; a mere assertion of it perfectly unconvincing. It explains nothing and is not a fact. It is, as just said, denied by every wink of our eyes, by every breath of our lungs, by every beat of our hearts. We want that which will combine and harmonise both change and changelessness. We want to reduce each into terms of the other.

Many have been the efforts to shut up the world-process into something which can be held in a single hand, which shall be but one single act of consciousness. Fichte could not do it in less than three successive, unsimultaneous and therefore change-involving steps, and then too but incompletely. The great mystic school of Rosicrucians has endeavoured to do so in one thought and sentence, "I am that I am"; but this propounds mere changelessness and makes no provision for change. The Veda-texts belonging to the penultimate stage have exclaimed separately, as said before: "I am Brahman" and then: "the Many is not at all"; but these too are insufficient for our purpose; they too establish changelessness alone and explain not change.

What we seek shall be obtained by compressing the three steps of Fichte into one; by combining the two separate scripture-utterances into a unity—a small change perhaps, at first sight, but almost as radical and important in result as an alteration of the mere order of letters composing a word, an alteration which makes a completely new word with an entirely new meaning.

NOTE.—It may be mentioned here that the Western philosophers especially selected in the text to serve as landmarks on the path of enquiry have been so selected because their special way of thought, arising out of modern conditions, is the freshest and most suited to the modern student and best fitted for the purpose in hand. Otherwise, indeed, the same subjects of enquiry have been and are being investigated by hundreds of the finest intellects of the human race from the most ancient times up to the present day, and different aspects of the same truths and propositions and solutions may be found in the works of the ancient Greek philosophers, Plato, Aristotle, and the Neo-Platonists especially, of Descartes, Spinoza, Leibnitz, of the mystics, Scheffler, Eckhart, Albrecht, and Bœhme, of Bruno and Bacon, and, again, Schopenhauer and Spencer, and many others. Each philosopher worthy of the name, and to whom the name has been given by public recognition, has undoubtedly left the world's stock of philosophical knowledge richer by at least some definite piece of work, a fuller and deeper view of some law, or a new application and use of it, or a new aspect of a question, or fact, or law. Indeed, as may appear later on, the most erroneous-seeming opinion ever held by any thinker will appear, from an all-embracing standpoint, and in a certain sense, to be a not inaccurate description of one aspect of a world-fact, one half of a truth. But some of the latest German thinkers seem to have succeeded better than any of their precursors in Europe in the attempt to systematise and unify. And even amongst these, from such accounts and translations of his writings into English as are available, Fichte appears to be an almost indispensable help to the students of true Vedânta and the higher metaphysic—the higher metaphysic which would enclose so-called occult and superphysical science within its principles as well as physical science; which claims to be a science because it offers to be tested in the same way as every particular science is tested, *viz.*, by endeavouring to show that its hypotheses agree with present facts, and also enable prediction to be made correctly, of results in the future; which, indeed, claims to be the very science of sciences by providing a great system, a great hypothesis, which, while special sciences systematise and unify limited groups of facts, would systematise and unify all possible world-facts, past, present, and to come.

CHAPTER VII.

The Last Answer.

सर्वे वेदा यत्पदमामनंति
तपांसि सर्वाणि च यद्वदंति ।
यदिच्छंतो ब्रह्मचर्यं चरंति
तत्ते पदं संग्रहेण ब्रवीमि ॥
ओमित्येतत् ॥

Yama, Lord of Death, than whom, as Nachiketâ said, there could be no better giver of assurance against mortality, no truer teacher of the truth of life and death, gives this last answer: "That which all the scriptures ponder and repeat; that which all the shining sufferers declare; that for which (the pure ones) follow Brahmacharya (the life of holiness, of sacrifice to Brahman); that do I declare to thee in brief, it is AUM."[1]

---

[1] *Kaṭha-Upanishat.* I. ii. 15.

What is the meaning of this mysterious statement repeated over and over again in a hundred ways in all Saṃskṛit literature, sacred and secular? Thus:

The *Prashna-Upaniṣhat* says: "This, O Satyakâma, desiror of truth, is the higher and the lower Brahman—this (that is known as) the Aum. Therefore, (strong-based) in that as (his) home (and central refuge), the knower may reach out to any thing (that he deems fit to follow after, and shall obtain it)."[1]

The *Chhândogya* says: "The Aum is all this; the Aum is all this."[2]

The *Taittirîya* says: "Aum is Brahman; Aum is all this."[3]

The *Mâṇḍûkya* says: "This, the imperishable Aum is all this; the unfolding thereof is the past, the present and the future; all is Aum."[4]

The *Târa-sâra* repeats these words of the *Mâṇḍûkya* and says again: "The Aum—this is

---

[1] एतद्वै सत्यकाम परं चापरं च ब्रह्म यदोंकारस्तस्माद्विद्वानेतेनैवायतनेनैकतरमन्वेति । v. 2.

[2] ओंकार एवेदं सर्वमोंकार एवेदं सर्वं । II. xxiii. 3.

[3] ओमिति ब्रह्म, ओमितीदं सर्वं । I. viii.

[4] ओमित्येतदक्षरमिदं सर्वं तस्योपव्याख्यानं भूतं भवद्भविष्यदिति सर्वमोंकार एव । i.

the imperishable, the supreme Brahman; it alone should be worshipped."[1]

Patañjali says: "The declarer Thereof is the Praṇava."[2]

Such quotations may be multiplied a hundredfold. What is the meaning of these mysterious and fanciful-looking statements? Many profound and occult interpretations of this triune sound have been given expressly in the Upanishats themselves, also in the *Gopatha Brâhmaṇa*, and in the books on Tantra, but the deepest and most luminous of all remains implicit only. For if the above seemingly exaggerated statements are to be justified in all their fulness, then, in view of all that has gone before, Aum must include within itself the Self, the Not-Self, and the mysterious Relation between them which has not yet been discovered in any of the preceding answers—that mysterious Relation, which being discovered, the whole darkness will be lighted up as with a sun, the Relation wherein will be combined changelessness and change. If it does this, then truly is the Indian tradition justified that all knowledge, all science, is summed up in the Vedas, all the Vedas in the Gâyatrî and

---

[1] ओमित्येदक्षरं परं ब्रह्म तदेवोपासितव्यं। i. 27.

[2] *Yoga-Sûtras.* i. 27.

the Gâyatrî in the Aum; then truly are all the Vedas and all possible knowledge there, for all the world-process is there. The Self, the Not-Self, and their mutual Relation—these three, the primal trinity, the root-base of all possible trinities, exhaust the whole of thought, the whole of knowledge, the whole of the world-process. There is nothing left that is beyond and outside of this primal trinity, which in its unity, its tri-une-ness, constitutes the Absolute which is, and wherein is, the totality of the world-process—the world-process which is nothing else than the Self or Pratyag-âtmâ, the Not-Self or Mûla-prakṛiti, and their Interplay.

But how can these three be said to be expressed by a single word? The immemorial custom of summing up a series, or of expressing a fact, in a single letter, and then of joining letters thus significant into a single word—of which many examples are to be found in the Upanishats—here gives the clue.[1] Each letter

[1] This ancient method of expressing a profound truth by assigning to each of its factors a letter, and then writing down the letters as a word, meaningless, a mere sound, except for the meanings thus indicated, is one which is not familiar to, and therefore may not commend itself to, modern thought. These "mystic words," of which so many are found in ancient writings, and later in Gnostic and Kabbalistic works, are regarded as jargon by the modern mind. And yet in these same words ancient wisdom has imbedded its profoundest conceptions, and the Aum is just such a word.

of this word must be the expression of a complete fact, and we are thus compelled to an inevitable conclusion.

The first letter of the sacred word, A, signifies the Self; the second letter, U, signifies the Not-Self; and the third letter, M, signifies the *everlasting Relation, the unbreakable nexus*—of Negation by the Self of the Not-Self—between them.

According to this interpretation of the Aum, the full meaning of it would be the proposition: Ego—Non-Ego—Non (est), or I—Not-I—Not (am), which sums up all the three factors of the world-process into a single proposition and a single act of consciousness.

The nearest approach to this *résumé* occurs in the *Chhândogya*[1]: "The name of Brahman is truth, सत्यं, satyam, which consists of three letters, स, sa, and ति, ti, and यं, yam. That which is sa is the unperishing; that which is ti is the perishing; that which is yam holds and binds the two together." The unperishing here means nothing else than the unlimited universal Self, Pratyag-âtmâ; the perishing is the endlessly

---

[1] एतस्य ब्रह्मणो नाम सत्यमिति। तानि ह वा एतानि त्रीण्यक्षराणि स ति यमिति। तद्यत्सत्तदमृतमथ यत्ति तन्मर्त्यमथ यद्यं तेनोभे यच्छति। VIII. iii. 5.

perishing, ever-renewed, and ever-dying, ever-limited Not-Self or Mûla-prakṛiti; the nexus, that which holds and binds the two together, is the unending relation of Negation by the One of the Many other, in which the two are constantly and inseparably tied to each other in such a way that the two together make only the numberless Absolute.

A similar statement, again using almost the same words, is made in the *Bṛihad-Âraṇyaka*.[1] "Truth, satyam, verily is Brahman. . . . The Gods contemplate and worship the truth, satyam, only. Three-lettered is this satyam; स, sa, is one letter, and ति, ti, is one letter, and यं, yam, is one letter. The first and the last letters, imperishables, are true; in the middle is the false (and fleeting). The false is encompassed round on both sides by the true. The true is the more (the greater, the prevailing). He that knoweth this—he may not be overpowered by the false." Here sa, the first truth, is Being;

[1] सत्यं ब्रह्मेति सत्यं ह्येव ब्रह्म । ते देवाः सत्यमेवोपासते । तदेतत्त्र्यक्षरं सत्यमिति । स इत्येकमक्षरं ति इत्येकमक्षरं यमित्येकमक्षरं । प्रथमोत्तमे अक्षरे सत्यं मध्यतोऽनृतं । तदेतदनृतमुभयतः सत्येन परिगृहीतं सत्यभूयमेव भवति । नैनं विद्वांसमनृतं हिनस्ति । V. v. 1.

and yam, the second truth, is Nothing, for both are imperishable; the middle is becoming, the ever-fleeting and ever-false.

The *Deví-Bhâgavata* says[1]: "Why, by what means and substance (has all this world arisen)? How may I know all (at once, by a single act of knowledge)?—Thus Mukunda (Vishṇu) pondered (within himself, in the beginning). Unto him that sovereign deity, Bhagavatî, uttered that which giveth all explanations in a single half-verse, *viz.*: 'I, not another, is (*i.e.*, am) alone verily this eternal all.'" This, it seems, is the plainest statement available in the Purâṇa literature, after the Veda, in which an endeavour is expressly made to sum up the world-process in a single sentence.

The *Yoga Vâsishṭha* says[2]: "I, pure con-

---

1 किमर्थं केन द्रव्येण कथं जानामि चाखिलं ।
इत्येव चिंत्यमानाय मुकुंदाय महात्मने ॥
श्लोकार्धेन तया प्रोक्तं भगवत्याऽखिलार्थदम् ।
सर्वं खल्विदमेवाहं नान्यदस्ति सनातनम् ॥
I. xv. 51-52.

2 अकिंचिन्मात्रचिन्मात्ररूपोस्मि गगनादणुः ।
इति या शाश्वती बुद्धिस्सा न संसारबंधनी ॥
Nirvâṇa-prakaraṇa, Purvârdha. cxviii. 9.

sciousness, subtler than space, am not anything limited—such is the eternal buddhi (idea) that freeth from the bonds of saṃsâra, the world-process."

The great hymn, Pushpadanta's *Mahima-stuti*, refers to the Supreme in these words:[1]

> "Thou whom the dazzled scripture doth describe
> As being negation of what thou art not."

Put into one sentence such description can take no other form than that of the logion, Ego Non-Ego Non (est).

Such are a very few of the utterances of sacred literature that at once become lighted up when the light of this summation is brought to bear on them. Thus does the Praṇava, the Aum, the sacred word, embody in itself the universe; thus does it include all previous tentative summations; thus is it the very heart and essence of the scriptures; so only is the tradition justified that all the universe is in the Praṇava. Herein we find that what before were the wheels of a machine, apart and dead, are now together and powerful and active as an organism. Herein we find the two great scripture-texts combined into one statement, that gives a new and all-satisfactory significance

---

[1] अतद्व्यावृत्त्या यं चकितमभिधत्ते श्रुतिरपि । Shl. 2.

to them. Herein we see the whole finding of Hegel, and far more besides, included. Herein we see the three propositions of Fichte compressed into one single proposition, which is a re-arrangement of his second proposition.

And it is not only a re-arrangement of it, though that is important enough, but more. If the statement that 'Being is Nothing' is not only external to us but unintelligible, the statement that 'Ego is not Non-Ego' is not yet quite internal, though certainly intelligible. It does not yet quite come home to us. The verb 'is,' and the order of the words in the sentence, make us feel that the statement embodies a cut-and-dry fact in which there is no movement, and which is there, *before* us, but *away* from us, not *in* us. The negative 'not' entirely over-powers the affirmative 'is,' and appropriates all the possibility of significance to itself, so that the rhythmic swing between the Ego and the Non-Ego, between us and our surroundings, which would be gained by also emphasising and bringing out the force of the affirmative 'is,' is entirely hidden out of sight, and only a bare dead negation is left. But now we change the order of the words, and the spirit of the old languages, the natural law underlying their construction, comes to our help. We place the Ego and the Non-Ego in juxtaposition, and an affirmative Relation *appears* between them first, to be followed afterwards by the development of the negative relation in consequence of the negative particle. And, more than this, we replace the 'is' by 'am,' the 'est' by 'sum,' as we have every right to do, for in connection with the Self, with I, अहं, Aham, 'is' has no other sense than 'am'; and in place of the Non-Ego, अनहं, Anaham, we substitute 'this,' एतत्, Etat, for we have seen their equivalence before (*vide* Ch. IV.), and will do so again later, in the section on Mûla-prakṛiti. Our logion therefore now runs as अहं एतत् न, "Aham Etat Na," "I This Not (am)." In the Saṃskṛit form the word corresponding to 'am,' *viz.*, अस्मि, asmi, is not needed at all, for it is thoroughly implied and understood. But as soon as we have the logion in this new form, "Aham Etat Na," we see that there is a whole world more of significance in it than the dry statement of the logical law of contradiction, "A is not not-A," "Ego is not Non-Ego." The one law of all laws, the pulse of the world-process, the very heart-beat of all life is here, now. The rhythm between the Self and the Not-Self, their coming together and going apart, the essence of all change, is expressed by it; and yet, when we take the three constituents of it at once, it expresses changelessness also.

As a man seeking for the vale of happiness, may toil for days and nights through a maze of mountain-ranges and come at last to a dead wall of rock and find himself despairing, and a sudden casual push of the arm may move aside a bush, or a slab of stone, and disclose à passage through which he may rush eagerly to the top of the highest peak, wondering how he had failed to see it all this while, it looks so unmistakable now, and may behold spread clear and still before him the panorama of the scenes of his toilsome journey, on the one side, completed and finished by the scenes of that happy vale of smiling flowers and fruits and crystal waters on the other—such is the finding of this great summation. All the problems that bewildered him before now receive easy solution, and many statements that puzzled him formerly, in the scriptural literature of the nations, begin to become intelligible.

After finding the truth of this great logion for himself the enquirer will find confirmation of it everywhere in the old books, as well as the world around him.

NOTE.—It should be noted here that the references to the Upanișhats, Purâṇas, &c., are not made with any idea of supporting the logion by 'appeals to scripture.' Rather, the intention is to suggest a new way of working with the sacred books, which may be of use to some readers. Whether any definite proofs will or will not be found by experts and scholars, that the logion is and was really meant by the Aum, does not affect its importance as an explanation and summation of the world-process. The logion came to the present writer first in 1887, as the needed explanation of the universe, in the course of his studies in Indian and western philosophy. He then endeavoured to find confirmation of it in Saṃskṛit works, but vainly, for thirteen years. Till the summer of 1900, when these chapters were first drafted, it remained for him only a guess and a possibility that the Aum meant the logion. This guess was justified, for him, in the autumn of 1900, in a most remarkable manner, the story of which will probably be told in a future publication. As to whether that 'remarkable manner' will prove convincing to others is for the future to decide. In the meanwhile, it should be repeated here that the logion should be judged on its own merits, and that the main purpose of quoting from the Upanișhats, &c., is to help on the thought of the reader by placing before him the thought embodied in those quotations as at least working in the direction of the logion.

CHAPTER VIII.

BRAHMAN OR THE ABSOLUTE—THE DVANDV-ÂTÎTAM.[1]

Let us see now if this summation will give us all we want, if it will withstand and resolve all doubts and queries and objections, even as the rod of power wielded by Vasiṣhṭha swallowed up and made nought of all the weapons of Vishvâmittra. Let us test it with questions the most wild and weird and fanciful. If it fails to answer one, it fails to answer all, and we must seek again for another summing up.

Aham Etat Na—this logion, in its entirety, represents with the greatest accuracy that it is possible for words to attain, the nature of the Absolute, the Absolute which so many names and words endeavour to describe—the unconditioned; the transcendent; consciousness that includes unconsciousness; the compactness,

---

[1] द्वन्द्वातीतं, beyond the pairs, *i.e.*, beyond the relative.

solidity, plenum of cognition, knowledge, or thought; the supreme; the indescribable; the unknowable.[1]

This timeless thought, this spaceless idea, taken *as a whole*, changelessly constitutes and is the nature of Brahman. So taken, it is one thought, one knowledge, one cognition, *one single act or mood of consciousness*, in which there is no particular content, but which yet contains the totality of all possible particulars; it is unbroken, pieceless; there is no motion in it, no space, no time, no change, no shifting, no unevenness, but all equality, an all-complete condition of balance and repose, pure, stainless and formless.[2] We can call it unconsciousness also, the absence of thought or cognition or action or any mood at all. For where the This is the whole of the Not-Self, and even that is negated, the consciousness that is left may well be called unconsciousness, as that of the state of sound slumber; it is clearly not

---

[1] अनवच्छिन्नं, अतीतं, परासंवित्, ज्ञानं, ज्ञानघनं, परं, अनिर्देश्यं.

[2] एकाकारं ज्ञानं, निर्विशेषं, अखंडं, निष्क्रियं, कालातीतं, देशातीतं, निर्विकारं, समं, साम्यं, शान्तं, नीरूपं, निरंजनं, &c., are the descriptive words used in Saṃskṛit.

any particular consciousness such as that wherein the particularity of *the* This, as *a* this, *a* that, defines both the subject Self and the object Not-Self. And yet it includes the totality of all such particular consciousnesses, for the Not-Self includes all particular this's.

Taken in two parts the same thought gives: (1) aham etat, I this, *i.e.*, I am this something other than I, a piece of matter, a material or physical body; and (2) (aham) etat na, (I am) not this thing which is other than I, this piece of matter, this material or physical body. Here, in these two sub-propositions, inseparable parts and constituents of the one logion, we have, as we shall see later in detail, the whole process of saṃsâra, saṃsâra which means a *process*, a process of alternation, a movement of rotation, for it is made up of the alternation of opposites: birth and death; growth and decay; inbreathing and outbreathing; waking and sleeping; acceptance and rejection; greed and surfeit; pursuit and renunciation; evolution and involution; formation and dissolution; integration and disintegration; identification and differentiation; differentiation and remergence—such is the essence and the whole of the world-process, at whatever point of space or time we examine it, in whatever aspect we look at it, animate or so-called inanimate, chemical, or mechanical, or physical, or organic, the birth and death of an insect and also each rhythmic wing-beat of that insect, or the birth and death of a solar system and also each vast cyclic sweep in space and time of that system. Why the logion has to be taken in parts and also as a whole, will appear when we study further the nature of the This.

This single logion thus includes within itself both changelessness and change. It includes the fulness of the Absolute-consciousness or unconsciousness, from the all-embracing timeless and spaceless standpoint of which the Self has eternally negated, abolished, and annihilated the Not-Self, in its totality, without remainder, and so left behind a pure strifelessness of perfect balance and repose and utmost peace. It also includes the pseudo-eternal, the pseudo-infinite, the in-de-finite, and, technically, the illusive, mâyâvic, endlessness of incessant identifications and separations, on the smallest and the largest scales, of the Self and the Not-Self, each identification being immediately balanced up by a separation, each separation immediately balanced up by an identification, सर्ग sarga, creation, and प्रलय pralaya, dissolution, following each other in untiring and ceaseless rotation, in order to imitate and show out in time, in an ever-futile and ever-renewed endeavour, that which is complete, always and at once, in the Absolute.

Thus it comes about that the method of the true Vedânta, the repeated super-imposition of an attribute upon the Supreme (object of enquiry and definition), and then the refutation and striking away of it, till all particular attributes have been struck away and the Supreme remains defined as the un-de-*fin*able—that method is also the method of all thought, and the method of the world-process, which is the embodiment of the endeavour to impose material attributes upon the attributeless throughout all time, the endless endeavour to de*fine* Spirit in terms of Matter.

अहं एतत् न, Aham Etat Na—this transcendent संवित्, samvit, thought, consciousness, idea, then, timelessly, spacelessly and changelessly constitutes and is the स्वभाव, svabhâva, the own-being, the nature, of the Absolute, which is also, therefore, identical with the totality of the world-process; such totality being attained not by the endless addition of parts and pieces of time and space as *outside* of us, but by the grasping of the whole of the Not-Self with all space and time as *within* us, so that past and future, behind and before, collapse into the now and the here, and parts are summed up, by *abolition*, in the whole.

What merits and qualifications, or absence of merits and qualifications, that may rightly be sought in and required of the Absolute, without which the Absolute would not be what its name implies, are missing from this? Is not the thought independent of all else? Does it not contain all in itself? The Absolute is the unconditioned. What condition limits this perfect cognition, this complete idea, which is its own end and looks to no end beyond itself, which is also its own means and seeks no means out of itself for its realisation? It is one single act of consciousness, which looks not before or after, to past or future, but is *complete*, and complete *now*, in the eternal present, complete *here*, in the infinite point. The 'I,' holding the whole of the 'Not-I' before itself, denies, in one single moment which includes all time, at one single point which exhausts all space, in one single act which sums up the whole of the world-process in itself, the whole of that 'Not-I,' denies that itself is anything other-than-I, a mighty truism which abolishes and yet covers all possible details of knowledge, for all possible 'not-I's' that may be known are summed up in the 'Not-I' so denied. All possible conditions are within this Absolute idea. All contradictions are within it. All the Relative and all relatives are within it. And yet it is not opposed to them or outside of them, for it indeed is the very substratum and possibility of them, nay, it *is* them, in their entirety, for so taken all together they counterbalance and abolish each other wholly. All divisions are within it, and yet it is unbroken, undivided, consistent, partless and numberless, the beyond number, for the One and the Many are both within it; addition neutralising subtraction, subtraction nullifying addition, multiplication counteracting division, and division completely balancing multiplication; all the possible opposites that constitute the factors of saṃsâra are present in it in equation and equilibration. It is the reconciliation of all opposites. It is निर्गुणं, nirguṇam, attributeless. Being is in it; Nothing or Non-Being is in it too. It is beyond Being and Nothing. It is Being; it is Nothing; it is both; it is neither.[1] And yet it is there, within us, around us, unmistakable. It is the whole, the constant, process of our daily life. "It moveth and it moveth not, far is it and yet near; it is within the heart of

---

[1] नासदासीन्नो सदासीत्. *Rig-veda.* X. cxxix. 1, 2.

नासन्न सन्न सदसन्न महन्न चाणु.

Hymn by Shañkarâchârya.

all, and yet apart from all."[1] It is the all. All is in it. Assertion by it and in it gives existence to the अनात्मा Anâtmâ, the Not-Self; rejection and denial by it and within it impose non-existence on that same Anâtmâ. It sayeth: I (am) This; and the This, the Not-Self, is. It sayeth: (I this) Not-Self (am) not; and the Not-Self is no more. But it sayeth both these things in the same breath, simultaneously. What is the result? This endless process that is ever coming out of nothing into being and vanishing out of being into nothing. We *see* it plainly and yet may not describe it adequately. Truly indescribable, अनिर्वचनीय anirvachanîya, has it been called, as also the world-process which is it. It is the vacuum, the shûnya, शून्य, of the shûnyavâdî,[2] when the Self and the Not-Self are regarded as having neutralised each other in a mutual negation. It is the plenum which is ever full of both, in the affirmation that ever lies implicit and hidden in the heart of the Negation. Two eternals are here in this Absolute, the eternal 'I' and the

---

1 तदेजति तन्नैजति तद्दूरे तदु अन्तिके ।
तदंतरस्य सर्वस्य तदु सर्वस्यास्य बाह्यतः ॥

Îsha-Upanishat. 5.

2 "He who holds the doctrine that all is nothing, a mere vacuum, or that all arises from and goes back into nothing."

pseudo-eternal 'Not-I,' eternal Being and pseudo-eternal Nothing; and yet they do not limit or restrict each other in any way, for there *is* only one eternal, and the other pseudo-eternal *is not*. Beyond space and time are they yet, and therefore beyond limits; and neither limits the other but rather each necessarily fits into the other, or, yet rather, the other is entirely lost in the one. None can take objection to the eternity of a pure Nothing beside the eternity of pure Being; and yet the two are opposed and not identical; and yet also both inhere in and make up the Absolute. If we are inclined to feel that the 'I' holding up to itself and denying the 'Not-I' implies a duality, let us remember what the 'Not-I' is, *essentially*, and what this denial of it by the 'I' amounts to. The 'Not-I' is the Negation of the 'I,' and this denial of it is the Negation of a negation of itself by the 'I.' What objection can there be to the statement that "I am not Not-I," "I am nothing else than I"? Is it not purely equivalent to the statement "I am only I"? And if so, where is the duality in it? A difficulty seems to arise when we think that the pure 'Not-I' is not equivalent to the totality of all particular 'Not-I's.' This difficulty will be dealt with later in an endeavour to show that the pure 'Not-I' *is* equivalent to the totality of all particular 'Not-I's.'

Such, then, is the indescribable of which the totality of the world-process is the endless description. Exact and rigorous and scientific description here perforce becomes a hymn, which may seem mystic to the unscrutinising observer, and yet is strictly accurate. The indescribability of the absolute Brahman is not the result of a powerlessness of thought, but of thought's completion. It is indescribable if we will use only one of the two sets of thought-counters, terms of Being or terms of Nothing, such as are used in dealing with things relative and limited; but it is fully describable if we will use both sets at once.

The names of this Absolute are many, as said before. To fix the nomenclature and prevent confusion, the English word used to describe it in future in this work will ordinarily be the Absolute, and the Saṃskṛit Brahman. Para-brahmaṇ is the same word as the last, with only the intensive and eulogistic para, *i.e.*, supreme, added. One other common and significant Saṃskṛit name for it which should be specially noted here, is the Param-âtmâ—the Supreme Âtmâ, the Supreme Self. In strictness the Absolute is as much the whole of Not-Self as the Self; but it is given the name of the 'Supreme *Self*' especially because the human Jîva, as will be apparent from what has been said before in Chapters IV. and V., arrives *first* at the Pratyag-âtmâ, the inward Self, the universal Self, and being established there, it then includes the pseudo-universal Not-Self within itself, and thus realises ultimately its identity with the Absolute, which it then calls the Param-âtmâ—the Supreme *Self*, because first seen through the universal Self, though now seen also to contain the Not-Self; and because the Self is the element, the factor, of *Being* in the triune Absolute.

As the *Shvetâshvatara* says[1]: "This udgîta, this music-sound, the Aum, is the supreme Brahman. In it are the three, well indicated by the (three) letters. Knowing the secret hidden between them, knowers of Brahman merge therein and (gradually) become free from rebirth." And again: "When with the lamp of the Âtmâ, (the Jîva) beholds the Brahman with all-intentness, Brahman, the unborn, the timeless, the pure of all tattvas, then he becometh free from all bonds."

---

[1] उद्गीतमेतत्परमं तु ब्रह्म तस्मिंस्त्रयं सुप्रतिष्ठाक्षरं च ।
अत्रान्तरं ब्रह्मविदो विदित्वा लीना ब्रह्मणि तत्परा योनिमुक्ताः॥
i. 7.

यदात्मतत्त्वेन तु ब्रह्मतत्त्वं दीपोपमेनेह युक्तः प्रपश्येत् ।
अजं ध्रुवं सर्वतत्त्वैर्विशुद्धं ज्ञात्वा देवं मुच्यते सर्वपाशैः ॥
i. 15.

CHAPTER IX.

THE DVANDVAM[1]—THE RELATIVE.

(*A*) THE PRATYAG-ÂTMÂ—THE SELF.

The Aham, the I, the Self, in the logion is the Pratyag-âtmâ. It is the inward, abstract, universal Self or Spirit, eternal Subject, wherein all Jîvas, individual, particular, concrete spirits, selves, or subjects, inhere. It pervades them all, as the genus pervades all individuals. It *is* all those individuals. The appearance of separateness, the individuation, the differentiation, is caused by matter, Mûla-prakṛiti, as will appear later. In itself, it is the avyakta, the unmanifest, the unspecialised, the unindividualised. It is the One एक, eka, in a special degree. It is the essence, the source and substratum of all similarity, sameness, unity, all oneness. It is Îshvara in the abstract sense, the one Îshvara of all particular Îshvaras—their Self, as also the Self of, and as much as of, the Jîvas that have not yet arrived at the state of Îshvara-hood. It is some-

[1] द्वंद्व the two-and-two, the paired, the double.

times called the Mâyâ-shabalam Brahman, or Saguṇam Brahman, the Brahman conjoined with attributes, enwrapped in, coloured with, Mâyâ. The Upanishats mostly describe it, this Pratyag-âtmâ, and, leading the enquirer to it, finally state that it is identical with Brahman. Such aphoristic utterances, apparently, have led to the confusion which prevails at the present day amongst the vedântîs of the various schools, as to the relation between Pratyag-âtmâ and Param-âtmâ, or Brahman. The great words of the Upanishats refer to the Pratyag-âtmâ: "Unmoving, it outstrippeth the wind; the Gods themselves may not attain to it; it goeth beyond all limitations; by knowledge of it, the Jîva attains to the (first) peace of unity; the white, the bodiless, the pure; the Self-born; smaller than the smallest, yet vaster than the vastest; which cannot be spoken of or seen or heard or breathed, but which itself speaks and sees and hears and breathes; which espouses the enquirer and appears within him of its own law, and may not be taught by another; ever it hides in the cave of the heart; it upholds the three worlds; it divides itself and appears in all these endless forms, and yet is best described by saying, 'not this,' 'not this.'"[1]

[1] *Vide* the *Îsha*, *Kena*, and *Kaṭha Upanishats.*

And then comes the addition: "This Âtmâ is the Brahman."[1] The meaning is that the one *so described* is the Âtmâ, but the same Âtmâ *plus the description, viz., 'not this'*—that is to say, plus the consciousness that 'I am not other than I,' which consciousness is inseparable from, nay, *is* the very being, and the whole being, and the whole nature of the Self—is Brahman.

This Pratyag-âtmâ is the true नित्य, nitya, constant, eternal; the कूटस्थनित्य, kûṭastha-nitya, the changelessly movelessly permanent, as opposed to the परिणामिनित्य, pariṇâmi-nitya, the changefully persistent and everlasting; it is the eternal. While the Absolute may be said to be beyond eternity as well as time—or rather to include them both as eternity *plus* time, seeing that eternity is opposed to time, and the Absolute is not opposed to anything else and outside of it, but contains all opposites within itself—the word eternal, as opposed to temporal, may properly be assigned to the Pratyag-âtmâ in its abstract aspect. As such it is ever-complete and undergoes no change, but is the substratum and support of all changing things and of time, even as an actor of his theatrical attires.

---

[1] *Mâṇḍûkya.* 2.

For concrete illustration, take the case of सुषुप्ति, sushupti, sound slumber, awaking from which the man says: "I slept well, I knew nothing." Knowing *nothing*, *i.e.*, the Not-Self, he was out of time literally, he was at complete rest in the eternal, wherein he felt perfect repose after the day's turn of fatiguing work; whereout he comes back again into time and to the cognition of *somethings*, when the restlessness of desire for the experiences of saṃsâra again overpowers him. The further special meaning of suṣhupti, the meaning of sleep, as of death, may appear later. In the present connection it is enough to refer to this one aspect of it, and to point out that the inner significance of the expression, "the Self knows *nothing* during suṣhupti," is that it, in that condition, positively knows what is technically called Nothing, *i.e.*, the Not-Self as a whole, for the potency, the necessity, of the Being of the Self maintains constantly, in one unbroken act or fact of consciousness, this Nothing or pure Not-Self before that Self. In other words the Jîva, in the short moment of suṣhupti passes almost entirely (for, strictly speaking, it cannot pass entirely, for reasons that will appear on studying the nature of the Jîva) out of the region of the many experiences of particular not-selves, of successive somethings, into the other side, the other facet (and yet not other but rather all-including aspect), of that region, *viz.*, into the region of the single underlying ever-present one experience, one consciousness by the universal Self of the pseudo-universal Not-Self. That the Jîva does not pass entirely out of the state of cognition, a consciousness which is its very nature and essence, is the reason why the thread and continuity of his identity reappears unbroken after the suṣhupti.

As with reference to time, the Self obtains the name of the eternal, co-existently present at every point of time—for all the endlessly successive points of time are co-existent to, and in, its eternal and universal all-embracing consciousness—so with reference to space, its name is the विभु, vibhu, all-pervading, infinite, unextended, or extensionless; and again the सर्वव्यापी, sarva-vyâpî, all-pervading, omnipresent, the simultaneously present at every point of space, for all the endlessly co-existent points of space are simultaneously present in that same consciousness.

Lastly, with reference to motion, its best name seems to be the कूटस्थ, kûṭastha, the rock-seated, or the अविकारी, avikârî, the unchanging, the fixed, or, again, the अंतर्यामी, antaryâmî, the inner watcher or ruler.

Out of the relation of the Self to the Not-Self, as embodied in the logion, there arises a triplicity of attributes in both. The triune nature of the Absolute—the one constant and timeless moment thereof which contains within it three incessant moments—imposes severally on the Self and the Not-Self, three guṇas, गुणाः attributes, properties, or qualities. These three inseparable moments in the Absolute may be thus distinguished: (*a*) The 'I' holds the 'Not-I' before itself, and, so facing it, denies it, *i.e.*, *cognises* the Not-Self's non-entity, its nothingness. This face-to-faceness constitutes the moment of cognition (including sub-divisions to appear later). (*b*) This cognition of the Not-Self by the Self is due to, and is of the nature of, a self-definition by the Self, a constant definition of its own nature to itself as being actually different from all Not-Self, from all things other than the pure Self, which might *possibly* be regarded as identical with itself. *Implied* therefore in this Self-consciousness is the *action* of an identification and a separation of the Self with and from the Not-Self. This is the moment of action, having its sub-divisions also. (*c*) The third moment is that which intervenes between the other two, the inner condition, so to say (for there is no real distinction of inner and outer here), of the 'I,' its tendency or *desire*, between the holding of the 'Not-I' before itself, on the one hand, and its movement into or out of it, on the other. This third moment, of desire, also has sub-divisions, to be developed later. These three moments manifest in the individual Jîva as ज्ञान, jñâna, क्रिया, kriyâ, and इच्छा, ichchhâ respectively.[1] They will be treated of in detail further on. Here it is enough to say that these three moments in the Absolute Brahman appear in the universal Pratyag-âtmâ as the three attributes of चित्, chit, सत्, sat, and आनंद, ânanda, respectively, which are the seeds, the principia, the possibilities and potencies, the universal and abstract aspects, of what in the individual Jîva manifest as jñâna, kriyâ and ichchhâ.[2] Sat, being in a special sense and degree, the principle in consciousness of *act*ual (self-) *assert*ion and (other-) denial, *act*ual identification and separation, putting together and taking apart, corresponds to kriyâ, which alone gives or takes away existence, or particularised being. Chit, con-

---

[1] The English words 'know, con, ken, cognise,' 'create' and 'wish' are apparently derived from the same roots, *viz.*, 'jñâ,' 'kṛi' and 'iṣh,' respectively.

[2] In current Vedânta works the meaning, as generally accepted, of sat, chit, and ânanda, is explained to be being, consciousness, and bliss respectively.

sciousness in its special aspect of cognition, mere holding before oneself of a Not-Self and ignoring it, denying it, knowing it to be not, corresponds to jñâna, which enables a thing to be known as existent or non-existent, true or false. Ânanda, the inner condition of the Self between cognition and action, is that principle of consciousness which connects the other two, is the basis of desire, which leads the Jîva from knowledge into action. It should be borne in mind that these three aspects, sat, chit, and ânanda, are not prior in time to kriyâ, jñâna, and ichchhâ, nor are they in any sense external causes or creators of the latter. They are co-eval with each other in their universal and unmanifested aspect, and are identical with the second triplet, which is only their particular and manifested aspect; even as universal and particular, abstract and concrete, substance and attribute, may be said to be identical. The two cannot be separated, but only distinguished, as before pointed out. Pratyag-âtmâ cannot and does not exist without and apart from Jîvas, and Jîvas cannot and do not exist without and apart from Pratyag-âtmâ. But while in Pratyag-âtmâ consciousness is self-consciousness, which, against the foil of the Not-Self, is self-assertion, self-knowledge and self-desire all in one, all evenly balanced and equal, none greater than the other, all merging into each—so that the Pratyag-âtmâ is often exclusively referred to in the Upanishats by only one of the three attributes, as only ânanda, or chit, or sat—the Jîva is a compound of jñâna, ichchhâ and kriyâ, which, by the necesssary fact of their confinement to particulars, realise their inseparable contemporaneousness only in an endless succession, rotating one after the other, two being always latent, but never absent, while one is patent.

How and why three moments come to be distinguishable in what is partless will appear on fully considering the nature of the second factor in the triune Absolute.[1]

Such then is the Sat-chid-ânanda, the Saguṇa-Brahman, having three attributes as the constituent principles of its being, the three potentialities which are necessarily present in it with reference to the necessary nature of its two co-factors in the Absolute. But we see clearly all the while that it is not personal, not individual, not some one that is separate from other ones, not the single ruler of any one particular kosmic system, but the universal Self, that is the very substratum of and is

---

[1] See the next chapter.

immanent in all such particular Îshvaras, *i.e.*, Jîvas risen to be rulers of world-systems, and all other Jîvas whatsoever.

We may note that the triplicity of attributes in the Self is a reflection of the triuneness of the Absolute: Self, with reference to the Self, whose very being is constant awareness of itself, developes chit; with reference to the Not-Self, which it *posits*—therefore creates, *i.e.*, gives to it the appearance of existence—and denies, sat; with reference to the Negation, ceasing from the restless turmoil of the Many, it shows forth ânanda and the bliss of peace.

This Pratyag-âtmâ is in a sense capable of being worshipped. Worship and devotion may be directed to it in the shape of constant study and recognition of its nature; of constant desire to see and feel by universal love its presence everywhere, and as all selves and in all not-selves; of constant endeavour to realise such presence by acts of compassion and helpfulness and service. Such is the worship of the Âtmâ by the Jîva who, having finished (for that cycle) his journey on the path of प्रवृत्ति, pravṛitti, pursuit, marked out by the first half of the logion, is now treading (for that cycle) the return-path of निवृत्ति nivṛitti and renunciation, which is laid down by the second half of that same logion. To such a Jîva the special Îshvara of his own particular world-system is the higher individuality—of which his own individuality is, in one respect, an integral part—the father of his material sheaths, and the high ideal of renunciation and self-sacrifice whom he is lovingly and devotedly to serve and closely to imitate, as far as may be within his own infinitesimal sphere.

Students who cannot yet quite clearly grasp the nature of the relation between the Self and the Not-Self in its purity and nakedness, cannot yet clearly distinguish the Pratyag-âtmâ from its veil of Mûla-prakṛiti, and yet more or less vaguely realise the universality of the Self, who are in short at the stage of the Vishiṣhṭâdvaita — such students worship the particular Îshvara of their world-system in a vaguely universalised aspect. Still other Jîvas, at the stage of the Dvaita and of the theory of creation, worship only and wholly the individual ruler of their world-system, or a subordinate deity, regarding him as the final explanation of the universe.

The absolute Brahman transcends and includes all worship.

CHAPTER X.

THE DVANDVAM—THE RELATIVE (*continued*).

(*B*) MÛLA-PRAKṚITI OR MATTER—THE NOT-SELF.

We have dealt with the first factor of the triune Absolute, namely the Self. The second factor is the Not-Self. Its many names, each significant of a special aspect, are: अनात्मा Anâtmâ, the Not-Self; अचित्, achit, the non-conscious; जड, jaḍa, the non-intelligent or the inert; नाना, nânâ, the many; ज्ञेय, jñeya, or विषय, viṣhaya, the object; अनृत, anṛita, the false; भेदमूल, bhedamûla, root of separateness; मूलप्रकृति, mûla-prakṛiti, root-nature; प्रधान, pradhâna, the chief, the root-base, of all the elements; मात्रा mâtrâ, the measurer, the mother, matter; and अव्यक्त, avyakta, the unmanifest.[1]

This Not-Self is—by the necessity of the

---

[1] The word मात्रा has, regrettably, dropped out of current use somehow; it deserves restoration, being the same as the well-known English word matter. It is used in this sense in the *Bhagavad-Gîtâ*: मात्रास्पर्शास्तु कौन्तेय शीतोष्णसुखदुःखदाः ii. 14.

Negation of it by the Self, which is the very nature of the Absolute—the opposite of the Self in every possible respect and aspect, as is indicated in the fact that some of its most characteristic names are made up by prefixing a negative to the names of the Self. Because of this fact, as the essential characteristic of the Self is unity, the very essence of the Not-Self is manyness, separateness ; and as the marks of the Self are universality and unlimitedness, so the marks of the Not-Self are limitedness, particularity, ever-specifiedness. As Fichte has said[1] : "All reality is in consciousness, and of this reality that part is to be ascribed to the Non-Ego which is not to be ascribed to the Ego, and *vice versâ*......The Non-Ego is what the Ego is not, and *vice versâ*." Or, as reported by Schwegler[2] : " Whatever belongs to the Ego, the counterpart of that must, by virtue of simple contraposition, belong to the Non-Ego."

This characteristic opposition of the Self and the Not-Self should be carefully considered, together with other aspects of the nature of the Absolute. The solution of the various difficulties, alluded to before, from time to time hinges upon it.

---

[1] *The Science of Knowledge*. P. 83 (Kroeger's English translation). [2] P. 246.

Because nothing particular can be said of the Ego, therefore everything particular, all possible particulars, must be assigned to the Non-Ego. But yet again, lest the totality of these particulars should become a fact different from the Non-Ego instead of identical with it, even as positive is different from negative, these particulars are paired off into opposites. These opposites, again, because particular and definite, are more than presence *and absence*; both factors have the appearance of *presence*, of positiveness, as debt and loan, as pleasure and pain. The pain of a debt is as much a positive burden on the consciousness of the debtor, as the pleasure of a loan is a weight on that of the creditor.

When we are dealing with the ultimate universal and pseudo-universal, *viz.*, Self and Not-Self, Being and Nothing, then even presence and absence are adequately opposed; it is enough to prefix a negative particle to Self and Being. But when we are in the region of particulars, this is not so; positive cold, in order to be neutralised, must be opposed by positive heat, and not merely by no-cold: a positive debt is not sufficiently set off and balanced by a no-debt, but only by an asset; *plus* is not nullified by zero, but by *minus*; a colour is not abolished by no-colour, but by another equally positive complementary colour. It should also be borne in mind, in this connection, that the positiveness of particulars, the reality of concrete things, is, after all, not so very definite and indefeasible as it seems at first sight, but on the contrary, a very elusive and illusive fact. In the ultimate analysis its whole essence is found to be nothing else than consciousness; the more consciousness we put into a thing, the more real it becomes, and *vice versâ*. That a house, a garden, an institution, falls out of repair, or order, and gradually disappears, loses its reality, its existence, if it is neglected by the proprietor or manager—that is to say, if the latter withdraws his consciousness from it—is only an illustration of this on the physical plane. The essential fact is always the same, consciousness upholding itself as well as its object, though the details differ; thus, to maintain its objects on the physical plane, consciousness employs the 'bahish-karaṇa,' the 'outer,' or physical, senses, organs, instruments and means in repairs, &c., while on the mental plane it employs the 'antaḥ-karaṇa,' the 'inner instrument.' As in the case of the individual and his house on the small scale, so, on the large scale, when Brahmâ 'falls asleep' and withdraws his consciousness from it, his brahmaṇḍa, world-egg or system, disappears. We should remember here that the *arrangement* of materials which is the *house*, the *garden*, &c., is, for all purposes, the *creation* of the maker's individual consciousness, and that the other *arrangements* of material which he uses as senses, means and instruments, &c., are also evolved and created by his life or consciousness; and finally that that material, ultimately the Not-Self, over which he as an individual has no power, is the creation of, the result of positing or affirmation by, the universal consciousness, the Self. If these facts are duly taken into account, then the presence of all possible kinds of mutually-destructive pairs of 'reals,' 'concretes,' 'particulars,' within and as making up the total of the Not-Self, equivalent to Nothing or Non-being in its totality, will not appear altogether incomprehensible.

The negative Not-Self thus appears as a mass of paired positives, the द्वंद्व, dvam-dvam, 'two-and-two,' which, while particular and positive from the standpoint of the limited, are yet by the fact of their being paired into opposites by the affirmation and negation contained in the Absolute, always destroying each other by internecine controversy, and so always maintaining and leaving intact the negativity of the negative, considered from the standpoint of totality. This feature of Mûla-prakṛiti is only a reproduction and reflection therein of the essential constitution of the Absolute, which is necessarily the supreme archetype and paradigm for all constitutions within it, there being nothing outside it to borrow from. This being clearly grasped, the famous quill of Krug may now be deduced easily. Where everything must be, the quill also may be, nay, shall be; and not only the quill, but the agencies that destroy the quill. All arbitrariness, all caprice, is done away with by this one statement. Arbitrariness means nothing more nor less than this: one thing *more* than another, one thing *rather* than another, *without due reason*. Where *all are equally*, and none more than another, there is no arbitrariness, no caprice. If we ask why this particular thing at this particular point of space and time, the reply is: In the first place, the particular space and time of the question have no particularity apart from the particular thing which defines them; so that the particular thing and the particular time and space are inseparable, are almost indistinguishable, are one thing in fact and not three. In the second place, all possible orders or arrangements, all possible particulars, cannot *actually* be at the same point of space and time to *one limited* Jîva; and yet they are all there also to him, one *actually* and the rest *potentially*, to satisfy even such a demand; and they are there also actually, *turn by turn*, to that same Jîva. On the other hand, *all* possible orders and arrangements and things are *actually* present also at any one point of space and time; but they are so only when we take into consideration all possible constitutions and kinds of Jîvas, and see that any one order corresponds to one particular kind of Jîva, and thus, the extreme demand that "everything must be everywhere and always"[1] is also justified. Such is the reconciliation of the opposites involved in saṃsâra, and the explanation of its endless flow and flux, its anâdi-pravâha, beginningless flow, as well as its ever-completeness and rock-like fixity. The significance of this will appear more and more as we proceed, for while all laws exist and operate and interpenetrate simultaneously, they cannot, owing to the limitations and exigencies of speech, be described simultaneously. "Speech proceeds only in succession."[2]

We see, then, that the negative Not-Self is a

---

[1] सर्वं सर्वत्र सर्वदा. *Yoga-Vâsiṣhṭha.*

[2] वाक् किल क्रमवर्तिनी। *Yoga-Vâsiṣhṭha.*

mass of positive particulars, and that at the same time, because of its being in inseparable connection with the Self, it necessarily takes on the appearance of the characteristics of the Self, and becomes pseudo-eternal, pseudo-infinite, pseudo-unlimited, so that matter appears as indestructible through all its changes.

Though essentially asat, Nothing, Mûla-prakṛiti is yet pseudo-Being, *i.e.*, existent, sat; though many and particular, yet it has a pseudo-oneness and a pseudo-universality; though limited, it is yet pseudo-unlimited; though finite, it is also pseudo-infinite; though dying, it is also pseudo-eternal. It is pseudo-eternal, because it is not only dying but *always* dying; *always*, in order to keep pace, as it must because of inseparability from it, with the eternal Self. It is pseudo-infinite, because it is not only finite but *everywhere* finite; *everywhere*, in order to avoid separation from that same infinite and omni-present Self from which it may never be separated. The same is the case with all the other characteristics.

Let us now pass on to the question why the logion has to be taken *in parts* as well as in the whole.

By opposition to the unity and unlimitedness of the Self, the Not-Self is many and limited. Under these necessary conditions the Self denies the Not-Self. But while pure Non-Being, *i.e.*, the *whole* of the Not-Self, in being denied, and in order to be effectively denied, becomes simultaneously affirmed, and so becomes a multitude of passing and mutually-destructive particulars, any one of these particulars, by the very reason of its being limited, defined in time and space and motion, is incapable of simultaneous affirmation and denial. Pure Non-Being may without objection be affirmed and denied in the same breath; but a particular limited something, which is *asat* and yet *sat*, which is sad-asat, existent and non-existent, cannot be both simultaneously. And yet it must be both, for Absolute-consciousness contains both the affirmation and the negation. The reconciliation of these contradictory necessities, these two antinomies of the reason, the solution of this apparently insuperable logical difficulty, is found in the 'successive' existence and non-existence of each limited something. This 'succession' is मिथ्या, mithyâ, mythical, a mere illusion, an appearance, because true only from the standpoint of the limited. Pass into the non-limitation of the Self, by turning the consciousness inwards, whenever and wherever you like, and thence into the fulness of the Absolute, and there is no succession. The *whole* of the limited, past, present and future, is *in* that unconditioned thought *at once.* The ever-complete and perfect balance of the Absolute *appears*, to the limited and from its own standpoint, as the successive and continuous balancing of things in saṃsâra. And this *continuity* of succession, this resurrection and rebirth between life and death, this recurrence between existence and non-existence, this becoming between Being and Nothing, this equivocation between affirmation and denial, may itself be regarded as a third part in the logion, completing the triplicity found everywhere because of the tri-uneness of the Absolute.

But lest this appearance of succession should seem to introduce something new and foreign to the svabhâva, the nature, of the Absolute, the safeguard, already mentioned in other words, is provided. While each one of a pair of opposites is succeeded in a later time in the same place (or space) by the other, it is also co-existed with in the same time in another place by that other; for the endless limited positives that make up the pseudo-unlimited negativity or non-being of the Not-Self, in order to do so, must be constantly paired as opposites so that they always counterbalance each other, and so actually leave behind a cipher only, whenever the totality of them may be summed up. Thus a *constant* balance too appears in the world-process, wherein the many co-exist with, as well as succeed, each other. The truth of this may be verified in the daily life of human beings as well as the life of kosmic systems. Life to one means and necessarily implies death to another simultaneously, at the same time, and to that one itself successively, *i.e.*, at a later time. Pleasure to one is pain to another and, again, to that one, in the same way. So with the rise and decay of solar systems. That this must be so is due to the fact that the totality of paired and opposed matter (positive and negative) is fixed, once for all, as the whole, by that unconditioned thought which is the Absolute, and cannot newly be added to or taken away from. Matter is uncreatable as well as indestructible. Therefore what appears as an increase in one place or moment is necessarily due to a decrease in another place and moment, and *vice versâ*. This will appear further in treating of the law of action and reaction.

In these facts, co-existent and successive, combined with the infinity and eternity of the Self—against which they are outlined and which they constantly endeavour to reflect and reproduce in themselves—we find embodied and manifested the continuous movement of all and everything from place to place and moment to moment; and also the recurring return of all and everything, though only in appearance and not in actuality, to the same position in co-existent surroundings amidst its companion-objects, and also to the same position in the successive order and arrangement of those objects.

This thought, if properly followed out, explains the why of recurring cycles in individual as well as kosmic life; why every Jîva and all Jîvas must pass though all experiences and the same experiences, turn after turn; how every finite thing, even a passing thought, an atom vibration, the most evanescent phenomenon, is pseudo-infinite and pseudo-eternal, *i.e.*, endless and everlasting; why there must be an endlessness of veils upon veils, planes within planes, senses beside senses, and elements after elements; why nothing and no one, atom-dust or solar system, on the whole, is really more important than any other; why and how the immortality of the Self is assured to all; and how all are yet always graded to each other and bound up, in ever higher and higher range of unity, in (the) one consciousness.

The considerations which explain why the logion is taken in two, or rather, three parts, also explain how three moments are distinguishable in the Absolute. Indeed, the difference between the three parts and the three moments is only the difference between the third person, on the one hand, and the first and second, on the other, between looking at the Self and Not-Self as Being and Nothing, or as 'I' and 'This.' The simultaneity of past, present, and future; the compression into one point of behind, here, and before; the absence of all movement—these are congenial to the whole, but are not possible to and in the part and the particular. The positing (while denying) of the Not-Self by the Self, the op-posing (while affirming) of the same by the same, the com-posing of (while negating all connection between) the two by means of the Negation —these three facts, while simultaneous in the Absolute, where the whole Self deals with the whole Not-Self, cannot be such where a particular, limited, not-self or 'this' is concerned. They can appear only in succession: first the positing, the moment of jñâna; then the op-posing (after identifying), the moment of kriyâ; and, intervening between them, or, indeed, enveloping them both and holding them together, the com-position, the moment of ichchhâ. And yet, even while so succeeding one another, these moments cannot, as pointed out in the previous chapter, altogether lose the contemporaneousness which belongs to them by right of being in the timeless and successionless Absolute, and which appears in the fact that they succeed not only one another but each other, and in incessant rotation.[1]

Thus is the world-process one vast device, or, rather, one vast mass of devices, for reconciling the opposed necessities of the reason.

Another of the more important consequences issuing from the essential nature, the limitedness, the particularity and manyness, of Mûla-prakṛiti may also be noted here.

The distinctions between thought and thing, ideal and real, abstract and concrete, are all immediately due to this characteristic, and are in reality nothing more than the distinction between whole and part. From the standpoint of the whole, the Absolute, or even from that of the universal Pratyag-âtmâ, all possible varieties of the Not-Self are 'ideal,' are 'thought,' are parts of the 'abstract' Not-Self, *thought* by the Self as negated; but each such variety, from

[1] These facts constitute the metaphysical 'why' of the continuum of consciousness, the theory of which has been propounded by James Ward, and is being elaborated by Stout and others.

its own standpoint, to itself, is 'real,' is 'thing,' is 'concrete.' The present, to that which is present, is the real, while the past and the future are ideal; but to the eternal, wherein past, present and future are all present, all is ideal, or all real. Because all is present in the Pratyag-âtmâ, therefore memory of the past and expectation of the future become possible in the Jîv-âtmâ. All this will be discussed more fully, later on, in connection with the nature of cognition.

We may now consider those special attributes of the Not-Self which stand out with prominence in the Saṃskṛit books. They are सत्त्व, sattva, रजः, rajaḥ, and तमः, tamaḥ. They correspond exactly to the three attributes of the Pratyag-âtmâ, and arise also from the same compulsion of the constitution, the svabhâva, the essential nature, of the Absolute, as described by the logion. It is unnecessary to repeat here all that has been said in this reference before. It will be enough to say that: *(a)* as sat is the principle of action in the Self, so rajas is the corresponding principle in the Not-Self, which makes it capable of being acted on, makes it amenable and responsive to all activity, gives it the tendency to active movement; *(b)* as chit is the principle of cognition in the One, so sattva is the principle of cognisability in the Many; and (c) as ânanda is the principle of desire in the enjoyer, the Subject, so tamas is the principle of desirability in the enjoyed, the Object. They correspond, respectively, to what appears in the particular as कर्म karma, movement, गुण, guṇa, quality, and द्रव्य, dravya, substance[1]; and, again, to the Etat, the Aham, and the Na, respectively, in the Absolute.[2]

---

[1] सात्त्विकस्य ज्ञानशक्ती राजसस्य क्रियात्मिका ।
द्रव्यशक्तिस्तामसस्य तिस्रश्च कथितास्तव ॥
Devi-Bhâgavata. III. vii. 26.

[2] The ordinary current, and, so far, almost exclusively accepted meaning of sattva, rajas, and tamas is different, as in the case of sat, chit, and ânanda. The eighteenth chapter of the *Bhagavad-Gîtâ* deals largely with these three qualities of Mûla-prakṛiti: and they are also defined in the *Sâṅkhya-Kârikâ*. At first sight there seems to be no connection between the meanings assigned here to the two triplets of qualities belonging to the Self and the Not-Self and the meaning assigned in current Saṃskṛit works. When the ordinary vedântî wishes to describe the opposites of sat-chid-ânanda, which he vaguely ascribes to Brahman (without making any definite distinction between Brahman and Pratyag-âtmâ), he speaks of anṛita-jaḍa-duhkha, untrue-unconscious-pain, as characterising what he, again vaguely, calls saṃsâra, the world-process, or prapañcha, the 'quintuplicate' or the 'tangled.' This is, *f.i.*, the phraseology employed in the *Saṅkṣhepa-Shârîraka*. These current acceptations are by no means incorrect, but they are not the 'whole truth.' They are correct only if regarded as expressing one, and a compara-

Such are the three guṇas, rajas, sattva and tamas, or, in the order in which they are usually mentioned sattva, rajas, and tamas—the great qualities of Mûla-prakṛiti. They are here slightly diverted from the order in which the attributes of Pratyag-âtmâ, sat-chid-ânanda, are usually spoken of in order to bring out the opposition and alliance between sat and sattva, or action and cognisability, and chit and rajas or cognition and movement, and finally ânanda and tamas, or desire and substance. With regard to these it has been said that "there is

---

tively less important, aspect or portion of the full significance. A little reflection will show how they naturally arise out of, and are connected with, the interpretations given here. The following statement of the various senses in which each of these six words is used in Saṃskṛit will help to show how thought has passed from one shade of meaning to another:

सत्, sat, is good, true, being, existent, real, asserted or assertable, actual.

चित्, chit, is living, conscious, aware, cognisant.

आनंद, ânanda, is peace, feeling of satisfaction, joy, bliss, pleasure, realisation of desire.

सत्त्व, sattva, is goodness, truth, being, existence, living being, energy, illuminating power, vital power.

रजस्, rajas, is dust, stain, blood, passion, restlessness, activity.

तमस्, tamas, is darkness, dulness, inertia, confusion, chaos, pain, faintness, sleep.

no individual or thing either on earth here or in heaven amongst the Gods, which is free of any one of these three qualities."[1] Their inseparability from each other and from the Not-Self, and therefore from the Self, follows naturally from all that has gone before. The *Devî-Bhâgavata*[2] shows and states clearly how while one quality may, nay must, predominate in a certain individual, the others are never, and can never be, entirely absent, even in the case of the high Gods, Brahmâ, Viṣhṇu and Shiva, who are ordinarily regarded as wholly râjasic, sâttvic, and tâmasic respectively.

The manifestations and results, but not the causes, of these guṇas are spoken of largely in the current Saṃskṛit works. Nor are any detailed statements as to the correspondences between these triplets of attributes, sat-chid-ânanda, rajas-sattva-tamas, kriyâ-jñâna-ichchhâ, and karma-guṇa-dravya, available in the extant books. Of course, it is enough, in a certain sense, to group the contents of the world-process under sattva, rajas and tamas, because, at present, the Mûla-prakṛiti or material aspect is the most prominent in human life; but the full understanding of their significance

---

[1] *Bhagavad-Gîtâ.* xviii. 40.

[2] III. vi. vii. viii. ix.

necessarily requires knowledge of the other triplets.

This Not-Self, the second of the three ultimates of the world-process, is not capable of receiving worship, or of being made the basis of religious practice, except in the way of study, as the object But even so, because it is one of the ultimates, it will necessarily lead in the end to a recognition of the other two, and so to peace. To single-minded, disinterested and unselfish scientists and students of the world of material objects may be applied the words of Kṛiṣhṇa: "They also, ever desirous of the good of all creatures, come ultimately to the Self",[1] as witness the instinctive recognition of the Self in these statements by a man of science: "Science serves life, not life science;" "The world is an idea, or a sum of ideas;" "The actual problem . . . consists not in explaining psychical by physical phenomena, but rather in reducing to its psychical elements physical, like all other psychical, phenomena."[2] It is but natural that such recognition should often be imperfect and often distorted, as witness

---

[1] *Bhagavad-Gîtâ.* xii. 4.

[2] Max Verworn. *General Physiology*, translated into English by F. S. Lee (1899). Pp. 2, 37 and 38.

this other statement of the same man of science: ". . . this monistic conception . . . alone holds strictly to experience . . . and necessarily sets aside the ancient doctrine . . . of the wandering of the soul."[1] But still it is much to have advanced to a recognition of the Self; the correction of inaccurate and hasty deductions is possible only on due study of the nature of that Self, which will show how there may be, or, rather, must be, one Self and monism, and yet also many selves and 'wanderings of souls,' at the same time.

[1] *Ibid.* P. 39.

CHAPTER XI.

THE DVANDVAM—THE RELATIVE (*continued*).

(*C.*—i.) SHAKTI-ENERGY AND NEGATION—AS THE RELATION AND THE CAUSE OF THE INTERPLAY BETWEEN THE SELF AND THE NOT-SELF.

The third factor in the स्वभाव, sva-bhâva, own-being of the Absolute is the Negation, the denial, the 'Not,' or rather the connecting of the 'Not' with the 'Not-I' by the 'I.' From the standpoint of the Absolute this third factor is not a third, any more than the second is a second—for the third is a negation of the second which is Nothing, Not-Being—and where this is so, it also follows that the first is not a first, for there is nothing left to recognise it by as a first, the resultant being a purity of peace as regards which nothing can be said and no exception taken. The full significance of this Negation, which is the nexus between the Self and the Not-Self, will appear when we consider the different interpretations, which turn upon it, of the logion, each correct and illustrated in the universe around us. Thus, the logion Aham Etat Na may mean:

(a) M U A. Not (the) Not-Self (but only the) Self (is).

(b) U A M. (The) Not-self (is, and the) Self (is) Not.

(c) M A U. (Only vacuity, nothingness is, and) Not Self (or) Not-Self.

(d) A M U. (The) Self (is) Not (the) Not-Self; or, (the) Self (is) Not (, to the) Not-Self.

(e) U M A. (The) Not-Self (is) Not (the) Self; or, (the) Not-Self (is) Not (, to the) Self.

(f) A U M. (The) Self (is the) Not-Self (and also) Not (it).

(g) A—U—M. Self——Not Self— Not, the Absolute wherein all possible permutations are.[1]

Such permutations and combinations of the Self and the Not-Self and the Negation, give rise to the actual varieties of facts in the universe and to the corresponding beliefs of man; now to the prevalence of spirit, now to

---

[1] These permutations are based on statements made in the *Praṇava-Vâda*, an unpublished Saṃskṛit MS., referred to in the note at the end of Ch. VII.

the triumph of matter, again to the reign of pralaya; to dreaming, waking, and sleeping; to idealism, materialism, shûnyavâda, pantheism (corresponding to *a*, *b*, *c*, &c., above, respectively) and all other possible forms of belief. But in every case we find the peace of the Absolute left untouched; because the nett result of the three being taken in combination is always a neutralising and a balancing of opposition, which may indifferently be called fulness or emptiness, peace or blankness, the voice, the music, the resonance of the silence; because the three, A, U, and M, are verily simultaneous, are in inseparable combination, are not amenable to arrangements and rearrangements, to permutations and combinations, and these last appear, and appear inevitably, only when the *whole* is looked at from the standpoint of a *part—an* A, *a* U, or *an* M, which is necessarily bound to an order, a succession, an arrangement. And yet also the whole multitude and turmoil of the world-process is in that peace, for 'No-thing,' Not-Self, is 'all things destroying each other,' and Negation is abolition of 'all these particular things,' and the 'I' is that for the sake of which, and in and by the consciousness of which, all this abolition takes place. This is the true significance of the Sâñkhya doctrine that Prakṛiti, the Not-Self, displays herself and hides herself incessantly, only in order to provide an endless foil for the self-realisation, the amusement, of Purusha, the Self. In such interplay, both find everlasting and inevitable fulness of manifestation, fulness of realisation and unfettered recreation.

The why of the movement of this interplay, of to and fro, identification and separation, action and reaction, has been already dealt with, in one aspect, in the previous chapter. It will have appeared from what was said then that the Negation appears in the limited as, first, an affirmation and, then, a negation.

We may now consider a little more fully the nature of the affirmation and the negation. The statement, repeated from time to time, that negation hides affirmation *within* it, and as *preceding* it in time, should be clearly grasped. In the logion, Ego Non-ego Non (est), the bracketed *est*, or *sum*, as it becomes later, is the hidden affirmation. A little reflection shows that it should be so, and must be so, quite unobjectionably, that thought can detect no fault in the fact. Take away the *est* not only from the sentence but really from consciousness, and the remaining three words lose all coherent meaning. To deny a thing it is necessary first to describe it, to allege it as at least a supposition; and to describe it is to give it at least a false, a hypothetical, a suppositious, existence. In order that the Non-Ego may be denied, it must first be alleged as at least a supposition. For this reason, and for the reason that affirmation and negation cannot be contemporaneous in a single, particular, limited, thing, it comes about, as we have seen, that the logion necessarily falls into two parts, (*a*) Ego Non-Ego, and (*b*) Non-Ego Non. The first contains within its expression the implicit word *est* or *sum*, otherwise it has no meaning; and the second part also similarly contains implicitly within it the same word, *est* or *sum*, which alone gives it any significance. For the reasons already partially explained in chapters VII. and IX., the affirmation and negation respectively take on the form of an identification of the Self with the Not-Self, and a separation from it. The mere indifferent assertion, in the third person, of the being or the non-being of the Non-Ego has no interest for the Self; it has no motive for making such an indifferent assertion. Such mere statement about another would have no reason to justify it, to make it necessary, to explain why it came to be made at all. It cannot be said that the Not-Self is a fact, and so has an existence independent of the motives and reasons and interests of the Self, because it has been settled at the outset that the Not-Self is not independent of the Self, but very dependent thereon for all such existence as it has. Therefore it follows necessarily that the assertion and denial of that Not-Self by the Self should be connected with a purpose in the Self, should immediately subserve some interest in that Self. The only purpose and interest that there can be is self-recognition, self-definition, self-realisation. The eternal Self requires nothing in reality from outside of itself; it is only ever engaged in the one pastime of asking: "What am I? what am I? am I this? am I this?" and assuring itself: "No, I am not this, I am not this, but only Myself." This pastime, it must be remembered, which from the standpoint of the 'this' is repeated again and again, is from the standpoint of the 'I' but one single, eternal, and changeless act of consciousness in which there is no movement. Thus, therefore, the affirmation necessarily takes on the form of an identification of the 'I' with the 'Not-I,' and the negation that of the dis-identification, the separation, of the 'I' from the 'Not-I'; and the logion is not merely an indifferent statement of the nonentity of the 'Not-I.'

The affirmation, then, Ego est Non-Ego, not only imposes on the 'Not-I' the Being which belongs inherently to the Self, but also, for the time, makes it identical with the Self, *i.e*, a self; and at this stage, that is to say, in the separation of the two parts of the logion, because the 'Not-I' is always a particular limited something, it takes on its most significant character and name, *viz.*, 'this,' 'idam,' or 'etat,' as it is called in the Saṃskṛit books. Side by side, also, with this change of name of the Not-Self, which does not mean any change of nature, but only the special and most important aspect and manifestation of the nature of the Not-Self, the bracketed *est* becomes *sum*, and the first part of the logion becomes: "I (am) this." In continued consequence of that same reason, the second part of the logion becomes: "This not (am I)," having the same meaning as, "I am not this," with a special significance, *viz.*, that in the actual world-process, in every cycle—whether it be the daily waking and falling to sleep of the individual human being, or the sarga and pralaya, creation and dissolution, of world-systems—the I-consciousness begins as well as ends the day, the period of activity and manifestation. The new-born baby's first shut-eyed feeling in the morning is the vague feeling of a self, in which of course a not-self is also present, though a little more vaguely; and his last shut-eyed feeling in the evening is the same vague feeling of a self returning from all the outward and gradually dimming not-self into its own inwardness and sleep. The order of the words in Saṃskṛit, Aham-Etat-Na (asmi), expresses this fact; and it expresses something additional also, for *asmi*, (I) am, indicates that the individual 'I' at the end of the day's work is, as it were, fuller, has more deliberate and definite self-consciousness, than it had at the beginning thereof.

The 'this,' it now appears, is, in the first place, the upâdhi, the body, the sheath, or the organism, which the individualised spirit occupies and owns and identifies itself with, and again rejects and casts away; and, in the second place, it is all the world of 'objects' with which the spirit *may* identify itself, which it *may* possess and own as part of itself, as belonging to itself, and again renounce, in possibility.

Thus, through the dual nature of the Negation, dual by reflection of the being of the Self and the non-being of the Not-Self, is kept incessantly moving that revolving wheel of saṃsâra of which it has been declared: "That wherein all find living, that wherein all find rest, that which is boundless and shoreless—in that tire-less wheel of Brahman turneth round and round the हंस, ham-sa, the swan, because, and so long as, it believeth itself to be separate from the mover of the wheel; but, recognising its own oneness with that Self that ever turneth the wheel, it forthwith attaineth the peace of immortality."[1] 'Soham,' सोऽहम्, is the Jîva that recognises the identity of the universal Ego with the individual ego in the words सः अहम्, "Saḥ aham," "That am I;" whereas 'ham-sa' (which as an ordinary word, means the migrating swan or flamingo) is the reversal and contradiction of this recognition, and indicates the Jîva that does not recognise its identity with the 'I.' Two arcs and two only, and always, are there in the endless revolution of this wheel. On the first arc, that which is not, the 'this,' appears as if it is; it takes 'name and form,' a 'local habitation and a name,' and predominates over the Self. This is the pravṛitti-mârga, the path of pursuit, whereon the Jîva, the individualised self, feels its identity more and more with the Not-Self, separates itself more and more from the universal Self, runs after the things of sense, and takes them on to itself more and more. But when the end of this first arc of his particular cycle comes, then the Jîva

---

[1] सर्वाजीवे सर्वसंस्थे बृहन्ते तस्मिन् हंसो भ्राम्यते ब्रह्मचक्रे।
पृथगात्मानं प्रेरितारं च मत्वा जुष्टस्ततोऽमृतत्वमेति ॥

Shvetâshvatara, i. 6.

inevitably undergoes viveka and vairagya, thought and surfeit, and turns round on to the other arc, the nivṛitti-mârga, the path of renunciation, when, realising more and more its identity with the universal Self, it separates itself more and more from the things of sense, and gradually and continually gives away all that it has acquired of the not-self to the other Jivas who are on the pravṛitti-mârga and need them. Thus while on the first arc the not-self, falsely masquerading as a self, prevails, and the true Self is hidden, on the second arc the true Self prevails, and that not-self, or the false self, is hidden and slowly passes out of sight. To him who sees with the eye of matter only, incognisant yet of the true Self, the Jîva seems to live and grow on the first arc and to decay and die on the second, and be no more at the end of it. The reverse is the case to the eye of spirit only. What the truth is, of both and in both, is clear to him who knows the svabhâva of the Absolute, and the perfect balance between spirit and matter..

It should be noted here that, inasmuch as the 'this's' are endless in number and extent of temporal and spatial limitation, cycles are also endless in number and extent, ranging from the smallest to the largest, and yet there are no smallest and largest, for there are always smaller and larger; and again cycles and periods of activity are always and necessarily being equally balanced by corresponding periods of non-activity and *vice-versâ*, further reasons for which may appear later on in connection with the law of action and reaction, and the nature of death. Thus sarga is succeeded by pralaya and pralaya by sarga endlessly, on all possible scales, and their minute intermixture and complication is pseudo-infinite; so that the names are justified of नित्यसर्ग, nitya-sarga, constant creation, and नित्यप्रलय, nitya-pralaya, constant destruction. From this complication it results that there is no law belonging to any one cosmic system, small or large, which *the limited Jîva* can divine and work out, *on limited data*, with the lower reason, *i.e.*, the understanding or मनः, manaḥ, of which there is no breach and to which there is no exception; and, again, there is no breach which will not come under a higher law belonging to another and larger system. The pure reason, or बुद्धिः, buddhi, sees the necessity of both, the particular law and the breach of that law, from the standpoint of the all-inclusive Absolute.

Having thus very cursorily indicated some of the most important features of the interplay of the Self and the Not-Self in the world-process, as arising out of the affirmative-negative nature of the third factor of the Absolute, we may next deal with the *cause* of the interplay from another standpoint than that taken up in chapter X, in connection with the question why parts appear in the logion.

It has been said that this multitudinous process of saṃsâra takes place though the Negation, and the word 'necessary' and its derivatives have been used from time to time all along in accounting for step after step of the deduction. It is clear that the Negation, with its included affirmation, is only a description of the Relation between the Self and the Not-Self. It stands between them as a nexus between two termini. It inheres in the two and is nothing apart and separate from them; by itself it can do nothing; but, as being the combined nature of the two, it explains, expounds, accounts for, and supports the infinitely complex process of saṃsâra. This combination of the nature of the two into the dual Negation is the *necessity* of the movement involved in the logion. This necessity requires no support or justification; it is self-evident at every step of the deduction; it plainly inheres in, and is part of the nature of, the three factors of the triune Absolute, which have been sufficiently explained and justified and established before. For, remember, this nature is not three separate natures—or even two separate natures, belonging to three or two separate, or even separable, factors of the Absolute—but is only *one single and changeless nature*, the nature of the 'I' *denying that it is the 'Not-I.'* Whatever may be distinguished or said of the Not-Self and the Negation, or of their nature, can be said only by the courtesy of that supreme nature which is the source, the essence, and the whole, indeed the very nature of what we call their natures. Bearing this in mind, we may easily see that this supreme and changeless nature is *necessity*, *i.e.*, the nature of the *Whole*, that which must be always, that which cannot be changed and avoided. This necessity is the one law of all laws, because it is the nature of the changeless, timeless, spaceless, Absolute; all laws flow from it, inhere in it, and are included within it. It is the primal power, the one force, the supreme energy, in and of the world-process, from which all forces are derived and into which they all return, being inseparate from it, being only its endless manifestations and forms. Its unbreakable and unalterable oneness and completeness appears in the facts of the conservation of energy and motion and the indestructibility of matter, manifesting in ever-new ways, ever-new qualities, but never changed in quantity, for the Absolute may not be added to nor substracted from. It is the absolute free-will which is called in the sacred books by the name of Mâyâ-Shakti, the impersonal Goddess of a hundred hymns and a thousand names. It includes in itself the characters, or rather the single character, of all the three ultimates, and it thereby becomes another expression for and of the Absolute, *viz.*, becoming; thus, Shañkara, for the immediate purpose of his hymn, personifying Shakti in imagination, utterly inseparable though she is from the Absolute, exclaims:[1] "Thou art the consort of the most high Brahman." This necessity is the cause of all causes, **कारणं कारणानां**, kâraṇam kâraṇânâm, and all other so-called necessities are but reflections of it.

We may appropriately consider the meaning of the word cause in this connection. From the standpoint of psychology, as has been shown over and over again by various acute and accurate thinkers in many lands, the world is an endless succession of sense-impressions, and the idea of absolute necessity, which we associate with the successions that are described as cause and effect, is a mere hallucination produced by the fact that a certain succession has been

---

[1] **त्वमसि परमब्रह्ममहिषी**, *Ânanda-Laharî.*

invariable so far as our experience has gone. This view is correct so far as it goes; but only so far as it goes. It does not go far enough. It does not explain satisfactorily the 'why' of the hallucination. Indeed some holders of the view refuse to deal with a 'why' at all. They content themselves with a mere description, a 'how.' But others will not rest within such restrictions. They must understand how and why there come to be a 'how' and a 'why' at all in our consciousness; how and why we talk of 'because' and 'therefore' and 'for this reason.' It is true that every so-called law of nature is only "a *résumé*, a brief description, of a wide range of perceptions"[1], but why is there any uniformity in the world at all, such as makes possible any such *résumé* or brief description?

The explanation of all this is that each 'why,' each generalisation, each law, is subsumed under a wider and wider law, till we come to that final and widest law, the logion, which is the *résumé*, the svabhâva, the nature, of the Absolute, which because of its changelessness requires no further 'why.'

A cause is asked for by the human mind only when there is an effect, a change. We do not ask 'why?' otherwise. We ask it because the very

---

[1] Pearson's *Grammar of Science*. P. 132. 1st edn.

constitution of our being, our inmost nature of unbroken unity as the one Self, "I am I," "A is A," revolts against the creation of something *new*, against A disappearing and not-A appearing, against A becoming not-A. We cannot assimilate such an innovation; there is nothing in that inmost nature of ours to respond to it. We therefore inevitably break out with a 'why?' whenever we see a change. And the answer we receive is a 'because,' which endeavours to resolve the effect into the cause in the various aspects of matter, motion, force, &c., and shows that the effect is really not different from the cause. And we are satisfied, our sense of unbroken unity is soothed. Causality is the reconciliation between the necessity, the fixed unity, of the Self on the one hand, and the accidentality, the flow and flux, the manyness, of the Not-Self, on the other.

But, all the same, it is only a subterfuge, an evasion, a mâyâvic illusion, it is only 'the next best thing' and not the best. For, in strictness, the merest change, the passing of something into nothing and of nothing into something, is impossible, and impossible to understand. True satisfaction is found only when we have reduced change to changelessness. Then we see that there are no effects and no causes, but only steadfastness, rockboundness, and such steadfastness or rockboundness is its own necessity, and requires not any external support. Such rockboundness we find in the logion, wherein all possible sense-impressions, all possible conjunctions and disjunctions of the Self and the Not-Self, are present *once for all*, and therefore in all possible successions. These pseudo-infinite and mutually subversive successions make up the multitudinous *order* as well as *disorder* of saṃsâra, the world-process, which is the contents of the logion. And the shadow of the ever-present necessity of the logion on each one of these successions is the fact, and the source, of the belief about 'cause and effect,' 'reason,' 'why,' 'therefore,' etc. Each one of these successions, because included in the necessity of the logion, *appears* as necessary also, as a necessary relation of cause and effect. And yet it never is in reality necessary, for every law has an exception, and every exception is under another law, as said before; it is only an *imitation* of the one real necessity. The counterpart of this truth is that every particular free-will, while not in reality free at all, *appears* free by imitation of the absolute free-will; and necessity and free-will obviously mean exactly the same thing in the Absolute, Aham-Etat-Na, which is and includes the totality of endless becoming. We may express the same idea in other words, thus: each one of the endless flow of sense-impressions, of motions, of successions, is an effect, of which the totality of them is the one constant cause; or again, the Absolute, or the universe, is its own cause; or still again, the necessity of the nature of the triune Absolute is the *one cause* of all the possible variations and details and movements which fall within and make up that triune, all that endlessness of becoming, as *one effect.*

The whole is the cause of each part within it. This is what we have to studiously realise in this connection, in order to understand the nature of cause, necessity, or Shakti-energy. The simultaneous, the changeless, the ever-complete, the Absolute, is the cause of the successive, the changing, the partial, which, in its full totality as the Not-Self, is always contained within that Absolute. When we so put it, the idea of causation presents no difficulty. But it may be said that the difficulty disappears because the essential idea of causation—one thing *preceding* and giving rise, by some inherent, mysterious, unintelligible power, to another thing which *succeeds*—is surreptitiously subtracted from the problem. To this the reply is that there is no such surreptitious subtraction, but an entirely above-board abolition and refutation of that so-called essential idea, and of every thing and fact that may be supposed to be the basis and foundation of that idea. We show that the idea of necessary causation by some limited thing of some other limited thing is only an illusion, and a necessary illusion, in the same way in which the idea of any one of many individuals being a free agent, having free-will, is an illusion and a necessary illusion. The one universal Self is free, obviously, because there is nothing else to limit and compel it. Here the word 'free' may, from one point of view, be well said to have no significance at all; but from another, it has a whole world of significance. Now, because every self is *the* Self, therefore it also must be free by inalienable birthright. And yet, being limited, being hemmed in on all sides, being not only the Self, but also a not-self, how can it be free? The reconciliation is that every individual Jîva *feels* free, but *is not* free; it is free so far as it is the one Self, and it is not free so far as it has made the 'mistake,' avidyâ, of identifying itself with a piece of the Not-Self. It is now generally recognised, and so need not be proved in detail here newly, that the idea of *necessity* present in our idea of causation is a purely subjective factor, not justified by anything or any experience outside of us. The outside world shows only a repeated succession, which by itself is never sufficient to substantiate any notion of invariable, inherent, *necessary*, power of causation. This element of the idea comes from within us, from the Self, from our self as willing, as exercising a power of causation, from our indefeasible feeling of an exercise of *free-will*, though that again, because limited and dealing with the limited, the material, is naturally always resolvable, on analysis and scrutiny, into physical forces. We thus see that the two ideas are intimately connected, nay, are different aspects of the same fact—the idea of necessary causation and the idea of causation by free-will. And as the one is an illusion, so is the other, neither more nor less. And we can *understand* both only by understanding how the changing is contained in the changeless—that there is in reality no change; that there is in reality no succedence and no precedence, but only simultaneity; no causation of one part by another part, but only the unarbitrary co-existence of all possible parts, by the one changeless necessity of the nature of the Absolute; and that whatever appears as a particular necessity of any special relation between one part and another part is only an illusive reflection, appearing from the standpoint of the particular parts concerned, of the One in that particular many. The necessity of the changeless we can understand; indeed we can understand it so well that we are almost inclined to call it a truism. The necessity of the changing is what we cannot understand, and are very anxious to understand; but we can *never* understand it, as we imagine and describe the fact of change to ourselves, because it is the very reverse of a truism, its opposite extreme, because it is false, not a fact, because *there is no change.* And only by understanding this can we understand the whole situation, by reducing change to changelessness, by realising that while from the standpoint of the successive particular 'this' there *appears* change, from the standpoint of the transcendental universal Self it *disappears* altogether in the rock-like fixity of the constant negation of the whole Not-Self, *i.e.*, of *all* the parts of the many Not-Self, at once, by the Self.

A slight illustration may perhaps help to make the thought clearer. A large library contains millions of different permutations and combinations of the words of a language, each permutation or combination having a connected serial as well as individual meaning. The library, as a whole, contains all these *at once* in an ever-complete and finished condition. Yet if any individual character out of the thousands whose life-story the library contains endeavoured to picture out its own life-story, realise it in every point, it would do so in what would appear to it, from its own standpoint, only a *succession*. In the library of the universe, the number of volumes is endless, and each volume is a life-story without beginning or end, the sole author is the one Self, the readers are also pseudo-infinite in number and pseudo-eternal in time, and they also are all only the author himself, the one Self, and each volume, again, tells only one and the same story, but in an order different from that of every other. Or take this other case, which may come even nearer home. Each one of us is living in the *whole* of his body, at every point of it, and at every moment of time. But let him try to define, to realise, to throw into distinct relief, his consciousness of every one of these points of his body. So far as he can do so at all, he will be able to do it only in succession. The whole of the universe, the whole of the Not-Self, is the body of the Self. It lives in it at each point of it, completely, at once, and in the way of innumerable mutually contradictory and therefore neutralising and counterbalancing functions; and it lives in each one of these points in the same way as in every other. Each point, to itself, therefore, *seems* to live in these innumerable ways and functions, in an endless succession which constitutes its immortal life.

The nature of this endless becoming, this endless world-process, this cause and effect combined, is embodied in that most common and most significant name of Shakti-energy, *viz.*, माया, Mâyâ, even as the whole nature of the Absolute is embodied in the Praṇava.

Mâyâ, as explained by the books on Tantra,[1] is या मा, yâ-mâ, reversed, yâ and mâ being two complete Saṃskṛit words meaning, when put together as a sentence, 'that which is not,' *is* as well as *not*, sad-asat, existent and not-existent, truly mysterious to the outer view. The extant Tantra-books, dealing with Shakti in a personal aspect, give to it a hidden name consisting of the single letter इ, 'i,' even as they call various other Gods by single letters.[2] This letter stands naturally between 'a' and 'u,' as should also 'm' being only the outer sheath of 'i,' though it is thrown to the end because of the fact that it appears as negation *after* affirmation. But this 'i' placed between 'a' and 'u' coalesces with and disappears entirely into the 'a,' in the conjunction which brings out of the joined vowel-

[1] The Tantra-shâstra is a very important class of Saṃskṛit literature. of which only the veriest fragments are now extant. It seems to have dealt with many departments of physical science, especially in their bearing on yoga-practice.

[2] See the *Târasâropaniṣhat* for instances.

sounds, 'a' and 'u,' the vowel-sound 'o,' for Aum is pronounced as *Ōm.*[1] This is in accordance with the grammatical rules, allowing of a double sandhi[2] (coalescence of letters), of archaic Saṃskṛit, the deliberately 'well-constructed,' the 'perfected' language, the complete grammar of which, if we only had it, would show, as tradition says, in the articulate development of vibration after vibration, sound after sound, letter after letter, word after word, and sentence after sentence, the corresponding articulate development of the world-system to which that language belongs. That this coalescence and disappearance is just, is plain from all that has been said as to the nature of Shakti, which ever hides in the Self, and disappears into the Not-Self whenever the Self acts[3] upon that Not-Self, and goes back again

---

[1] This is taken from the *Praṇava-vâda*, mentioned before.

[2] Instances of this are frequently met with in such ancient works as the *Râmâyana*, the *Mahâbhârata*, and the Purâṇas.

[3] This it does, it must be remembered, in the one single way of lending to, and at the same time withdrawing from, the Not-Self its own being. प्रकृतिं पश्यति पुरुषः प्रेक्षकवदुपस्थितः सुस्थः । "Purusha, fixed, self-contained, like a spectator, *witnesseth* Prakṛiti."—*Sâṅkhya-Kârikâ.* Verse 65. This *beholding*, this *witnessing*, by the Self is the *affirmation* by it of Prakṛiti, the Not-Self, which affirmation alone gives to it all the existence it has; it is Consciousness which energises and makes possible all the phenomena that physical science deals with.

to the Self through and after the Negation. When we endeavour to consider it apart from the others it will still not be separated from the 'm,' and then, too, it will identify itself with the *hidden affirmative*, whereby power *manifests* and *appears forth* in many-formed results and effects, rather than with the overt negative. This has been indicated in exoteric Hinduism in the relation between Shiva and His consort Gaurî; Gaurî, in her many forms, is the implied and affirmative aspect of ichchhâ, while Shiva is its overt aspect of destruction and negation only; in His being this Gaurî hides inseparably as veritable half of His frame, so that the hymns addressed to her declare that "it is only when conjoined with her, the primal Shakti, that Shiva becomes able to prevail and energise, and otherwise knows not even to stir."[1]

Because of its special connection with the Negation is this necessity, this Shakti, treated of together with the Negation, and not as a fourth ultimate. This ever-present *necessity*, the nature of the triune Absolute, of the succession of the world-process, *appears as* and is that which we call Shakti, might, ability, power,

---

[1] शिवः शक्त्या युक्तो यदि भवति शक्तः प्रभवितुं ।
न चेदेवं देवो न खलु कुशलः स्पंदितुमपि ॥

Saundarya-Laharî.

force, energy, etc. In other words, as negation is the *nature* of the relation between the Self and the Not-Self, so this necessity, which inheres in the combination of the three and is not separable from any, may be regarded as the *power* of that nature of the Self and the Not-Self which makes inevitable that relation. This relation immediately flows from, or better, is only another form of that necessity, and the necessity is therefore treated as being more closely connected with the relation, *i.e.*, Negation, than with the other two factors of the Absolute. In this Mâyâ-Shakti we see repeated the trinity of the Absolute, the primal impress of which is always appearing and reappearing endlessly everywhere. Each of the factors of the Absolute repeats in itself, over again, that trinity in the shape of corresponding aspects. In the Pratyag-âtmâ, the sat corresponds to Etat, the manifest seat of action, whereby the existence of the Self appears; the chit corresponds to the Aham, which is the manifest seat of knowledge; and ânanda to the Na (asmi) wherein lies the principle of affirmation-negation, attraction-repulsion, *i.e.*, desire. In Mûla-prakṛiti again, rajas, activity, corresponds to Etat; sattva, illumination, knowability, to Aham; and tamas to Na (asmi), denial, darkness, inertia, substantiality, possessibility. In the

Mâyâ-Shakti of the Negation, the triplicity appears as the energy of: (*a*) affirmation, attraction, enjoyability, आवरण, âvaraṇa, enveloping, corresponding to the Aham; (*b*) negation, repulsion, distraction, flinging away, विक्षेप, vikṣhepa, corresponding to the Etat; and, (*c*) the revolution-process of alternation, balancing, साम्य, sâmya, corresponding to ânanda, the spiral dance of Shiva, tamas and the Na.[1] The meaning of this may become fuller and fuller as we proceed, for no work, that endeavours to describe the essence of the world-process, can help imitating that process more or less, combining the simultaneity of all and everything in the Absolute with its gradual development in fuller and fuller

---

[1] There is no current triplet of Saṃskṛit words, like sat-chid-ânanda, or sattva-rajas-tamas, to express the three guṇas, or aspects, of Shakti spoken of in the text above. The words used here, at least the first two of them, are met with in the extant works of Advaita-Vedânta, as describing aspects of Mâyâ-Shakti, but in a somewhat different sense. Possibly the powers of सृष्टि, sṛiṣhṭi, emanation, throwing forth, स्थिति, sthiti, maintenance, keeping together, and लय or संहार, laya or samhâra, reabsorption, destruction, neutralisation, balancing up, which are currently ascribed to Brahmâ, Viṣhṇu, and Shiva, or rajas, sattva, and tamas, respectively, mean the same three aspects in essence. Looked at in another way, samhâra would be reabsorption or attraction, sṛiṣhti would be throwing forth or repulsion, and sthiti would be maintenance or the balancing of the two. In this view, the correspondences of the triplets would also have to be read differently. As to these variations see the remarks in the next chapter.

repetition in the succession of 'the relative' of the world-process.

This Mâyâ-Shakti is said to be the movement and the intelligence of all the worlds;[1] it is their whole wisdom and whole wealth; it is the power of desire for the maintenance of the worlds' things, and also for their destruction. Many are its aspects and corresponding names. One half of it—that appears in the affirmation, "I (am) this"—is the अविद्या, avidyâ, the nescience, the error, the illusion, the imperfect knowledge, the separative intelligence, that binds the Jîva to the first arc of the wheel of saṃsâra. The other half—that is embodied in the negation—appears as the vairâgya and the विद्या, vidyâ, the satiation with the pleasures and the sorrow over the pains of the world, and the discrimination, the knowledge, the clear understanding, of the distinction between the permanent and the transient, that lead the same Jîva on to the second arc of the wheel. In its completeness, it is the महाविद्या, mahâ-vidyâ, the fulfilled and perfected knowledge, the unifying wisdom of buddhi and pure reason, that frees the Jîva from all bondage, makes of him an Îshvara (in the strict and technical sense), and guides his life on that second arc in that condition of yoga, union, of reason with desire,

---

[1] Symbolised as राधा and दुर्गा respectively (vide *Devî-Bhâgavata.* L. ix.)

which makes the true free-will of a deliberately universal love and so confers true liberty, true mukti.

They that desire to grasp or fling away the things of the world, physical or subtle, worship Shakti in her form of avidyâ, or vidyâ, in one or other of their many aspects; they that desire the wealth and fulness of the spirit worship her as महाविद्या, mahâ-vidyâ, the great wisdom. Each worship leads on, in course of time, by cyclic necessity, to the next. The worship of mahâ-vidyâ is the same as the worship of Shakti's true lord, the Pratyag-âtmâ, whose supremacy she ever insists on, and, in dutiful and loving subordination to whom and for the fulfilment of whose universal law of compassion to all selves, she—as Gâyatrî, the mother of the Vedas, the wisdom-illumined will that knows how to draw upon the inexhaustible stores of nature—confides high sciences and powers gradually to the Jîvas walking on the path of renunciation, for the humble service and helping of all fellow-Jîvas.

One point should be specially noted here. As there is much confusion in the extant Saṃskṛit works between the Pratyag-âtmâ and the Param-âtmâ, so there is also much confusion as regards Shakti and Mûla-prakṛiti or Prakṛiti. Because Shakti is connected with both Pratyag-âtmâ and Mûla-prakṛiti and is herself hidden, there is a natural tendency to regard her only as the one or the other. Throughout the *Deví-Bhâgavata*, for instance, she is now identified with the Self, mentioned under the epithet of Shiva, and now with Mûla-prakṛiti. Thus Shakti, personified, is made to say: "Always are He and I the same, never is there any difference betwixt us. What He is, that am I; what I am, that is He; difference is due only to perversion of thought." But the distinction is also pointed out at the same time: "He who knows the very subtle distinction between us two, he is truly wise, he will be freed from saṃsâra, he is freed in truth."[1] Again it is said: "At the beginning of creation, there were born two shaktis, *viz.*, prâṇa and buddhi, from samvit, consciousness, wearing the form of Mûla-prakṛiti."[2] Of course it is true, in the deepest sense,

---

[1] सदैकत्वं न भेदोस्ति सर्वदैव ममास्य च ।
योसौ साहमहं योसौ भेदोस्ति मतिविभ्रमात् ॥
आवयोरंतरं सूक्ष्मं यो वेद मतिमान् हि सः ।
विमुक्तः स तु संसारान्मुच्यते नात्र संशयः ॥ III. vi. 2, 3.

[2] मूलप्रकृतिरूपिण्याः संविदो जगदुद्भवे ॥
प्रादुर्भूतं शक्तियुग्मं प्राणबुद्ध्यधिदैवतम् ।
IX. 1. 6, 7.

that Shakti is *not* different from the Absolute, but only its very nature, svabhâva, and, as Mûla-prakṛiti is included in the Absolute, therefore Shakti may also be identified with Mûla-prakṛiti, without which it cannot manifest and truly would not *be*. At the same time it is desirable and profitable to make the distinction—even though a distinction without a difference—from the standpoint of the limited, wherein thought must be, and has deliberately to be, taken in its 'perverted,' successive and partial form.

In the *Bhagavad-Gîtâ*,[1] also, Kṛishṇa speaks of his दैवी माया daivî mâyâ, 'difficult to cross,' 'difficult to escape and transcend;' his दैवी प्रकृति, daivî prakṛiti, divine nature or power; and again of his two prakṛitis, अपरा aparâ, the lower, and परा, parâ, the higher, describing the former as consisting of the various elements which the Sâñkhya describes as issuing from Mûla-prakṛiti, and the latter as being the life of the Jîvas that upholds the world. The meaning of such passages would probably be easier to follow if what has been said above as to the nature of the Self, the Not-Self, and the Energy which is born of, or, rather, *is*, the necessity of the nature of these two, is borne in mind. As avidyâ, this primal

---

[1] *Bhagavad-Gîtâ*. vii. 14; ix. 13; vii. 5.

Energy turns more towards the Not-Self and becomes the aparâ-prakṛiti, which name is used to cover not only the force which leads the Jîva outwards, but also the manifestations of the Not-Self which it especially brings out and into which it leads the Jîva. As vidyâ, it turns more towards the Self, and is the parâ-prakṛiti, the source of life, nay; which, as consciousness, in the Self of the Not-Self, *is* life, and so includes all Jîvas. As the two together she is daivî-prakṛiti, in which vidyâ and avidyâ coalesce into the mahâ-vidyâ, regarded not as knowledge, but rather as the Shakti, the Energy, which utilises all-knowledge, for the carrying on of the world-process.

CHAPTER XII.

THE DVANDVAM—THE RELATIVE (*continued*).

(*C.—ii.*) SHAKTI-ENERGY AND NEGATION—AS THE CONDITION OF THE INTER-PLAY BETWEEN THE SELF AND THE NOT-SELF.

In the last chapter we dealt with the affirmative aspect of the Negation, as the energy which links together in an endless chain of causality the factors of the succession of the world-process, as the necessity of the whole which appears as the *cause* of each part, the *relation* of cause and effect between all the parts. We turn now to the negative aspect of the Negation, wherein it appears as the *condition*, or conditions, of the interplay between the Self and the Not-Self, the *conditions* in which the succession of the factors of the world-process appears and takes place.

A little reflection will show that *cause* and *condition* are only the positive and negative aspects of the same thing. A cause may be said to be a positive condition, and a condition a negative cause.

Let not the objection be taken here that we are transporting, by an anachronism, the notions of our life at the present day to a primal stage wherein pure ultimates and subtle undeveloped essentials of the universe only should be discussed. It has been pointed out over and over again that there is no gradation, no development in time, from the abstract to the concrete. The two underlie and overlie one another and are co-existent. And even were it otherwise, that which appears in development must have been in the seed all along. The world-process is in and is the Absolute. Metaphysic only endeavours to trace each abstract and concrete fact of our life, taking it, as it stands before us, back into its proper place in the Absolute, in the changeless whole, and so freeing us from the night-mare of change. Therefore taking the words 'cause' and 'condition' in the sense in which we find them used to-day, we may legitimately try to show that these senses correspond to aspects of the ultimates.

We find, then, as just said, that a cause and a condition may be regarded as the positive and the negative aspects of whatever is required to bring about an event. Other ways of looking at them are to regard causes as persisting conditions, and conditions as co-existing causes; or to say that causes are conditions which cease to exist when the effect begins to exist, and that conditions are causes which persist throughout the existence of the effect as well as before and after; and so on. Looked at from the standpoint of the Absolute, inasmuch as everything is necessarily connected with everything else, and the whole only is the source of each part, all these various ways of describing cause and condition resolve themselves into merely various ways of describing the different relations, all equally necessary, of facts, or parts, to each other. Out of these various ways we have the many distinctions between final cause, efficient cause, material cause, formal cause, instrumental cause, movement or action, motive, &c., in western philosophy; and between निमित्त, nimitta, समवायि or उपादान, samavâyi or upâdâna, असमवायि, asamavâyi, सहकारि, sahakâri, असाधारणनिमित्त or अमुख्य, asâdhârana-nimitta or amukhya, उद्देश्य, uddeshya, कर्ता, kartâ, क्रिया, kriyâ, कार्य, kârya, प्रयोजन, prayojana, etc., with their divisions and sub-divisions, in the eastern systems.

The one common characteristic of cause, running throughout all these, is that which is given by the old Nayyâyikas: that "which being, the effect becomes, and, which not being, the effect does not become,"[1] the principle of concomitant variations, in short, as called in western philosophy. The first half represents the positive aspect, the one true universal cause, corresponding to the Self, the affirmation, the Shakti element of the Negation; and the second half the negative aspect, the one true universal condition, corresponding to the Not-Self, the denial, the negative element of the Negation; whereas all other so-called particular causes or conditions are in reality only so many *effects*, which have taken on a false appearance of cause or condition by reflection—in the *succession* of the world-process—of the true universal necessity which makes each particular a necessary fact, and so a cause and a condition, with reference to all other particulars; that is to say, makes each particular appear as the necessary effect of preceding, and the necessary cause of succeeding, particulars, in an endless and unbreakable chain, the whole of which chain, however, is only *one effect* which is identical with its *one cause*, the necessity of the Absolute.

We thus see that the Self or spirit and the Not-Self or matter are, neither of them, either cause or effect; but that the *changes* of cogni-

---

[1] Bhîmâchârya. *Nyâyaskosha.* P. 197. Article कारणम्, kâraṇam, cause.

tion, desire and action, and of qualities, substance, and movement, of which they are the forum or substratum, are causes or conditions, and effects or results, of one another in turn, and that the totality of these changes, being regarded as one effect and result, has for *one cause* the Shakti-energy, and for *one condition* the Negation, embodied in the third factor of the Absolute.

This Shakti-energy, we have seen, has three aspects: attraction, repulsion, and rhythmic alternation or revolution—or creation, preservation, and destruction. The Negation proper has also three aspects: देश, desha, space, काल, kâla, time, and अयन, ayana, motion. These are the triple guṇas, or aspects, of the Negation, in the same way as sat-chid-ânanda and sattva-rajas-tamas are the guṇas of Pratyag-âtmâ and Mûla-prakṛiti respectively. The Negation, with respect to the one limitless Self, in whose consciousness the Not-Self, the endless many, are co-existent, is negation *everywhere*, is the utter blankness of pseudo-infinite and kûṭastha-seeming *space*. The Negation, with respect to the Not-Self, the pseudo-infinite many, which find themselves realised in that consciousness turn by turn, is negation in *succession*, is pseudo-infinite and flowing *time*. The Negation with respect to Negation, is the endeavour to affirm, to justify, the consciousness of the inseparable connection between Self and Not-Self *everywhere* and *always*; this can be done only in and by means of an endless *motion*, which is the one way to encompass all space and time—motion, in and by which only space and time are joined together and realised, even as the Self and the Not-Self are realised in and by the Negation.

Let us dwell for a moment on the fact that space, time and motion are the guṇas, the qualities, of the Negation. We see readily, on even slight reflection, that space and time are mere emptinesses, vacua, which may appropriately be regarded as phases of the Na, the Not, the naught. Motion presents a little more difficulty. We seem to feel that it is something positive. Yet this is due only to the fact that we are thinking more of the *moving thing* than of its *motion*. Let us try to think of motion as separate from the moving thing, even as we think of space and time as separate from extended or enduring things, and we shall see at once that it is as much an emptiness as the latter; indeed is nothing else than an emptiness which combines in itself the emptinesses of the other two, since we know space and time only by motion. It is thus doubly empty. Space seems, time seems, to leave a trace behind. More, we feel as if space *is*, *there*, always, before us; we feel that even time *is*, *there*, always. We speak of even the past and the future as if they were something positive, something recoverable, something contained, locked away, in the present which we hold in our hands. But motion?—it is gone and has left no trace; lines traced on running water. Of course the moving or the moved *thing* may remain, but that is not motion, any more than it is space or time. Motion, then, is verily the most negative of negations.

Another point. Space, time, and motion have been shown here as corresponding to Self, Not-Self and Negation respectively. But too much stress should not be laid on, nor too much precision expected in, these correspondences. Where everything is connected with everything, the distinguishing of such correspondences can only mean that certain facts, as viewed from a certain standpoint, are seen to be more specially in connection with each other than with others. Change the standpoint slightly, and new connections are thrown into relief and old ones retire into the shade. This is seen to be the case more and more as we proceed from the simple to the complex. In the very instance now before us, for example, with reference to the fact that the

Negation is the nexus between the Self and the Not-Self, motion may be said to correspond to Negation, as also being a nexus between space and time. But take another triplet into consideration now: jñâna-ichchhâ-kriyâ. Here, while it may be said that the condition of chit or jñâna is space, implied in the co-existence of subject and object, knower and known, it does not seem quite fitting to say that the condition corresponding to sat or kriyâ is time, and to ânanda or ichchhâ is motion. Of course it would not be altogether incorrect to say even this; yet it seems more obvious to say that kriyâ corresponds to motion, and ichchhâ to time, which, in terms of consciousness, is memory of past pleasure and pain, and present expectation or wish to secure the one and avoid the other again in the future. On the other hand, we may not unjustifiably say that motion corresponds to ichchhâ, because ichchhâ implies a movement from the past through the present towards the future; and that the succession involved in kriyâ is time. Or, again, we may consider the matter without inaccuracy in this manner: space is something overt, almost visible one may say; motion is also overt, something visible; but time is hidden, it is a matter for the inner consciousness only, as ichchhâ is the hidden desire between an overt cognition and an overt action; therefore, while space and motion may correspond with the overt Self and Not-Self, time should correspond with the hidden Negation. Arguing from the mere words also, one may say that the Self and the Not meet in the Not-Self, therefore space and time, meeting in motion, should be assigned to Self and Negation, respectively, while motion should be assigned to the Not-Self. Still again we may correctly say that time is realised only by change, *i.e.*, motion, and motion is possible only in space, therefore space is the meeting-point of the two and so should correspond to the nexus, *i.e.*, the Negation. And so on. We see thus that from different points of view, one and the same thing appears in different aspects. For the present, seing that motion has almost unanimously been regarded, in the east and in the west, as incorporating both space and time, we may accept the correspondence noted first, *viz.*, that of space, time and motion, to Self, Not-Self and Negation, respectively, as the most prominent.

Let us now take up each of these three separately.

(*A*) SPACE.

Space is the *co-existence*, सहास्तिता, sahâ-stitâ, सहभाव, saha-bhâva, of the many. It is the possibility of the co-existence of the many, and the actuality of their non-existence. The Self is one and opposed to the many at once and eternally; hence the co-existence of the countless not-selves as well as their endless succession. The form and result of their co-existence is mutual exclusion, which produces the duality of 'side by side,' 'one beside another,' with the intervening space 'between,' as the completing third which connects the two, one on each side. This triplicity of 'side, beside, and between,' पार्श्व or पक्ष, pârshva or pakṣha, अपरपार्श्व or अपरपक्ष apara-pârshva or apara-pakṣha, and अंतर, antara, appears in space as viewed from the standpoint of the Not-Self.

Viewed from the standpoint of the Self, space may also be said to be the co-existence of the Self and the Not-Self. But the co-existence of these two is scarcely a *co*-existence. Such co-existence can properly be ascribed only to things of the same kind and nature, on the same level, and side by side with each other; while Self and Not-Self are opposed in nature; the one is Being, the other is Non-Being. Their co-existence is only through and in the way of the third factor, Negation; *i.e.*, the Not-Self does not exactly *co*-exist with the Self; it rather exists *in* it, in its consciousness, and exists only to be denied. Hence we have another form, though not essentially different in nature, of spatial relations, than that described above as 'side, beside, and between.' This other form is that of 'in and out,' अन्तः, antaḥ, and बहिः bahiḥ, 'internal and external,' 'core and sheath,' both held together in the 'through and through,' सर्वतः, sarvataḥ, the 'pervading,' व्याप्त, vyâpta, the 'whole.' Thus we have another triplicity in space as with special reference to the Self. In this, again, from the standpoint of the universal Self, that Self is the enveloping space, pure, colourless, abstract, in which the etats live and move, and so it may be said to be the outer and the Not-Self the inner. It is this aspect of the Self, the Pratyag-âtmâ, which has probably given to the Param-âtmâ its best-known name of Brahman, boundless immensity, from the root बृह्, bṛih, to grow, to expand, to be vast. But from the standpoint of the individual, an aham limited by an etat, Self is the inner core and Not-Self the outer sheath.

We may distinguish another form of the triplicity of space, as with reference to the Negation, *viz.*, 'point, radii, sphere,' बिंदु, bindu, व्यास, vyâsa (strictly, व्यासार्ध, vyâsârdha), गोल, gola. The other triplets of words too express nothing else than emptiness and negation, but this mathematical triplet seems to be even more abstract, more empty of content, if possible;

hence the propriety of regarding it as arising from a view of space with special reference to Negation.

Other ways of expressing the triplicity involved in space may be said to be 'behind, here, before,' and 'length, breadth, and depth, which last is the best known and most commonly mentioned form of the dimensions of space.

As the mathematical kinds of motion are pseudo-infinite, as the standards and measures of time are pseudo-infinite, so the degrees and measures of space or extension are also pseudo-infinite. There are always, and *ad infinitum*, etats minuter than the minutest and vaster than the vastest. As minute vibrations of motion permeate grosser sweeps, as subtler standards of time permeate larger measures, so smaller sizes and dimensions permeate and pervade larger sizes and dimensions. In this sense, as with motion and time so with space, there are not only a certain number, but necessarily a pseudo-infinite number, of dimensions. Otherwise, the triplicity described above, in various triplets of words, represents the three dimensions proper of space, all other dimensions, subtler or grosser, being but permutations and combinations of these three.

The meaning of this will appear further in connection with the pseudo-infinite लोकाः, lokâḥ, *i.e.*, planes, grades, kinds or regions of matter, each made and marked by a differently vibrating atom; each supporting, serving as the आधार, âdhâra, the substratum, of the next so-called lower and grosser, and each supported in turn by the preceding so-called subtler and finer; each behaving in an apparently mysterious, superphysical and space-transcending way, because of the subtler and penetrative nature of its vibrations, from the standpoint of the lower, but becoming a part of, one step of, the ordinary, familiar and 'well-understood' scale of matter, including the lower planes, from the standpoint of the higher.

In the language of symbology, which yet seems intended to describe the literal facts of the subtler planes of matter also, this space may be regarded as meant by the garland of human heads, individual-points of consciousness and atom-points of matter, that Shiva, embodiment of the negative ichchhâ, ever bears upon his breast; each head separate from the other, each side by side with another, yet all united together by the strong single thread of the desire-consciousness of mutual desire. It may also be symbolised by the dark and giant mammoth-skin that is the outer envelope of that inner God, for ichchhâ cannot manifest except in space.

(*B*) TIME.

As the movement between the Self and the Not-Self is the basic principle of all motion, so the *succession*, क्रम, krama, of this movement, of the affirmation and the negation, is the basic principle of, indeed is, time. Time is nothing else than the succession of events. It may also be described as the possibility of the succession of events, changes in the conditions of objects, and the actuality of their non-cession, non-procession, non-duration, the ever-standing witness of their non-permanence, their non-existence. That is to say, as space is emptiness which is the possibility of the co-existence of objects, which, regarded in itself and as differing from these objects, is only *defined* and thrown into relief by them and *is not* them, which, indeed, looked at thus, is their absence and their opposite; so time is an emptiness, which is the possibility of the succession of events, is only defined and thrown into relief by those events, and is not them, but their absence and their opposite. As this succession of events, *i.e.*, experiences, identifications and separations, slackens or quickens or ceases (comparatively and apparently), so the standard of time changes; it appears to be long or short, or even disappears altogether as in the case of sound slumber, before mentioned, to the individual and limited consciousness. This is verifiable by anyone in the experience of dreams, reveries, and other extraordinary or abnormal psychic conditions, as in hypnotism and trance. The same is the case with the standard of time with reference to consciousness; quick steps make short distances, slow paces make long ones. In view of the increasing rapidity of means of transit, people speak of distances in terms of time—'it is so many hours' to a place—rather than in terms of space, so many hundred miles.

With reference to the Self, time may be said to present the triplicity of beginning, end, and middle; beginning, आदि or आरम्भ, âdi or ârambha, *i.e.*, the affirmation of the etat or its origin; 'end,' अन्त or अवसान, anta or avasâna, its negation; and the 'middle,' मध्य, madhya, which holds together both.

The constant appearance and disappearance, and disappearance and re-appearance, of each etat, necessarily due to the double necessity of being limited on the one hand, and yet being also, on the other hand, in the indissoluble relation of contact with the *eternal* Self, forces upon it a pseudo-eternal succession of its own, apart, as it were, from its identifications and disjunctions with the

Self, and gives us another aspect of the same thing. This is that most current form of the trinity inherent in time, *viz.*, 'past, present, and future,' भूत, bhûta, वर्तमान, vartamâna and भविष्यत्, bhavishyat, or 'before, now, and after,' as viewed from the standpoint of the Not-Self.

In this second aspect is contained the secret of personal inmortality in brief. Every etat, being once in touch with the eternal, must be marked with that eternity forever. There is no succession of once and twice and thrice, etc., in the *Eternal*; but every separate etat is under the sway of such succession, and there is a contradiction, an impossibility indeed, involved in the juxtaposition, the coming together and the contact, of the successionless and the successive. But the two *are* in contact, there, before us, all around us, irresistibly bound together by the nature of the Absolute. This antinomy of the reason is soluble only by imposing, on the successive, the false and illusive *appearance* of the successionless, the eternal, which simultaneously includes all moments of time, once, every etat pseudo-eternal, *for-ever*-eternal, twice, thrice, first, second, third, etc., by making everlasting, in short. Therefore, every etat appears and vanishes and reappears throughout all time (*i.e.*, in the endless consciousness of a Jîva), again and again, as a firefly in the black darkness of a cloud-shut night of the rain-time in the tropics. Hence, while in one sense mukti is eternal or even timeless, having no beginning and no end, as viewed from the standpoint of the Pratyag-âtmâ or the Param-âtmâ respectively, in another sense it is always beginning and always ending, from the standpoint of Mûla-prakṛiti. In other words, the individual Jîva, viewed as identical with the Pratyag-âtmâ, and so with the Param-âtmâ, is never bound and never freed; so that then it can scarcely be said even to have mukti; as such it is above and beyond both बंधन, bandhana, bondage, and मोक्ष mokṣha, liberation, indeed both are in it always rather than it in them ever. But viewed as identical with a *piece* of Mûla-prakṛiti, an etat, it is always, in literally endless repetition, falling into bondage, *i.e.*, into identification with, and voluntary imprisonment in, a body, and getting out of that bondage again into liberation, *i.e.*, separation from, and out of, that prison-house. This is why we read in the Purâṇas that the highest Gods and Ṛiṣhis, although all muktas, still, without exception, return again and again, cycle after cycle, kalpa after kalpa, passing and repassing endlessly through the spirals, retaining, every one of them, like all other Jîvas, their centres of individuality through the pralayas as through ordinary nights, despite the apparent loss (from the standpoint of lower planes of matter) of their defining and demarcating circumferences. But immense complications—which are indeed pseudo-infinite and therefore utterly unresolvable and incomprehensible in their entirety by any individual within limited time and space—are introduced into this incessant evolution and involution, because of the ever-mutable and ever-changing nature of every etat.

To illustrate the reflection and re-reflection of the triplicity of the Absolute everywhere, as of a light between two mirrors, and also the changes, in correspondence with changes in points of view, we may say that in this triplet of 'past, present, and future,' yielded to us by looking at time with reference to the Not-Self, the present is the nexus, or the Na, between the past as jñâna and the future as kriyâ; or, again, the future may be regarded as the nexus which will connect together and reproduce both past and present; or, the past may be thought of as having contained both the present and the future. The three are a circle, and we may start at any point in it.

Finally, time, viewed with reference to the Negation, may be said to yield the mathematical triplet of 'moment, period, and cycle,' क्षण, kṣhaṇa, समय, samaya, and युग, yuga.

In symbology, time is the Kâla, the 'dark,' the 'mover,' and the 'destroyer, death,' all three in one. It is pictured as the vast-sweeping Garuḍa that conveys, from place to place as need for giving help arises, the God of jñâna, Viṣhṇu; Garuḍa, the eagle with the two all-covering wings of the past and future, whose sole food and means of maintenance are the small cycle-serpents (that, though belonging to the family of the endless Ananta, form part of the retinue of Shiva, the God of ichchhâ), one of whom he eats up every day of his life by ordinance of the Creator. It may also be the vana-mâlâ, the wreath of forest-flowers, that Viṣhṇu wears, representing the endless chain of life-moments strung together by the thread of the cognitive consciousness. And yet again, it is the thousand-hooded serpent-king, Ananta, 'without end,' Sheṣha, 'the ever-remaining,' who on his countless heads and coils supports with ease the divine frame of Viṣhṇu as well as the globe of this earth, and whom alone of all the snakes the eagle Garuḍa is powerless to touch.

It may be noted here that the paurâṇic story assigns Garuḍa, here regarded as corresponding to time and the Not-Self, as vehicle to Viṣhṇu, the God of sattva and jñâna, corresponding to the Self. It similarly assigns the rosary of human heads, here said to correspond to space and the Self, to Shiva, the God of ichchhâ, corresponding to the Negation. Even more perplexing than these, it assigns Lakṣhmî-shakti, the Goddess of wealth and activity, to Viṣhṇu, and Sarasvatî-shakti, the Goddess of jñâna, to Brahmâ, the God of action. The shakti of Gaurî-Kâlî, (white-black, affirmation and negation), the Goddess of ichchhâ, is of course obviously assigned to Shiva, the God of destruction, and also of all 'auspiciousness' and blessings. In the *Rahasya-traya*,[1] Sarasvatî is said to be the sister of Viṣhṇu and Lakṣhmi the sister of Brahmâ; and Viṣhṇu takes Lakṣhmî in marriage and Sarasvatî is given to Brahmâ.[2] All these and similar other apparent inconsistencies may be reconciled by the consideration that while one factor of any trinity is predominant in any one individual, and is regarded as essential to that individual's being, as constituting his peculiar nature, still the other two factors are also necessarily present in or about him (otherwise

[1] Ch. i. See also Nîlakaṇṭha's commentary on the *Devî-Bhâgavata* III. 1. 85.

[2] *Devî-Bhâgavata*. III. vi.

his peculiar nature too could not manifest and would not be), and then they are symbolised as shaktis, vehicles, apparel, ornaments, &c.

(*C*) Motion.

We have seen above how the eternal negation of the Not-Self by the Self *appears* as a *movement*, चलन, chalana, गति, gati, अयन, ayana, of mergence and emergence between the two because of the limitation of the etat. The third which completes and binds together this duality of 'mergence and emergence' निमज्जन nimajjana, and उन्मज्जन, unmajjana, may be regarded as the 'continual recurrence' of the process, as continual juxtaposition, संमज्जन sammajjana, permeation, or संसरण samsaraṇa, procession. This movement, considered metaphysically, in the abstract, is the primary and essential principle which underlies and determines all the motion that appears in the world-process, and it gives us the triplicity inherent in motion as appearing from the standpoint of the Self.

From the standpoint of the Not-Self we derive another aspect of motion. It is embodied in, and derived from, the fact that each 'this,' etat, besides the movement into and out of the Self, which it is continuously subject to in consequence of the whole-law of the logion, has also a special motion of its own, in consequence of the part-law of that logion. The 'this' is the opposite of the 'I' in every respect, and the eternal completeness and fulness, the freedom from change and motion, of the 'I' is necessarily matched by the limitation and therefore imperfection of each separate 'this'; and the motion of each separate 'this' is the necessary expression of its endless want and changefulness. If the etats could be really steady and unmoving points in endless space, not feeling any want, and therefore not moving, then the contradiction would arise that the whole and each part were equal, being both perfect. Hence the whole, *i.e.*, the absolute Brahman, the Param-âtmâ, and, as identical with it, the Pratyag-âtmâ also, is often described as the centre without a circumference, or conversely, a circle without a centre, or as that which is all centres only, and so on. This is verifiable practically by everyone without much difficulty. Sitting in a quiet place, shutting in the senses, fixing the consciousness upon itself, *i.e.*, the Pratyag-âtmâ, the universal inward Self, and regarding and denying the whole mass of particulars summed up as a single Not-Self, the man loses all sense of time and space and motion, and the whole of the universe, Not-Self and himself, seems shut up into a single moveless point of consciousness. Space and time would not exist if such motion, as between a particular etat and another particular etat, and, indeed, between all possible etats, did not exist. In other words, this second motion is necessarily due to the fact that *each* etat, being opposed to the omnipresent, the infinite and eternal, the unlimited, 'I,' has to oppose it at *every point* of the whole of its endless being, and so reproduces and reflects in itself a pseudo-omnipresence. This pseudo-omnipresence of the limited etat takes shape as, becomes, is, endless and perpetual motion everywhere, from place to place, from point to point, of space. It cannot accomplish the law and achieve its nature in any other way.

Other ways of describing the fact are these: motion is the perpetual endeavour of the limited to become unlimited; of the successive to achieve simultaneity; of the finite to secure infinity; it is the constant struggle of space, or extension, and time, or intension, to coincide and collapse into the perfect rest, the single point, the rockboundness of the Absolute-consciousness.

This second view of motion, with reference to the Not-Self, gives us the triplet of 'approach, recess, and revolution,' or 'centripetal, centrifugal, and orbital motion,' उपसर्पण, upa-sarpaṇa, अपसर्पण, apa-sarpaṇa, and प्रसर्पण pra-sarpaṇa, or परिभ्रमण, pari-bhramaṇa.

Finally, with reference to the Negation, we have the mathematical triplet in motion of 'linear, rotatory and spiral,'[1] ऋजु, ṛiju, चक्र, chakra, and वक्र or कुटिलभ्रमण, vakra or kuṭila bhramaṇa, corresponding to Self, Not-Self and Negation. These three motions sum up in themselves all the possible movements of saṃsâra, as may be pictured by the diagram at p. 434, Vol. ii., of *The Secret Doctrine*, if the spines shown therein along the outer side of the single line, whose convolutions make up the whole diagram, were also made parts of, and continuous with, that same single line, and the line were shown as constantly coiling and turning round and round upon itself, like a spiral wire-spring, and all this line and process of coiling were produced and carried round and round pseudo-infinitely.

---

[1] Some physicists regard vibratory or oscillatory motion as a third primary form of motion, side by side with the translatory, freepath or linear, and the rotary or rather rotatory or circular. (*Vide* Dolbear. *Ether, Matter, and Motion.* iii.) But it will probably be found on analysis that vibratory motion is also made up of elements from the linear and the rotatory, as the undulatory is compounded out of the rectilinear and the vibratory.

This motion, the first factor of the second trinity, seems to be figured in the Purâṇas as the hamsa, the swan-vehicle of Brahmâ, the lord of action, which hamsa (under another interpretation of the Upanishat-text quoted before) circles with double beat of wing incessantly in the great wheel or cycle of Brahmâ. It may also be the rosary of crystal beads that Brahmâ ever turns around and tells in his right hand, in constant movement, weaving all single vibrations into one on the thread of the action-consciousness. It may, yet again, be the ever twisting, turning, rolling stream of holy Gañgâ stored within the same God's bowl of sacred waters, the kamaṇḍalu.[1]

Before passing on to our next subject of discussion, the individual self, or Jîva, we may note that although space and time and motion have, like Pratyag-âtmâ, Mûla-prakṛiti and Negation, been treated of in successive order,

---

[1] The statements made in this work as to symbology, it should be borne in mind, are only suggestive. They have no immediate importance here with reference to the general principles underlying the constitution of the kosmos, which alone are attempted to be outlined in this work. That they are made at all is only in the hope that the suggestions may be of use, and possibly give some clue to students who may take an interest in working out, with the help of paurâṇic legends, the details issuing out of the general principles described here.

this is only because of the limitations of speech, which, as has been said, can proceed only in succession : वाक् किल क्रमवर्तिनी. It must not be imagined, any more as regards the former trinity than as regards the latter, that there is any precedence or succedence amongst the three. They are perfectly synchronous, perfectly inseparable, all equally important and all equally dependent with and on each other, and also with and on the primal trinity, of Self, Not-Self, and Negation. And all these trinities again co-inhere in and are inseparable from the Jivâtmâ, the Jîva-atom, the Jîva-unit, which combines and manifests in itself all of them, and therefore is 'the immortal beyond doubt and fear,' if it will only so recognise itself.

He who grasps this secret of the heart of motion, time, and space, will understand Vasiṣhṭha's riddle that 'all is everywhere and always.' For the Jîva is the tireless weaver that, on the warp and woof of time and space, with the shuttle of motion, weaves eternally the endless-coloured tapestry of all this multifarious illusion-world, carrying the *whole* plan thereof incessantly *within himself*, and so carrying 'all' 'always' and 'everywhere' in one. If we turn our eyes to the warp and the woof and the shuttle, we see but the endless tapestry of Penelope that never progresses and never regresses, though worked incessantly. Law requires more law and that again more still; to fulfil and justify the opposed necessities, to reconcile the contradictions of the constitution of the Absolute, one process is invented; that shows defect, another is invented; that breeds only new grievances, they are amended; ten more start up, new laws appear to cover them! A laughable yet very serious, a fearful yet all-beautiful, an exceeding simple yet most awesome and stupendous लीला, lîlâ, pastime and child's-play. An untold and untellable, a veritably exhaustless richness of variety, which is yet but the thinnest mâyâ and pretence to hide the unruffled calm and sameness of the Self. A heart of utter peace within mock-features of infinite unrest and toil and turmoil. Thus ever goes on this endless, countless, strictly and truly pseudo-infinite complication, this repetition over repetition, reproduction of reproduction, and reflection within reflection. And yet is it ever reducible—at any moment of space and time and motion, as soon as the Jîva really chooses to reduce it so, by simply turning round its gaze upon itself—into the eternal peace of the simple formula of the logion: Aham Etat Na. And this is so, because the complications are not outside of the Jîva, but, as soon as it realises its identity with the universal Self, *within* it[1]; forgetting, as it were, its own true nature, it creates them in and by the very act of running after them till it becomes giddy, ready to fall down in despair with its own whirlings, all in vain, like a snake chasing its own tail, which it would find and seize more surely as part of its own self if it but gave up its mad gyrations, and turned back upon it quietly and peacefully and rested still. "The Self-born pierced the senses outwards, hence the Jîva seeth the outer world, and not the inner Âtmâ. A wise one here and there turneth back his gaze, desirous of immortality, and beholdeth the inward Self."

परांचि खानि व्यतृणत्स्वयंभूस्
तस्मात्पराङ् पश्यति नांतरात्मन् ।
कश्चिद्धीरः प्रत्यगात्मानमैक्षद्
आवृत्य चक्षुरमृतत्वमिच्छन् ॥

"O silent Sleeper in this seething Sea!
Plain we behold and yet speech may not be.
We wander, wonder, search and then we find,
But find it in the silence of the mind.
Who will believe the marvel, if we say,

[1] *Kaṭha*. iv. 1.

Though it be plain, plain as the light of day,
That on the boundless wall of nothingness,
A Painter full of skill but bodiless,
Limns phantom figures that will never fade,
Though to efface them time has e'er essayed,
Limns forms of countless colours ceaselessly,
O serene Sleeper of this stormy Sea!"

Tulasi Dâs. *Vinaya Patrikâ.* Hymn No. 112, to Keshava, *i.e.*, Vișhṇu 'sleeping in the waters'.

NOTE.—Many kind friends have suggested that the word 'pastime' is likely to jar the feelings of at least some earnest-minded thinkers, holders of serious views as to the destinies of man, his relation to God, and the general purpose of creation or evolution. Readers who, not content with the solutions now extant of the problems of life (as mentioned in the preface), find it worth their while to read to the end of this book systematically will I earnestly believe, find that the view of life advocated herein is not inconsistent with, or exclusive of, any, but rather includes all the deepest views of and the highest-reaching wishes for the future of man, so far as such may be ascertained from published writings. For an endless progressiveness, an infinite perfectibility, an ever closer approach to the ever-expanding Divine, are hoped for here also for the human race most sincerely and strongly. Only, in this work, this view is regarded as constituting not the whole, but only half the truth, as being that aspect of the truth which is visible from the standpoint of the individual Jîva. The other and supplementary half is that, from the standpoint of the universal Self, there is no progress and no regress, no change of any kind, so that if that condition may be described at all in terms of the changing, then the only words to use are 'pastime,' 'play,' 'unfettered will,' 'uncontrolled outgoing of life,' 'unresisted and irresistible manifestation of the inner nature,' 'the unquestionable will of God,' 'Thy will be done,' 'Who shall question

Him ?' etc. Are the free rompings of the child, and the vigorous games of youth, and the vast industries of peace and war of a nation's matured manhood, that are but as means to the child's rompings and the youth's games—are these such a slur upon life that the word 'pastime' should jar upon the serious-minded ? Are not rather the happy homes the very essence of a nation's life, and the child's bright smile and laugh and play the very essence of the home ? Play is a thing as serious at least as work, in the well-balanced life. And, while this idea is yielding up its full significance, let the reader bear in mind that, as shown by the above inadequate translation from Tulasi Dâs, a devotee of devotees, whose book, the *Râmâyaṇa*, is the Bible of a hundred millions of the Hindus, this idea of the world being the pastime of the Self has been entertained with loving fervour by at least some of the most earnest-minded of men. This book will truly have failed in its purpose if it leaves behind the impression that devotion to individual Îshvaras, embodying universal and impersonal ideals, has been scoffed at and belittled herein, rather than made infinitely stronger and deeper and more unshakeable by being placed on the firm foundations of reason.

CHAPTER XIII.

JÎVA-ATOMS.

(A) GENERALLY.

Before proceeding further we may make a brief retrospect.

From the confusion of the world we travelled slowly and laboriously to the Absolute. In that we saw the first trinity, of the Self, the Not-Self, and the Negation. We saw again that the Self was triple, sat-chid-ânanda; the Not-Self was triple, rajas-sattva-tamas; the affirmative Shakti-energy of the Negation was triple, sṛishṭi-sthiti-laya; and, finally, that the Negation itself was also triple, desha-kâla-ayana, which constitute almost the most prominent trinity of the world-process. We also saw that each one of this last trinity was again triple in its own turn. We may also have noticed, in passing, that the whole, the aggregate, of any three, might, in a sense, be regarded as a fourth which summarised and completed them all. We also had a glimpse of the fact that these trinities and triplets are all combined in the

Jîva-atom which, because of this fact, contains, in seed, the whole of the world-process in itself. After this brief *résumé* we may go on to consider Jîva-atoms in a little more detail.

By opposition to the *oneness* of the Aham, the 'I,' the Etat, the 'this,' is by necessity *many*; and each of these many, by opposition to the Self's unlimitedness and changelessness, and, again, by mutual exclusion and limitation, under the stress of the Negation, is limited, and trebly limited, in space, time, and motion; *i.e.*, it has got a परिमाण, parimâṇa, dimension, extension, size in space, by limitation on this side and on that; a स्पंद, or स्फुरण, spanda or sphuraṇa, a vibration in motion, a pendulum-swing, a revolution within a radius, a limited movement, which is necessarily made rhythmic by the fact of limitation in space and time; and an आयु, âyu,[1] a duration, a life-period, a limited succession, in time. Such is the general description of the atoms which make up Mûla-prakṛiti, the very essence of which is manyness, atomicity. The atom is an etat, a 'this,' having limited size, duration and motion; it cannot apparently be

---

[1] This word and आयाम, âyâma, extension, and अयन, ayana, movement, seem to be connected together in a suggestive and significant way, but the latter two are not very current now in the general meanings mentioned. Hence the other corresponding words have been given above.

defined more simply or comprehensively anywise else.

But an etat cannot exist apart from the Aham; Mûla-prakṛiti is inseparable from Pratyag-âtmâ. Each 'this' is indissolubly connected with the 'I,' by the double bond of 'am' and 'am not'—'am' representing the ascending phase of the metabolism of the life-process, and 'am not' the descending phase thereof. From all this it follows necessarily that the one Self becomes limited off into a pseudo-infinite number of ahams, Jîvas or Jîvâtmâs; that every aham is embodied in an etat, and every etat ensouled by an aham, and that every one of these pseudo-infinite atoms that make up Mûla-prakṛiti is therefore living. Each such living atom, combining in itself Pratyag-âtmâ and Mûla-prakṛiti, is an individual, an individualised Jîva-atom. And we may note that as each atom is a 'this,' having definite size, duration, and vibration, so is each Jîva an 'I,' having a definite extent or reach of consciousness, an age or lifetime, and a restless activity of mind. The Saṃskṛit words denoting these aspects of the Jîva are also the same as for the aspects of the atom, except that, in place of the word परिमाण, parimâṇa, dimension, the word क्षेत्र, kṣhetra, the 'field' (of consciousness) is more commonly used.

These attributes, it is clear, appear in the Jîva with reference to the primary attributes of the Negation, space, time, and motion.

With reference to the attributes of the Shakti-aspect of Negation, creation, preservation, and destruction, the attributes of the Jîva-atom may be said to be birth, life, and death; or, in other words, growth, decay, and stagnation, as corresponding to attraction, repulsion, and balancing.

In such a Jîva-atom the mutual imposition of the attributes of each, the Self and the Not-Self, is complete; in collapsing together they have taken on the properties of one another; and the Jîva-atom therefore shows, in its own individuality, the phenomenon of permanence in impermanence and impermanence in permanence, oneness in manyness and manyness in oneness. The one Pratyag-âtmâ becomes many individuals; the manifold Mûla-prakṛiti becomes organised ones, each indestructible, each having a personal immortality, or unending duration, and a pseudo-infinity of endless stretch of consciousness, as also the true eternity and infinity of the Pratyag-âtmâ. In strictness, the reflection of the One in the many should cause the appearance of pseudo-infinite geometrical 'points without magnitude,' true 'centres,' which make the '*singular* one,' as opposed to and yet reproducing the '*universal* One'; but as, because of the other law, operating simultaneously with equal force, *viz.*, that the etat is limited as against the unlimitedness of the Aham, the point must have *definite* limitation; therefore everywhere we have Jîva-atoms having size, etc., as said before, in place of points, which, however, always exist as possibilities, as abstract and theoretical centres. Such definite Jîva-atoms, considered with greater reference to the atom-aspect, may be called particulars; with greater reference to the Jîva-aspect, individuals; the individual, particular, or definite, being the reconciliation of the singular and the universal.

We see now what the real value of the distinction between animate matter and inanimate matter is. Here, as everywhere else, the truth lies in the mean, and error in the two extremes. There is absolutely no matter at all that is not en-*liven*ed by spirit; and also no spirit that is not in-*form*ed with, inclosed, inclothed in, matter. This—which is proved by its own irrefragable chain of deductions to the inner, the pure, reason, the reason which looks at facts from the standpoint of the universal Self, as opposed to the outer, the impure, reason which looks at them from the standpoint of the individual self—is now being proved even to the outward senses by the admirable industry of modern physical science. It has been shown by an elaborate and very instructive series of facts and arguments: "that a fundamental difference, *i.e.*, difference in the elementary materials and the elementary *forces*, between organic and inorganic bodies, does not exist,"[1] and that the differences between them "are no greater than the differences between many inorganic substances, and consist merely in the mode of union of the elements."[2] The scientists of to-day have collected facts and performed experiments which show conclusively that so-called inanimate and inorganic matter responds to stimulus and behaves generally in the same manner as animate and organic matter[3]. Hasty deductions from such facts, *e.g.*, "the soul is but an electric current in another form," "matter and spirit are identical," are liable to misconstruction, and rest really upon inaccuracy and misunderstanding. It would be almost truer to say that "the electric current is but soul in another form." Minds that have not yet learnt to look leisurely, calmly, and impartially, at both sides of a question, and are still at the stage of taking hurried, passionate and one-sided

---

[1] Max Verworn, *General Physiology*. P. 136. [2] *Ibid* P. 272.

[3] J. C. Bose, *Response in the Living and the Non-Living*.

views of it with a partisan-zeal, either emphasise matter too much and resolve spirit entirely into it, or emphasise spirit too much and resolve matter away entirely into it. This is the result of looking at only one aspect, at one half, of the two-sided whole. The truth is that all matter is living, and all life material; that the pseudo-eternal motion of all matter in all its endless complications is throughout accompanied, on an ineffaceable parallel, by the fact of consciousness, the fact of life, now higher and now lower in degree of manifestation, according to the increased or decreased elaboration of the complications. The Etat and the Aham can never be separated. And yet they are distinct and can never be identified literally, either, except as they both are ever merged by the Negation in the completeness and self-sameness of the Absolute. This psycho-physical parallelism is the inner meaning of the Sâñkhya-doctrine, referred to before, *viz.*, the constant concurrence of consciousness with all variations of motion in matter, which concurrence constitutes universal life and makes those motions possible. This is all that consciousness does; the Âtmâ is the âdhâra, the base, the support of all these motions; without it they would have no meaning and would not be. When all vital phenomena have been explained away into atomic affinities, as is being done by modern scientists anew, then the question arises: "Whence and how and why these affinities?" The only answer is: The universal consciousness imposes them on the atoms; and the result is that the whole series of explanations is reversed, that the belief in vital force is restored on a higher level, and all affinities become resolved into the vital phenomena of one universal Shakti. Of course, initiation of actions and movements by *individual* consciousnesses is abolished even so; but what the truth is on this point may be gathered partially from what has been already said about free-will, and may be discussed more fully later on.

The distinction between animate and inanimate then amounts to this, that to the person noting the distinction at any particular time and place, in the former the element of Pratyag-âtmâ is the more prominent and manifest, while in the latter the element of Mûlaprakṛiti is the more apparent.

The reason for this alternate predominance, now of the one and now of the other, is the alternation of the 'am' and the 'am not.' When the 'am' is strong we have the appearance of 'the living,' of crescent 'life,' of anabolism. When the 'am not' prevails, then we have the phenomenon of 'death,' 'the dying,' 'the dead, the inert,' of katabolism. In the strict sense of the words, 'life' and 'death' are not correct here; only living' and 'dying' are correct. The scientific doctrine of necrobiosis, of gradual death, is voucher for this fact. But like 'animate' and 'inanimate,' 'life' and 'death' have, as convenient words, a practical value, though the facts can never in reality be separated; living and dying are going on *constantly*, incessantly, *side by side*, and also *one after another*, because of the general principles which underlie, as explained before, the triple sub-divisions of time, space and motion; for, (1) to say, "I am this etat," is also to say at the same time, in the same space, and by the same motion, "I am not this other etat;" and so, to say, "I am not this etat," is also to say, "I am this other etat." Again, (2) to say, "I am this," is to say later, in another time, space, and motion, "I am not (the same) this," and *vice versâ*. And, finally, (3) it is unavoidable to be saying, everywhere and always, either "I am this," or "I am not this." Thus it comes about that every organism is living and dying, *i.e.*, changing, *at the same time*, and has also *successively* ascending and descending phases of metabolism. Thus are spirit and matter, life and death, ever connected like the two ends of the beam of a balance; if one rises, the other falls in equal degree; if the one falls, the other rises similarly, but entirely separated they never can be.

It may be gathered from the above, that the word 'life,' as currently employed, means 'living and dying,' and 'death' means 'dying and living.' Let us now see more fully what death really means. When we have done that, our information as to the essential significance of one prominent aspect of the Jîva-atom, the aspect of animate-inanimate, will have been rounded out and completed in a way.

By the law of अध्यास, adhyâsa, mutual superimposition of attributes between the Self and the Not-Self, the Jîva-atom must begin and end in time, *i.e.*, be impermanent, and, must at the same time be permanent. The reconciliation of this contradiction lies in ever-recurrent beginnings and endings. But how is this possible? How can a thing, an etat, having once *been*, ever cease to be, and if it once actually *ceased* to be, how could it be again? The necessity for the obviation of this objection creates at once new laws and facts. In the first place, the difficulty is solved by (apparent) dissociations of ensouling inner Jîva and ensheathing outer body, *i.e.*, the transfer of the individual consciousness from one body to another.

But having said this, it now becomes necessary to explain here what is meant by *inner* Jîva and *outer* sheath, where we have been speaking of a single and apparently homogeneous Jîva-atom so far. Although the Jîva-atom is a one, yet again within that one there is an irreducible and irrepressible duality—strictly speaking, indeed, a trinity, as may appear later in connection with the explanation of the metaphysic of the expression त्रिभुवन, tribhuvana, the triple-world. The 'I' is joined to the etat by the 'am' in "I (am) this"; and yet they are only *joined;* the two cannot be literally identified. The consequence of this is that we have an inner Jîva, self or soul, and an outer upâdhi, sheath or body. This inner self is something which by its very pratyag-âtmic nature and constitution is always eluding sensuous grasp and definition. "How and by what may the knower be known?" as the *Bṛihadâraṇyaka* says.[1] It is self-luminous. Whenever we seek, consciously or unconsciously, to *define* it, we at once find in its place an upâdhi, a sheath, as Indra found Umâ Haimavatî,[2] a sheath subtler than the previous one, from the standpoint of which as 'outer' we started to secure this 'inner' self; subtler no doubt, but yet as undoubtedly material. This 'inner' self, the 'abstract,' would lose its very nature and falsify itself, would no longer be

---

[1] II. iv. 14. [2] *Kena.* iii.

'inner' and 'abstract' if it could be grasped. To be grasped means to be outer. Therefore this self ever recedes further and further inwards, within a literally endless series of veil after veil, as we try to follow it with the eye of sense, while to the eye of the pure reason, that is to say, to itself, it is always present, immovably stationary. The physical reflection of this law, as found by physical science, is that "there exists upon earth at present no living substance that is homogeneous throughout," and that "the living substance that now exists upon the earth's surface is recognised only in the form of cells," each of which "contains, as its essential constituents, two different substances, the protoplasm and the nucleus;"[1] and the nucleus has been found, on further investigation, to contain still inner cores and sheaths, etc., *viz.*, the nucleolus and other substances.[2] The truth is that, as more or less openly described in the *Yoga Vâsiṣhṭha*[3] and other works on Yoga and Vedânta, and in theosophical literature, the constitution of man, and, indeed, of all living matter, is a plantain-like system of leaf-sheath within leaf-sheath, layer within layer, fold

[1] Max Verworn, *General Physiology*. P. 296.

[2] Ibid P. 91; see also H. W. Conn: *The Story of Life's Mechanism*.

[3] *Vide* the story of Lîlâ in the Utpatti-Prakaraṇa.

within fold, and shell within shell, all interpenetrating each other, but each distinct from each. And metaphysic adds that this must be so, not up to any limited extent or definite number, which would be arbitrary (except as regards any particular world-system which must necessarily deal with definite time, space and motion, and therefore definite numbers of layers and planes of matter), but pseudo-infinitely, which only is in accordance with reason, when the whole of the world-process is taken into account. More about this may appear later; in the meanwhile what has been said may suffice to show how we have the possibility, and therefore the necessity (for in the sight of metaphysic to be possible is to be), of the phenomenon of death by the passing of the Jîva from one body to another inner and subtler body. This outer body, which, then, is left behind, is called dead from the standpoint of the inner Jîva, which has now passed on to another sheath. And the inner Jîva may similarly be called dead from the point of view of the body. There is a reciprocal severance of association and reciprocal death, a reciprocal cessation of interchange, interplay and inter-vivification. The opposite of death in this sense is 'birth' and not 'life'; and it may be defined in the same terms. If 'death' is the transference of the individual consciousness from one plane of etat to another, birth is the same transference from another into the one. The same event means a death in one plane or world, and a birth in another. In other words, as death is reciprocal, so is birth; each dies to the other; each is born away from the other. The sleeping of the Jîva in the physical body, on the physical plane of the जाग्रत्, jâgrat, waking-consciousness, is its awakening in the astral body, on the astral plane of the स्वप्न, svapna, dreaming-consciousness; its sleeping in the latter, again, is its awakening in the कारण, kârana, causal body, on the corresponding plane of the सुषुप्ति, sushupti, 'deep-sleep'-consciousness; and so on pseudo-infinitely, and in the reverse order, *vice versâ*, also, pseudo-infinitely.

But, again, the totality of etats can never be really separated from the *one indivisible* Self, nor *an* etat from *an* aham, from its own particular aham, so to say, *viz.*, the one with which it was identified in the beginning of beginningless time, any more than it can be really unified and identified with such. There is no sufficient reason why an etat should be really separated—especially remembering that it has to be reunited with it as said before—from any aham with which it has once, at any time, been in junction. *Once*, therefore *ever*, is the requirement of the first principles of logic, the first laws of thought: 'A is A and not not-A.' The result of these acting and counteracting necessities of reason is that we have the periodic definite, overt, and *patent*, severance and connection of each aham with one particular etat in any one particular limited cycle of space and time; and the undefined, hidden, and *latent* connection of it constantly with *all* other etats, in the past, present and future. (Compare the teaching in *The Secret Doctrine* on the subject of the auric egg, and in the Vedânta on the subtle atomic sheaths carried by a Jîva in its passage from lower to successively higher worlds.)

In other words, the one Aham in its pseudo-infinite pseudo subdivisions is in unceasing and yet recurrent conjunction-disjunction, **संयोग-वियोग**, saṃyoga-viyoga, with all pseudo-infinite etats; each etat, or rather each conjunction and each disjunction of the pseudo-infinite number of such, representing, nay, being, a special experience, and the *whole* being one constant and changeless experience; so that we come back, as we shall always, again and again, with fuller and fuller knowledge of the content, to the fact that "all is everywhere and always."

One more statement seems to be needed before we pass on to other aspects of the Jîva-atom. What is the true significance of the words 'nature,' 'inanimate nature,' as ordinarily used to signify lands and mountains, clouds and rivers and oceans, the light and heat and fire of the earth's volcanoes and of the sun and the stars, the airs and gases of the atmosphere, and the ether of the spatial regions? These appear to stand out in sharp contrast, as vast masses of inanimate matter, to the human and other Jîvas deriving their sustenance from them? How are these *masses* to be explained? Where is the Aham in them? Or if it is there, why so latent in so much the larger portion of Mûla-prakṛiti? The question seems at first sight to be exclusively within the province of mere speculation; but a true metaphysic should include the principles of all physics and all sciences whatever, for the ideal standard thereof is that it is the system of universal principles which underlie all the world-process, as the architect's plan underlies the building. The explanation of this question may, therefore, properly be sought for in physical science. If found, it will help greatly to enlarge and confirm our grasp of the nature of Aham and Etat, and their pseudo-infinite variety of extent in space, time and motion, and therefore their pseudo-infinite overlappings.

Physiological science says: "individuals of the first order are *cells*; . . . of the second order are *tissues* . . . associations of individuals of the first order; . . . of the third order are *organs* . . . associations of individuals of the second order; of the fourth order are *persons* . . . associations of various individuals of the third order; of the fifth order are *communities* . . . associations of individuals of the fourth order."[1] There is no reason why this chain should not be lengthened pseudo-infinitely. It is very probable that physical science will some day discover definitely that the vital connections between the members of a community are of a nature exactly similar to, if, perhaps, weaker in intensity than, those between the organs in a person, the tissues in an organ, and the cells in a tissue. And thus it will discover that the solidarity of the human race, as made up of communities, is not a merely poetical metaphor or political abstraction or religious ideal but a physical fact; and, still further, that the various kingdoms, human, animal, vegetable, mineral, &c., have a common life as well as special lives, in endless continuity, so that even ordinary pantheism is vindicated, in a very literal sense, as being one part, but not the whole, of the body of truth which makes up metaphysic.

'Individuals' in the preceding paragraph

---

[1] Max Verworn. *General Physiology.* P. 62.

really signifies selves, and the quotation shows how larger and larger masses of 'animate nature' are included within larger and larger 'selves.' We may now select some other extracts which will show how large masses of '*in*animate nature' may be inspired by single 'selves,' while the preceding paragraph, by its explanation of the flux and elasticity of 'individuality' in animate nature, helps to make clear the possibility of 'individuality' in inanimate nature, and so helps to abolish the distinction between animate nature and inanimate nature. Preyer thought that "originally the whole molten mass of the earth's body was a single giant organism; the powerful movement that its substance possessed was its life."[1] Pflüger opined that "living proteid . . . is a huge molecule undergoing constant, never-ending formation and constant de-composition, and probably behaves towards the usual chemical molecules as the sun behaves towards small meteors."[2] Of course there is difference of opinion and mutual discussion going on amongst the holders and opponents of such views, but the result of the discussion can only be that new details and fuller significance will come to the surface, and the general truth pervading and reconciling all opposing

[1] *Ibid.* P. 303. [2] *Ibid.* P. 307.

views will be realised in a higher degree. Individual students of science may now and then secretly believe or openly call each other fanciful or unscientific, in the excusable heat of the race after truth, and under the influence of the zealous faith of each (which sometimes helps by putting vigour and energy into the chase) that his own path is the shortest cut. But truth lies in the net result of the whole, and, from this standpoint, the mere fact is enough, for the present, for our purposes, that such views are entertained by scientific men, in whose sobriety as a collective body the lay public implicitly believes. This fact softens, and makes possible the assimilation of, the view which otherwise would look exaggerated and weird and unsober, that the earth and the moon and the sun and the stars might each be—they *are*, by the deductions of the reason—as much individual beings as the matter-of-fact citizens of a civilised town of to-day; and again, not only individuals, but individuals within individuals, so that a large number, or, strictly speaking, a pseudo-infinite number, of distinct lives, *i.e.*, lines of consciousness, are being ministered to by apparently the same etat, while at the same time all the pseudo-infinite etats are, *vice versâ*, ministering to the one life of the one Self.

This will become clear when the student casts entirely away from him the associations of time, space, and motion, those arch magicians, mystifiers and illusion-makers in this Mâyâ's playhouse of the world-process. He should consider the facts solely in their mutual proportion and relation. Thus considered, millions of such heavenly bodies might as easily float in the veins of the 'Virât-Purusha with the thousand heads and thousand feet and hands,'[1] as leucocytes and phagocytes and bacilli and bacteria and microbes in the veins of a single human being; and they may very well discharge similar functions also. Each of such has its own life, and also forms part of the life of another which, in turn, has its own special as also a subordinate life, and so on in a chain which extends literally endlessly.

The apparently inanimate masses of material nature may thus all be regarded as parts of some one or other smaller and larger 'individual.' Their inanimateness is at the most no greater than the inanimateness of a human being's nails or hair or epidermis or blood or bone, each of which may, nay, does, harbour and nourish multifarious minute lives, while also connected on the descending or ascending phase of meta-

---

[1] *Puruṣha-Sûkta.* See also *Bhagavad-Gîtâ.* xi.

bolism with a larger life. This is but another illustration of the law that an etat cannot stay devoid of an aham; if one aham, one line of consciousness, deserts it, another or others take up its place immediately. In daily experience we see this, in the springing up of new lives in disintegrating organic forms that have served their purpose of sheath to a larger life and so 'died.' And what the Upanishat declares,[1] that "this world appears forth from the Unperishing as hair and nails from the man," is probably declared in a similar sense, with reference to the Virât-Purusha.

The result of all this in the words of physical science is that, as Preyer said: "as . . . the matter of the universe . . . is in eternal motion . . . so life, which itself is only a complex process of motion, is as old as matter."[2] The student of metaphysic has to read 'pseudo-eternal' in place of 'eternal,' and 'conscious motion' in place of 'motion.'

We have floated away very far on the stream of the discussion of animate and inanimate; but we have seen again in the course thereof, what was stated before, how law begets law and fact, and these more laws and facts, with prolific, indeed endless, multiplicity, and we are now in a position to understand how, if the necessary

---

[1] *Mundaka*. i. 7. [2] Max Verworn, *General Physiology*. P. 309.

means for the knowledge of concrete details, now said to be known to only occult physical science, were available, Krug's famous quill, before referred to, could be deduced with even complete minuteness of steps. Thus we may realise how the whole of the solid-seeming of this world is hung on to, or indeed is entirely made up of, the airiest of cobwebs of laws and principles (that are always getting metamorphosed into facts), which the silkworm of the Pratyag-âtmâ spins into an endless cocoon out of and around itself, and which disappears at once, together with the silkworm, replaced by the gorgeous and free-feeling and free-flying butterfly, as soon as it realises and undergoes the perishing, the death, the nothingness, of both, as soon as the individualised Pratyag-âtmâ understands the endless interplay of mutual termination and determination between the Self and the Not-Self, and so becomes the mukta, the liberated.

The Upaniṣhat-verse just referred to has thus another and deeper metaphysical significance besides the literal one before mentioned: "As the spider casteth forth its web and rolls it up again, as the herbs rise up from out of the earth, as hair and down grow from the life and being of the man, so doth this universe appear from and within the Unperishing and Unchanging."

CHAPTER XIV.

Jîva-Atoms—Objectively, *i.e.*, Atoms.

After the above general treatment of the Jîva-atom we may now take the two aspects of it separately and in a little more detail. And of these two we may dispose of the particular, the atom-aspect, first, leaving for later treatment the other aspect of the individual, the Jîva, the discussion of which is the main purpose of the rest of the work, reference to the material side of life being made only as necessary to explain and illustrate the spiritual side.

In the first place, the attributes common to the Jîva and the atom, *viz.*, size,[1] life, and vibration, may be further particularised with respect to the atom.

Size, in this reference, may be said to break up into the triplet of 'bulk or volume,' 'shape or form,' and 'measure, magnitude, or dimension,' as including both the others. And these again may be looked at as 'large, small,

[1] The significance of the word size in reference to the Jîva is explain d at the outset of the next chapter.

average,' 'long, round, ovoid,' 'linear, plane, cubical,' &c.

A hypothesis may be advanced here as to form.

It has been said above that, under the stress of the necessity embodied in the logion, etats appear in pseudo-infinite number as constituent points of the manifold Mûla-prakṛiti. It has also been said that by that same necessity they are never actually points without magnitude but points with magnitude, with definite volume and form and measure and are therefore atoms. Atoms would be without volume and form and measure if the Etat were not limited. But the Etat is limited, consequently they must have volume and form and measure. And if they must have these, or, rather, as is enough to say, form (for all three are only different ways of looking at the same thing, measure being limitation pure and simple, while form is limitation from outside, and volume limitation from within), the sphere ought, apparently, to be their primal form, because the only universally non-arbitrary form is the sphere. A form which embodies the essence of pointness—that it is the same however looked at—can only be a sphere, which presents the same appearance from whatever side it is seen. Of course the law of non-arbitrariness requires and necessitates the existence of all possible pseudo-infinite kinds of forms and figures in the world-process, but the difference between the non-arbitrariness of the sphere on the one hand, and that of 'all possible figures' on the other, is the difference (if such an expression may be used without fear of misunderstanding) between the Pratyag-âtmâ on the one hand, and the pseudo-infinite contents of its consciousness, the varieties of the Not-Self, on the other. The Pratyag-âtmâ is everywhere and always, but the contents of its consciousness, made up of interminable and intermixing not-selves, are in definite times, spaces, and motions; so the sphere (when we abolish the periphery of limitation) may be said to have its centre potentially everywhere and always, while its contents—all possible figures made up of the numberless interlacing radii, interlacing because the centre is everywhere, each corresponding to a not-self—are only in definite times, spaces, and motions. Because of this fact most figure-symbology represents the self-centred Pratyag-âtmâ as the point, differentiated matter, spirit-matter, as the line or the cross of two lines, and the whole, the Absolute, as the circle; the line or the cross of two lines and the circle being used to meet the exigencies of script in place of what ought, in strictness, to be, apparently, the cross of three lines meeting at right angles to each other, and the sphere, respectively. The correspondence of the point and the line to the Self and the Not-Self respectively should be noted, and may prove of use hereafter. It may appear at first sight that there is no such opposition between the line and the point as there is between the other pair, the Self and the Not-Self, inasmuch as the line is only a production, a prolongation, of the point. But the opposition is there. From all that has gone before it will be clear that the Not-Self is nothing independent of the Self, nothing else than a production and a lengthening, a limitation and definition, of the Self, that is to say, a going of the immovable Self out of itself into a denial, a negation, of itself. Even so the lines are the first denial of the non-magnitude of the point; and out of such denial all the endless multiplicity of figures grows in the metaphysic of the Negation, *i.e.*, mathematics, as all the endless multitude of not-selves grows out of the denial of the Self in the complete metaphysic. In describing these imaginary lines, by rushing to and fro, the point without magnitude may be said to be seeking to define itself, to give itself a magnitude, even as the Self appears to define itself by entering into, by imposing upon itself, imagined not-selves and saying, 'I am this,' 'I am this.'

Corresponding to this triple sub-division of size, we may note a triple sub-division under duration also. The words in this reference have not such a recognised standing as those connected with size. But we may distinguish 'period' corresponding to form as limited from without; 'filling' to volume as limited from within; and 'rate' as limitation proper corresponding to measure. Each of these again manifests as 'long, short, average,' 'well-filled, ill-filled, occupied,' 'fast, slow, even,' etc.

We may similarly distinguish under vibration (tentatively, as in the case of duration), the three aspects of 'extent, rate, and degree,' and subdivide each of these three again into 'great, little, mean,' 'high, low, even,' and 'intense, sluggish, equable,' etc.

In the above-mentioned arrangements of triplets we see illustrated the fact that all the things of the world-process fall into groups of three in accordance with the primal trinity that underlies and is the whole of the universe. And these groupings are not mechanical or empirical but organic. It may appear to the cursory observer that there is no 'why' apparent in them. But the 'why' is there, and in a very simple way too. Each member of a trinity reflects in itself each of the three and so produces three trinities; and this process is a pseudo-infinite one; hence the whole content of the world-process is only a pseudo-infinite number of groups of such trinities and triplets. All these, it must be remembered, are simultaneous from the standpoint of the Absolute, and not growing one out of another in time. If we would know why there is such a thing as this reflection, we should reconsider the arguments in the preceding chapters, whereby the necessity of both changelessness and change, of timelessness and time, spacelessness and space, simultaneity and succession, unity and diversity, the reality of non-separateness and the false appearance of separateness and distinguishability, are established. The three are one and yet three, and the result of this apparent antinomy is that they reflect each other, each carries the image of the others in its very heart, to prove its oneness with it, and all do this endlessly.

To show that these endless multiplications, seemingly so tangible in their multitude, are, in reality, on close scrutiny, found to be very unsubstantial, we may consider a little more fully what has been parenthetically hinted above, *viz.*, that volume and form mean the same thing. Form is nothing else than a negation of continuity, a denial, a limitation, a cutting short of continued existence on all sides.

Volume means evidently the same thing looked at from within; it is an inability to extend further. Hence only are form and volume liable to change. If they were anything real, actual, having *being*, then how could they change, *i.e.*, pass from being into nothing and from nothing into being? "There is no being to that which really is not, nor non-being to that which truly is."[1] And such change is apparent every second, every millionth of a second, of our lives. The solution lies in the fact that, in all change, what really changes is only mere form (and it will appear on analysis that all other aspects or qualities of the atom are also on the same level with form), which is simply negation looked at as above; and that what remains behind is the pseudo-thing-in-itself, the 'substance' which is 'indestructible,' the essence of which we regard as 'resistance.' Resistance is nothing else than the power of attraction and repulsion embodied in a Not-Self, an etat, as exclusiveness, separateness, separate self-maintenance. It is the reflection of the affirmative-negative, attractive-repulsive energy of ichchhâ in the Self. This 'resistance,' 'self-maintenance,' like desire (of which indeed it is but another name in the objective language

---

[1] *Bhagavad-Gîtâ*. ii. 16.

belonging to the atom, as distinguishable from the subjective language belonging to the Jîva), has no overt form of its own and therefore, in a strict and abstract sense, never changes, remaining ever the same in totality. It is the energy that physical science recognises as remaining constant in the universe. Its overt form is the multitude of changing forms and actions. And yet again, lest it should be said that even form is after all not pure and utter negation, but has an appearance at least, has an *ex-is*-tence, outer-being, and so should not be capable of destruction, the law makes provision for this also, and ordains that no form, however ephemeral, shall be destroyed beyond recall. As it has only pseudo-being, so it shall not have fixedness, but it shall have unending possibility, and therefore actuality, of recall and repetition. The remarks that apply to 'forms' apply also to 'actions,' 'motions,' 'movements,' which constitute the essence of change.

We see thus that these reflections *add* nothing to the primal trinity, but are included in it. Their details constitute all the universe, and may not be comprehended by any single individual mind and in any single particular book, however large they may be. As the extent of these is, such will be the amount of detail comprehended. But the main principles may be grasped, and as new details are brought forward by empirical experience, they may be classified and put away, as a matter of convenience, in accordance with those main principles.

We may conclude this line of observations by noticing another series of triplets very important in itself, and also illustrative in a high degree of the principle of reflections and re-reflections.

The attributes, size, life, and vibration, common to both aspects or halves of the Jîva-atom, all considered with special reference to the primal, twofold (or threefold) motion of alternation involved in the Negation, which constitutes the swing of the world-process, yield us these parallel triplets, *viz.*:

(1) 'increase, decrease, and equality' in respect of matter; and 'liberality, narrowness, and tolerance' in that of spirit;

(2) 'growth, decay, and continuance' in respect of body; and 'pursuit, renunciation, and indifference or equanimity,' in that of soul;

(3) 'expansion, contraction, and rhythm' in respect of the sheath; and 'pleasure, pain, and peace' in that of the Jîva.

We may also note that, in special relation to Mûla-prakṛiti, the triplet of size, etc., takes on the form of 'quantity, quality, and mode.' Its transformation with reference to Pratyag-âtmâ also may be described by the same three terms in the absence of other well-recognised ones, though the difference of connotation in the two cases is great; for they cover the different triplets mentioned by Kant under the heads of quantity, etc., in connection with the 'categories' and with 'logical judgments' respectively.

We may now proceed, in the second place, to specify the attributes that appear in the atom with reference to the primary attributes of Mûla-prakṛiti.

These are:—

(*a*) Dravya, द्रव्य, substance, or द्रव्यत्व, dravya-tva, substantiality, mass, power of self-maintenance, that which constitutes it a something having a separate existence, that which makes it 'capable of serving as the substratum of movement,' 'capable of being moved,'[1] the immediate manifestation of this substance, this 'compacted energy' being movement.

(*b*) Guṇa, गुण, all qualities whatsoever, and

(*c*) Karma, कर्म,[2] activity, vibration, incessant movement.

---

[1] द्रवितुं, or द्रावयितुं, योग्यं द्रव्यं ।

[2] These three terms belong specially to the Vaisheṣhika-system of Indian philosophy which deals with this part of metaphysic predominantly; but as with most of the other

This triplet of dravya, guṇa, and karma is, as has been already indicated more than once, a reflection and reproduction of more primal triplets. The mergence of Pratyag-âtmâ and Mûla-prakṛiti, producing the Jîva-atom, also reproduces therein their two triplets of attributes in this most familiar and therefore most important form. Sattva, rajas, and tamas become respectively transformed into guṇa, karma, aud dravya ; and sat, chit, and ânanda respectively into kriyâ, jñâna, and ichchhâ, which again correspond to karma, guṇa and dravya respectively. Jñâna, ichchhâ, and kriyâ will be treated of in the next section in connection with the Jîva-portion of the Jîva-atom.[1]

Saṃskṛit words used in this work, so with these, though they themselves are more or less current, yet the connotations that have been put into them here would often not be recognised, in some cases would be strongly repudiated, by the authors of most of the current Saṃskṛit works in which they are to be met with. The present writer believes, however, that these are the real original connotations, and that they were lost with the growth of the spirit of separateness and selfishness in the people, and the consequent gradual loss of the deeper metaphysic which unified and organised the various systems of philosophy as different chapters of a single work, clues to which are endeavoured to be rediscovered in these few pages, all too poor and fragmentary as they are.

[1] Hints, and more or less veiled statements, regarding these correspondences, are scattered over the *Devî-Bhâgavata*, especially in Pt. III. vi.—ix., VII. xxxii., and IX. l., and are also to be found in the *Kapila-Gîtâ* and other works on Tantra-Shâstra.

(i) Guṇa, then, is that in the atom which corresponds to the elements of chit or cognition, and sattva or cognisability, in Pratyag-âtmâ and Mûla-prakṛiti respectively. It is the *qualities* of matter, which alone we *know* and *can know*, and never the thing-in-itself, as that expression is used by western psychologists and philosophers; for that thing-in-itself, so far as it has a being at all, a pseudo-being, as substance, is the object of *desire* and not of *knowledge.* Guṇa may be subdivided again into three classes: (*a*) the मुख्य, mukhya, chief, व्यावर्तक, vyâvartaka, distinguishing or differentiating, स्वाभाविक or प्राकृतिक, svâbhâvika or prâkṛitika, natural, असाधारण, asâdhâraṇa, uncommon or special, or *essential, i.e.*, properties, or differentia, or propria, *e.g.*, special sensuous properties, sound, touch, colour, taste, or smell, etc., which would form part of definitions; (*b*) the गौण, gauṇa, secondary, आकस्मिक, âkasmika, accidental, साधारण, sâdhâraṇa, common, or *non-essential, i.e.*, qualities, which would form part of its descriptions; and (*c*) धर्म, dharma, लक्षण, lakṣhaṇa, attributes, which would generally include both, for, in reality, the distinction between essential and accidental rests only on greater or less persistence in space time and motion. We might perceive again in this triplet a general correspondence to the Self the Not-Self and the Negation respectively.

With reference to (*a*) we may note, that in our human race only five senses are working at the present time, and hence we have the five well-known sense-properties under the sub-head of 'essential'. The varieties of each of these again are many, and if we had the necessary information as to the details of the subject, we should be able to throw these into triplets, corresponding with and reflecting each other endlessly. Thus, under sound, we have: soft, harsh, grave, low, loud, rounded, shrill, sonorous, deep, light, heavy, even, piercing, rolling, crackling, bursting, tearing, thunderous, whistling, screaming, roaring, rushing, dashing, moaning, groaning, rasping, grinding, etc., etc., sounds. Tacts are smooth, rough, even, silky, flowery, velvety, hard, soft, firm, cool, warm, damp, dry, clammy, moist, etc. Colours are white, black, red, yellow, blue, brown, golden, violet, orange, grey, green, purple, etc., etc., with their endless shades and combinations. Tastes are sweet, salt, acid, astringent, hot, bitter, acrid, pungent, putrid, etc. Smells or scents are fragrant, malodorous, stimulating, rose, jasmine, violet, pârijâta, mâlatî, sugandha-râja, (the 'king of scents', also called rajanî-gandhâ the 'night-scent'), lemon, lily, lotus, the blooms of myrtle, neem, and mango, etc. These sub-varieties must necessarily be endless in accordance with the endlessness of the objects of the senses; but humanity possesses definite names only for those that it uses and experiences most frequently.

(*b*) The non-essential qualities are, by their very nature, more difficult to fix. They are, generally speaking, those which describe the relation and position of an object, to and amidst other objects; thus, well-built, ill-built, near, distant, commodious, insufficient, etc. Many of the properties mentioned above as amongst the essential, may, perhaps, on sifting, be found to be non-essential, or *vice versâ*. Reference to the purpose in hand decides generally whether a quality is non-essential or otherwise.

(*c*) Attributes, partaking of the characters of both, may be instanced as 'heat, cold, temperateness', 'lightness, heaviness, weightiness, softness, hardness, firmness, plasticity, rigidity, elasticity, pressure, suction, support, etc.,' 'shape, size, duration', etc. These attributes have an obvious reference to the latent and patent aspects of energy, and to Negation, as the others, properties and qualities, have to the Self in itself, and to the Not-Self as many, respectively. Such considerations are, clearly, capable of endless and useful elaboration. But we have not the opportunity and means for that elaboration here, and so must pass on.

From the psychological standpoint we may note in passing, every sense-property is something *sui generis*, on the same level and side by side with every other. As sense-properties, all are equal and independent, and none is grosser or subtler than any other, whence the current saying: "The experience of the musk's fragrance cannot be communicated by any amount of oaths and affirmations";[1] *i.e.*, it must be smelt personally to be known. Thus each sense-property, and each shade of it, must be experienced directly in order to come within the precise cognition and recognition of any Jîva. This is the manyness, the separateness and exclusiveness of sensations. The remarks made and figures given at p. 480, vol. iii., of *The Secret Doctrine* will be found very suggestive in this connection, and read together with what has gone before may help to show some consistency in the apparently very inconsistent statements made on this subject in the Purâṇas. Thus, it is declared that in our world-system, the first 'element' to come forth (to say nothing of the still earlier âdi or mahat-tattva, and the anupâdaka or buddhi tattva, which are only vaguely alluded to here and there) was âkâsha, with the guṇa of sound; then vâyu, with the

---

[1] नहि कस्तूरिकामोदः शपथेन विभाव्यते ।

guṇa of touch; then fire, with light and colour; then water, with taste; and, lastly, earth, with smell; and it is added that each succeeding one was derived from the next preceding, and retained the quality of its originator besides developing its own special quality. Again it is said that the order of evolution of the elements and qualities is entirely different in different cycles, mahâ-kalpas, of this and other world-systems. It is also said that the *number* of the elements and corresponding senses and sensations differs actually (as Voltaire only fancied in his *Zadig et Micromegas*) in different worlds, there being eighteen in some, thirty-six in others, and so forth,[1] as there are only five known to us in this world. Such also seems to be the meaning of the statement that "this world-system of ours is crowded round with infinite other systems governed by Brahmâs having five, six, seven and more up to thousands of *faces*."[2]. Still again, it is said, in the doctrine of पञ्चीकरण, pañchîkaraṇa,[3] quintuplication, the mixing of each of the five tattvas with each of the other four in certain proportions, that, at present, each material object has in it all five

[1] *Yoga-Vâsiṣhṭha.*

[2] *Tripâd-vibhûti-mahâ-nârâyaṇa-upaniṣhat.* vi.

[3] *Pañchadashî.* i. 26-30, and *Pañchîkaraṇa-vivaraṇa.*

elements, and, therefore, the possibility of being cognised by all five senses; but the most prevailing element gives it its best-recognised nature. And as a matter of fact we find that beings having different constitutions of the same sense, and the same being during different conditions of the same sense, receive different sensations from apparently the same sense-object. Thus it is now recognised that certain rays that are dark to men are luminous to ants, and *vice versâ*.

All this means again, in brief, that each atom having in it the common guṇa of sense-cognisibility, sensibility, has also therefore in it what is necessarily included in this universal quality, *viz.*, every possible particular guṇa; but only one or some are manifest and others latent, in different conditions of time, space, and motion, to different Jîvas, Jîvas being regarded as 'lines of consciousness.' That is to say, one kind of atom will mean one thing at one time and space to one kind of Jîva, and will, simultaneously and in that same position, mean a pseudo-infinite number of things to pseudo-infinite other kinds of Jîvas; and it will also mean pseudo-infinite kinds of things to the same kind of Jîva in the pseudo-infinite succession of time and space.

(ii) We may now turn to the karma-aspect

of the atom corresponding to the sat and rajas aspects of Pratyag-âtmâ and Mûla-prakṛiti respectively.

It may at first sight appear that sat, being, should correspond with dravya rather than karma. But if what has been said before, from time to time, on the nature of sat and ânanda, and again of rajas and tamas, is carefully considered, it will appear that sat properly corresponds to karma and not to dravya. 'Being' is what we are inclined to regard as the innermost, the most important, factor in the constitution of an object, because it *primâ facie* appears to be the most permanent; and dravya, as shown above, is such in the case of the atom; the idea therefore comes up strongly that dravya should be connected with 'being.' But the first premiss here is not accurate. It does not discriminate between 'being' and 'existence.' What is being, sat, in the Pratyag-âtmâ, is 'existence,' 'outer-is-ness,' in matter. And in the Pratyag-âtmâ (if such a distinction may be permitted where there is truly and strictly none possible, and where all are aspects and all absolutely equally necessary and important), ânanda, bliss, is even more 'inner' than 'being'; it is, so to say, the *feeling* of own-being; the difference between a man looking at himself with eyes open and again with eyes shut. In this sense ânanda may be said to be even more 'being' than is 'being' itself. And karma, therefore, corresponds not to this innermost being of ânanda, but to the outer being, the existence, the manifestation of sat. And existence, reality, appearance, manifestation, is all in and by action and movement. A very good physical illustration of this is the fact of natural history, that most insects and birds and quadrupeds, in wild life, are often so completely concealed by their mere protective colouring that their existence is not recognised at all, that they remain as it were non-existent, even when they are quite close to and right under the eye of the observer; but become manifest at once, *i.e.*, existent, with the slightest shake, motion, or action.[1]

Having thus shown that karma represents sat, we may proceed to note again that it is inseparable from the atom, is in fact one of its essential constituents. The consequence is that every atom is in unceasing motion.

Karma falls also into three kinds: (*a*) expansion, प्रसारण, prasâraṇa (corresponding to the boundlessness of the Self); (*b*) contraction, आकुञ्चन, âkuñchana (corresponding to the

[1] This point has lately been much emphasised in a psychological eference by the distinguished psychologist, Prof. Ladd, of America.

separate, mutual, repelling and restricting of not-selves); (*c*) आन्दोलन, ândolana, rhythmic vibration, corresponding to the (affirmative-) negation which sums up both movement and counter-movement in itself, and holds the two others together in the conjunction of alternation. The guṇas specially arising out of karma are: वेग, vega, speed, मांद्य, mândya, slowness or dulness, and गति, gati, velocity. Minor varieties under each of the three are endless, as in the case of guṇas: thus, rapid, slow, steady; ऊर्ध्वगमन, ûrdhvagamana, upward motion, अधोगमन adhogamana, downward motion, तिर्यग्गमन, tiryaggamana, sideways motion; उत्क्षेपण, ut-kṣhepaṇa, uplifting, अपक्षेपण apa-kṣhepaṇa, repulsing or casting away, अटन, aṭana, wandering; vertical horizontal, oblique; etc., etc.

(iii) Lastly we come to the dravya-aspect of the atom which, it is clear from the reasons already given, represents the ânanda and tamas aspects of the Self and the Not-Self respectively. It is the 'etat-ness,' the mere 'this-ness' of the atom, in a strict sense. It is that in the atom which is the heart of the thing, its substance, its inertia, its mass and weight and resistance, all that makes it a something existing in and for itself, so far as it can have such a pseudo-existence-in-itself at all. It appears mysterious and unresolvable only when and if, after asking:

"What is *this?*" we try fallaciously to answer the question in terms of something else than guṇa and karma. The answer to that question must always be in terms of guṇa and karma, or, otherwise, merely the reiteration: 'It is a *this*.' Three *aspects* make up the *fact* of the atom—इदम्, idam, '*this*' (dravya), इत्थम्, ittham, '*such*' a this (guṇa), and एवम्, evam, '*thus*' (karma), and they can never be separated from each other.

Dravya too may be sub-divided into: (*a*) substances with positive weight (predominant), in the aspect of attraction; गुरु, guru, heavy; (*b*) those with negative weight (predominant),[1] in the aspect of repulsion; लघु, laghu, buoyant; (*c*) those with inertia, dead weight, positive-negative or passive-active resistance to all change, self-maintenance, in whatever condition the thing happens to be; स्थिर, sthira, stable. The sub-divisions of these, as of the others, are endless: mahat, buddhi, âkâsha, vâyu, tejas, âpas, pṛithivî, solids, liquids, gases, ethers, metals, non-metals, organic, inorganic, minerals, vegetables, animal substances, etc., etc. Some of the qualities arising out of these sub-divisions have been already noticed before in the guṇa-aspect.

---

[1] See Dolbear *Matter, Ether, and Motion.* P. 91.

We have noted before that resistance is of the very essence and nature of dravya, and we see now that it has the dual form of attraction-repulsion. This makes further clear, if such clarification were needed, that dravya represents the ânanda and tamas aspects, which again correspond to the Shakti-energy of the first trinity. We *desire* a *thing*, we *know* its *qualities*, and we *act* upon, change or modify, its *movements*.

The three sub-divisions of dravya may also, as before, be regarded as corresponding, in the order in which they are stated above, to the Self and sattva, to the Not-Self and rajas, and to Negation and tamas respectively.

It will have come to the notice of the reader that the task of expressing these correspondences precisely becomes more and more difficult as we enter into greater and greater details and sub-divisions, and the same triplet is repeated under more than one head. The aspects become gradually so intermingled that they cannot be distinguished easily, and the assignment of triplets in a table of correspondences may naturally and reasonably vary, if the students differ in standpoint and in the amount of attention paid to each factor, some regarding one aspect as the predominant one and others another. In this last case, for example, if attraction be regarded as *active* affirmation, attention being specially directed to the activity, and repulsion as *passive* and steady negation of others, of manyness, then the two appear reasonably to correspond to rajas or Not-Self, and sattva or Self, respectively. But if attraction be regarded as unification, and repulsion as separation, it would be right to say, as said above, that they correspond to sattva or the Self, and rajas or the Not-Self respectively. Still again, if attention were paid to the fact that the unification of attraction, when it appears in the limited atom, is a false and not a true unification, that it is the assertion in reality of the Not-Self, which is then only masquerading as the Self, while the separation of repulsion is the diminution of such a false self and therefore an advancement of the true Self, then we would go back to the correspondence of attractive weight with the Not-Self, and of negative weight with the Self. The view of this particular correspondence put forward here as the main one, *viz.*, of positive weight to the Self, of repulsive weight to the Not-Self, and of inertia to the Negation, proceeds upon the consideration that the fact of the unity and of the principle of unification present in the atom is more characteristic, in the present reference, than the fact that the atom is only masquerading as a one and a self.

This should not confuse the careful student, but should only help him to look at every question from many sides and standpoints, and so recognise the harmonising elements of truth in each view rather than the discordant elements of error.

The laws previously ascertained apply to this triplet of aspects of the atom. As these three cannot be separated from each other, though, turn by turn, one is predominant and the others in the back-ground, so the three sub-divisions of each are also contemporaneous in this way: that one appears to be more manifest from one standpoint, while the other appears to be more manifest from another standpoint at the same time. This last statement applies especially to the sub-divisions of dravya and karma, as to which it is well-known that what is solid and immovable to one individual may be pliable as a liquid or a gas to another, and *vice versâ*; and, again, that what appears to be linear motion from one standpoint appears as rotatory or curved from another, and *vice versâ*. Provision for the limitation, in time, space, and motion, for the death and re-birth of these aspects of the atom, even in the midst of their persistent continuance, is made by the fact of change, absorption and transformation of each into other kinds of guṇas, karmas, and dravyas, and yet again recovery of their previous condition, in an endless manner. Ample illustration of this will be found in physical science, in connection with the doctrines of the pseudo-indestructibility of matter, the pseudo-eternity and conservation of energy and motion, showing how substances (energies proper), attributes, and vibration, are being constantly transformed, all the while retaining the possibility of recovering their older shapes.

The concomitance of these three aspects, dravya, guṇa, and karma, and, by inference, of all their subdivisions, from the metaphysical standpoint of the whole, is especially important and significant to bear in mind. It will help to show the underlying truth in each, and reconcile all, of many conflicting hypotheses of physical science. Thus: some hold the view that atoms are nothing substantial but *only* vortices, pure motion, vortices of *nothing*, one may fairly say, for even when the holders of this theory say that the atoms are vortices of *ether*, they, in order to avoid an obvious *petitio principii*, take care to describe ether in terms the opposite of those used in describing matter, and so practically reduce ether to *nothing*; others say that they are substantial, whether they have or have not a vortical or other motion besides. So too, the first theory of light was corpuscular, that light *is* corpuscles; then it was discarded in favour of the undulatory theory, that light *is* undulations; with the discovery of new metals, radium, etc., and observations of their behaviour, the radiatory theory is being reinstated again.[1] So again, one extreme view is that all sensations *are* merely vibrations of the objects sensed, transmitted to animal nerves; another extreme is that they have nothing to do with vibrations, which may or may not be a parallel coincident, but are things *sui generis*. The scientists who have trained themselves in philosophy also, as many are beginning to do now, look at the question impartially from both poiuts of view, and therefore readily see the defects of each extreme, and acknowledge that nothing yet known explains how a certain number of *vibrations* at one end of a nerve should appear as the *sensation* red, or blue, or yellow, at the other end of that nerve. The inconclusiveness of all such theories lies in their exaggeration, their one-sidedness, and their attempt to reduce

---

[1] Dr. Hübbe-Schleiden (of Döhren bei Hannover, Germany) suggests the following as a more exact statement of these theories:—"1. Light is emission of corpuscles (Newton). 2. Light is vibration of ether (Huyghens, Fresnel). 3. Light is emission of electrons."

all the aspects of the atom to only *one* aspect, guṇas and karmas to dravya only, or dravyas and karmas to guṇa only, or guṇas and dravyas to karma only. The truth is that all three aspects are always and inseparably concomitant; that an atom is ever a something, an etat, a this, which has always a certain motion, a certain kind of vibration, which motion or vibration again is always accompanied by a special sense-property. "The three aspects are inseparable and are the expression of all that happens in the physical world. Given one of the three in all its details, the other two would be known."[1]

A few more concrete, if somewhat cursory, observations may be of use to illustrate the simultaneity and concurrence of all aspects of the atom. Thus, though, at the present stage of evolution, volume and form appear to be specially, indeed, even almost exclusively, connected with the sense of vision amongst all the senses, yet it is not so, in reality. Even the current usage which employs words having a spatial reference, in connection with all senses, shows this, and is not merely metaphorical.

---

[1] Max Verworn. *General Physiology.* P. 546; *his* three aspects, however, are 'Substance, form, and transformation of energy,' form being substituted for sense-quality, and transformation of energy for motion.

We speak of bulky or extensive or voluminous or massive sounds and touches and tastes and smells; also of their forms. The words are so employed because of a fact in nature; sounds, touches, tastes, and smells also have volume and form; they belong to sense-objects, to etats, are in space, time, and motion. The words quantity, measure, magnitude, etc., apply to all sense-objects and with a clear meaning. The pitch and loudness and timbre of sounds; the freshness or staleness, strength or weakness, insipidity and vapidity or acuteness and intensity of tastes; lightness or heaviness of touches; sweet sounds, sweet sights, sweet scents, and sweet tastes; beautiful voices, beautiful forms and colours, beautiful smells; rough and smooth tones as well as touches; all these are illustrations of the fact. Because of such common features hiding behind diverse features, under guṇa as well as dravya and karma, is it possible to translate the sensations of one sense into those of another, under special circumstances and conditions, the manipulation of which belongs to that region of science which is only just opening up to the public, under the names of hypnotism, mesmerism, animal magnetism, psychism, telepathy, clairvoyance, etc. The cases of psychics able to experience any sensation with or at any part of the body are now recognised by most persons. The ill-understood vedântic doctrine of the quintuplication of the five tattvas or sense-elements, âkâsha (ether), vâyu (air), tejas (fire), âpas (water), and pṛithivî (earth), seems also to refer to this subject. It seems to be the completion of the physics of the universe begun by the Vaisheṣhika and the Nyâya systems in their statements as to अणु, aṇu, atoms, द्व्यणुक, dvyaṇuka, diatoms, त्रसरेणु, trasareṇu, tri-diatoms, etc. This is not clear now in the absence of details, but the suggestion that they are such completion comes unmistakably and unavoidably to everyone who will approach the old books in the genuine spirit of the even-minded student. Working at this suggestion and comparing the apparently conflicting statements in the Purâṇas, the student may succeed in making up some at least provisionally satisfactory system of the essential principles of chemistry, physiology, and cosmogony, pending knowledge of details through development of special faculty by yoga.[1]

We see, then, that all three aspects run on indefeasible parallels, even as thought, thing,

[1] The student will find much help and suggestion on this point in theosophical literature generally, and in *The Secret Doctrine* of H. P. Blavatsky, and Ch. I. of the *Ancient Wisdom* of Annie Besant especially.

and motion always accompany each other though distinguishable, and that change in any of the three will necessarily bring about a change in the other two also. In a sense, it is true, there should not be any change in the dravya; a mere 'this' will remain only 'this'; and dravya constitutes the pseudo-permanent element in the atom, as has been said before; yet, seeing that each etat is inseparably connected with a quality and a motion, it happens that there is, as common observation shows, a *sort* of change of *nature* in the substance also. The substance is no longer recognised as the same. The energy has also changed its form. Water becomes gas, and people naturally and not unreasonably say that the *substance* has changed, as well as motions and qualities. In this sense, the *tattva*, the 'that-ness,' the element, may properly be said to change. Rigorously speaking, there can be no change in mere, pure, 'this' (dravya); but no more can there be any change in mere, sheer, 'such' (guṇa), or in mere, abstract, 'thus' (karma). What changes is the particularised condition of each as limited and made concrete by necessary relativity to the others.

We have now generally defined and described the three universal attributes of the atom. Wherever an atom is, there must be present these three also. Whatever its variations, these must accompany it. Let us now try to find out something more about thc variations of the atom generally. These variations will naturally be most prominently connected with the guṇa and the karma, though change in these will cause the appearance of change in the dravya also.

Under guṇa, we have inferred that in respect of form, corresponding to the Not-Self, etats have, by reflection of the unity and completeness of the Self, one universal underlying form, the sphere, and a pseudo-infinity of other forms made up of the intermixture of points and lines. In respect of volume corresponding to the Self, the common fact is only this, that there must be 'bulk,' 'triple-dimension,' 'extension,' *some* size, and the detail is that the etat must have *every possible* size. Thus we have atoms of all possible sizes, each size of atom (with corresponding other qualities, vibrations, substantial nature, etc.) constituting one plane of matter, and each plane constituting the 'outer' sheath, the material, of a pseudo-infinite series of world-systems on the same level with each other, and the next minuter size constituting the 'inner' spiritual' or 'ideal' counterpart and core thereof and therein. The case is the same with special qualities. The presence of *some one quality*, of 'sense-cognisability,' is common and inevitable; but there is no restriction what that must be. Reason and the law of non-arbitrariness require that the whole of all possible qualities must be present in the whole and every part of the world-process, *manifesting*, of course, to *any one Jīva*, only in *succession*.

The main kinds of the karma-movements of atoms may be deduced, as a tentative hypothesis, as follows. We have seen that the basic ultimate atom everywhere, in whichever world-system we take it, would be a sphere, though size and quality may vary; for it is formed by the aham-consciousness revolving round itself in the circle of the logion. But, existing side by side as spheres, the forces of approach and recess work between them, as mutual attraction and repulsion. Every atom endeavours to approach and recede from every other simultaneously. The same atom would attract as well as repel another at the same time. In other words, every atom would try to *absorb* another into itself for its own growth (corresponding to the intensification and expansion of the consciousness 'aham—etat (asmi),' and at the same time to *resist* being absorbed into another, so losing instead of intensifying its own self-existence and identity. With attraction and repulsion coming into play, the self-revolving spheres would begin to move in straight lines towards or from each other. At this stage movements would become manifest. Before this (from the standpoint of the particular world-system we may be in) the self-revolution would not be apparent as movement; the atom would scarcely be apparent even as a something; that there would be in it, even then, a necessary movement of self-revolution, would be only a metaphysically necessary assumption. The next stage would be that after one atom has secured and subordinated another, absorbed it into itself (the why and how of which may appear afterwards), the two together, making a line, would now fall into the self-revolving movement of the stronger, and the circular-disc movement would result. Lastly, the disc revolving on its own axis would become the sphere again, but a sphere the sphericity and motion of which are manifest instead of hypothetical, as in the condition of the primary atom. We may consider here that as the shortest line is composed of two atom-points, and the smallest disc must be made of such a line circling around itself according to the motion of the stronger atom, so the smallest solid sphere should be made of at least, and also at most, three such lines crossing each other at the middle and revolving round that point on the axis made by the strongest line. In other words, the manifest sphere would consist of three double-atoms. Such is perhaps the metaphysic underlying the vague available statements of the Nyâya and Vaisheṣhika systems as to diatoms being first formed from atoms, then tri-diatoms from diatoms, and the world—our own world-system at least—from them. This order reproduces respectively, the Absolute, the duality of the Self and the Not-Self, and the triple duality of the Jîva-atom, —the individual, the definite one (which most systems of numerals express by a line), formed by the junction of the self with a not-self. The intermixtures and modifications of these main movements, *viz.*, the linear, circular, and revolutional or spiral, make up the necessary pseudo-infinite variations of movements in the world-process.

As to the variations of the dravya-aspect, it has been said that they accompany the variations of the other two. It need only be added that the greater the number and the more restricted the area of the rhythm-movements, the revolutions, of the atom and the derivative molecule, the more firm, rigid, gross, and exclusive and resistant for others, and attractive and existent for themselves, they would become; and *vice versâ*, the fewer the number and the wider the area of the movement, the subtler, more plastic and more evanescent they would be. The atom of each world-system being regarded as representing the mere 'objectivity,' the Not-Self, the Etat or This, it follows that it is uniform and unchanged throughout the life of that system. Differentiation probably begins with the diatoms, which may be regarded as coeval with the guṇas, these corresponding, in the Jîva-atom of a system, to what the तन्मात्र, tanmâtra, would be in the consciousness of the Îshvara of that system, as may be seen later. The guṇas referred to here are their special sense-qualities, sound, touch, etc., considered psychologically. The differentiation may be considered as definitely marked at the stage of tri-diatoms, corresponding to the elements, the sthûla-bhûtas, defined and characterised by these sensations, *viz.*, âkâsha, vâyu, etc., and to the respective outer sensory and motor organs of the living beings of that system. These tri-diatoms may, then, for practical purposes, be regarded as representing that dravya-aspect of each thing which is variable. Before the development of these tri-diatoms (in the Vaisheṣhika and not the modern chemical sense) there would be probably no manifest differentiation of the various tattvas, the sense-elements, one from the other. The variations of such ultimate molecules of a world-system, as physical science is now gradually showing (in terms of 'atoms,' however, rather than of 'molecules'), would correspond with variations of resistance and density, of number and kind of vibrations, and of special sense-qualities.

We see then that the atom is not an invariably fixed quantity. Its fixedness is only an appearance, and exists only in connection with world-systems taken singly. Just as a stone, a tree, an animal, a human being, have an appearance of permanence and continuance from day to day, and yet are changing incessantly from moment to moment; just as a whirling torch, or catherine-wheel, or gas-flame, has the appearance of a flat disc or sheet of fire, though something altogether different in reality; so an atom has only a pseudo-fixedness and sameness of size, duration, movement, etc., in space, time and motion. The appearance of fixedness in incessant change is due to the imposition of 'sameness' by a connected individual consciousness—the consciousness of the Brahmâ—in each world-system. In other words, the nature of the Jîva, as Self, imposes (according to its own necessities to be dealt with later), a certain sameness and continuance, while the nature of the atom, as Not-Self, requires incessant change; and the reconciliation is found in constant *repetition* of the vibrations which maintain the other attributes together with themselves. Apart from such appearance of fixity there is truly a pseudo-infinite variety in every aspect of the atom, and a pseudo-infinite pseudo-infinity, pseudo-infinity within pseudo-infinity. Thus each size of atom, together with all its attributes and qualities corresponding to that size, is necessarily pseudo-infinite in number, and would be found in every part of space and time. And yet, when the geometrical axiom, which applies to all things in space, says: "*Two* things cannot occupy the same space at once," how can all these pseudo-infinite sizes of atoms exist in the same space? The reconciliation is to be found in the fact that this apparent pseudo-infinity is a 'psychological,' an 'ideal,' infinity, entirely created and carried along with itself, wherever it goes, by the consciousness of the Self as a foil to its own infinite-infinity. The geometrical axiom does not apply to the Absolute-consciousness which transcends and includes space and time and motion, and creates all the infinite overlappings of individuality which have been mentioned before, and which correspond to the apparent overlappings of the atoms. And yet again, lest there should be even the appearance of a violation of the geometrical axiom, the various sizes, whenever and wherever examined by any one individual consciousness, would be found to fit one into another and constitute the different and inter-penetrating planes of the world-systems.

Thus it happens that what is an atom to one Jîva, within the limits, spatial and durational, of a solar system, may contain whole worlds within itself to a Jîva sufficiently minute. And, *vice versâ*, what is a solar system to us may form only an atom to a Jîva sufficiently vast. The repeated and much emphasised statement in the *Yoga Vâsiṣhṭha*, that a world contains atoms, and each of these atoms a world, and that world atoms again, and so on *ad infinitum*, is justified in this manner in a very literal sense. Consider here what was said before, as to the chain of individualities in a single organism, and as to the Virât-Puruṣha, and the thought may become quite clear. The student will also be greatly helped here by the latest researches of physical science, going to show that what has till now been regarded as the indivisibly ultimate atom consists of hundreds of 'corpuscles,'[1] and by the tentative results

---

[1] The word 'atom' has been used here throughout as equivalent to the words 'aṇu' or 'param-âṇu' of Saṃskṛit. The new word 'ion' is, it seems, nearer to 'aṇu'; but it has

of enquiry by budding superphysical senses so far as they are publicly available.[1]

How order is imposed on this infinity of disorder; how the world-process is ever an organic whole, within whatever limits of space and time and motion we take it; and how this pseudo-infinity of pseudo-infinities is held together in co-ordination, in a system of planes within planes, lokas within lokas, by the mighty stress of the principle of the individuality and oneness of the universal Self—this may all appear in the next chapter on the Jîva.

---

not yet got a recognised position in western science and philosophy, and is still competing with 'corpuscles', 'electrons', etc. When the ideas and words have settled down in the course of a few years, it may perhaps be useful to change our nomenclature also. In the meanwhile the idea intended to be conveyed by the word 'atom' here is that of a piece or particle of 'etat', 'this', 'matter', which, for the time and in the particular world-system and from the standpoint with which we may be concerned at the moment, is ultimate and 'indivisible'. Sometimes, though very rarely, the word has been used here as equivalent to 'sheath' or 'body', and this has been done because, in the particular connection in which the word has been so used, the sheath or body is the irreducible minimum which the Jîva requires for its manifestation.

[1] Vide Annie Besant's paper on "Occult Chemistry" in *Lucifer* (now *The Theosophical Review*) for November, 1895 (xvii. 216).

CHAPTER XV.

Jîva-Atoms—Subjectively, *i.e.*, Jîvas.

At the outset of this chapter we may note that the aspects of size specialised with reference to the Jîva would be 'range or extent of consciousness in all its manifestations, cognition, desire, and action,' 'its definiteness or intensity,' and its 'calibre or scope generally'. These would sub-divide into 'broad-mindedness, narrow-mindedness, rationality or common sense', 'vagueness or weakness, clearness or strength, distinctness or firmness', 'long-headedness or far-sightedness, width of interests, depth', etc., etc.

As to the specialisations of duration and vibration, it need only be said that the words used in connection with matter in the preceding chapter apply, by ordinary usage, to corresponding features of mind also.

With these brief suggestions, we may pass on to the features more prominently characteristic of the Jîva, as the embodiment of consciousness.

The entire nature of consciousness is exhaustively described by and contained in the words: "I-this-not (am)." This is the

Absolute-consciousness, the true चिद्घन, *chid-ghana*, compacted chit, महासंवित्, mahâ-saṃvit, great consciousness, which, in its transcendence of numbers, limitations and relations, includes all that is governed by numbers, limitations and relations, and indeed is all. This consciousness is the Absolute, and includes both the factors of what is ordinarily distinguished as the द्वंद्वं, dvandvam, the pair, of चित्, chit, the conscious (corresponding to Pratyag-âtmâ) and जड jaḍa, the unconscious (corresponding to Mûla-prakṛiti). It may not unreasonably be objected, because of this fact, that the word 'consciousness' is not altogether suitable as an epithet for the Absolute, even with qualificatory adjectives. But it becomes unavoidable, now and again, to describe the Absolute in special terms borrowed from the triplets of the attributes of Pratyag-âtmâ and Mûla-prakṛiti, which are the penultimates of the world-process, as the Absolute is the very ultimate and the all. The nearest approach to the ultimate is obviously by the penultimates, hence the necessity of speaking in terms of the latter; and this is why Brahman is described, in the Upanishats and other works on Vedânta, now as pure or shuddha-chit, again as the mahâ-sat or boundless being, and finally as the ânanda-ghana or ânanda-maya, composed or compacted of bliss; also as the tamas beyond the tamas, the darkness beyond the darkness, the shuddha or pure sattva, and the paro-rajas, the transcending-rajas. And so, for our present purposes, we have to speak of Brahman as the Absolute-consciousness, slightly emphasising the pratyag-âtmic aspect thereof rather than the mûla-prâkṛitic, but carefully guarding the while against possible misconstruction by openly stating that fact at the outset.

In its unique completeness, then, this Absolute-consciousness includes every possible cognition, every possible desire, every possible action, all at once and for ever; even as it includes all possible objects of cognition, desire and action, namely qualities, substances and movements. But taken as consisting of successive and separable parts in the pseudo-infinity of the world-process, it appears as broken up into the three aspects of jñâna or cognition, ichchhâ or desire, and kriyâ or action. How these three and only three aspects arise in the Jîva, on the collision of the Self and the Not-Self, has been already outlined in the chapter on Pratyag-âtmâ where the genesis of sat, chit, and ânanda is explained. It may be briefly restated thus.

An ego bound to a non-ego in the bond of the logion is necessarily bound by a triple bond at three points in contact with three corresponding points in the non-ego, *viz.*, jñâna, ichchhâ and kriyâ on the one hand, and guṇa, dravya, and karma, respectively, on the other. "I-this-(am)not"—in this fact we see the following:

(1) The 'I' and the 'this,' being placed opposite to each other, are either turning face towards face, or face away from face. The ego cognises, perceives the non-ego, receives into itself the *reflection* and the imprint of that non-ego (metaphorically as well as literally, as will appear later), or ignores and forgets it. This is (dual or rather triple) jñâna.

(2) The 'I' *tends* to move *towards* or *away from* the 'not-I.' This *tendency* is desire, corresponding to the affirmation-negation of Shakti. It is (dual or rather triple) ichchhâ.

(3) The ego *actually* moves towards or away from, the non-ego. This is (dual or rather triple) kriyâ.

All these are but modifications, forms, aspects, or degrees of the main fact of identification or separation between the Self and the Not-Self.

Fichte seems to have endeavoured to express the same or a similar idea thus: "(1) The ego exhibits itself as limited by the non-ego (that is to say, the ego is cognitive); (2) conversely, the ego exhibits the non-ego as limited by the ego (that is to say, the ego is active)."[1]

---

[1] Stirling's *Schwegler*. P. 265.

In other words, we may say that there is a mutual action and cognition between the ego and the non-ego: the action of the non-ego upon the ego is the cognition of the non-ego by the ego; and the cognition (if the expression may be used) by the non-ego of the ego is conversely the action of the ego on the non-ego. When the ego impresses itself on the non-ego, we have action from the standpoint of the ego and cognition from that of the non-ego. When the non-ego imprints itself on the ego, we have cognition from the standpoint of the ego and action from that of the non-ego. To this it should be added that the condition intermediate between cognition and action, intermediate between the ego's 'being influenced and shaped' by the non-ego, on the one hand, and its 'influencing and shaping' the non-ego, on the other, is desire. The corresponding condition of the non-ego would probably be best described by the word *tension*. This desire is always hidden, while cognition and action are manifest.

Multifarious triplets arise under cognition, desire, and action. (1) 'Waking, sleeping, dreaming;' 'presentation, oblivion, representation;' 'knowing, forgetting, recollection;' truth, error, illusion;' 'sensation, conception, perception;' 'term, proposition, syllogism;' 'पद, pada, वाक्य, vâkya, मान, mâna;' 'concept or notion, judgment, reasoning;' 'reasonableness or sobriety, fancy, imagination;' 'real or actual, unreal or fanciful, ideal;' 'observation, thought, science;' 'concentration, meditation, attention;' 'attention, distraction, research, or rapport, or union, or hate, indifference;' 'partiality, carelessness, justice;' 'desire, emotion, will;' etc. (3) 'Action, yoga,' etc. (2) 'Like, dislike, toleration;' 'love, reaction, balance;' 'activity, indolence, effort;' 'restlessness, fatigue, perseverance;' 'act, labour, industry;' 'action, plan, scheme;' 'evolution, involution, revolution;' etc. These may be treated of in detail later on. In the meanwhile, some observations as to the general relations of subject and object, individuals and the surroundings they live amidst, the more prominent conditions of the *life* of the world-process, may be recorded here.

It has been said that an ego is literally imprinted with and modelled to the shape of a cognised non-ego, and that cognition by an ego means and is the action of a non-ego upon it. It might be questioned how it is that action, cognition, and even desire, which are the attributes of Self, subject, can ever belong, or be spoken of as belonging, to Not-Self, object; and, conversely, how the capabilities of being acted on, cognised, and desired, which are the attributes of Not-Self, can ever belong, or be spoken of, as belonging to Self. The answer is this. If we were speaking of the universal Self or the pseudo-universal Not-Self, then it would be perfectly correct to say that jñâna, ichchhâ, and kriyâ, or rather their root-principles, chit, ânanda, and sat, belong exclusively to the Self; and guṇa, karma, and dravya, or rather their root-principles, sattva, rajas, and tamas, belong exclusively to the Not-Self. But we are now in the domain of the limited and the particular, and are dealing not with abstract Pratyag-âtmâ and pseudo-abstract Mûla-prakṛiti, but with limited, separate, selves and not-selves; and it has been amply shown in the last two chapters that a limited self means a composite of Self and Not-Self, a Jîva-atom, wherein the Jîva-aspect is predominant; while a limited not-self equally means a composite of Self and Not-Self, but a composite in which the atom-aspect is predominant. The consequence of this is that we find both the triplets of attributes present in every such composite, although of course one triplet always predominates over the other, thereby giving rise to the distinction between animate and inanimate.

Thus it comes about that each separate not-self, being ensouled by a self and therefore being a pseudo-self, assumes by the connection of identity with the universal Self, the characteristics of the latter, and this assumption takes on the form of a pseudo-infinite endeavour to find, and therefore to spread and impose, itself everywhere and always. Hence a pseudo-infinite radiation, by vibration, of each and every not-self, that is to say, of each and every piece or mass whatsoever of Mûla-prakṛiti, out of the pseudo-infinite permutations and combinations of all possible sizes of such pieces or masses, to which it is at all possible to apply the adjectives 'each' and 'every.' In other words, each and every not-self is endeavouring pseudo-infinitely to reproduce itself and fill infinity with its own form, as is now nearly established even by physical science in the doctrine of the incessant and endless mutual radiation and registration by all objects of their own and of all others' pictures of all qualities whatsoever, sights, sounds, smells, etc.; and this is the *action* of the not-selves upon the selves, which action, *in* the selves, appears as cognition.

This reproduction, it is obvious, takes place literally. When we see an object, the picture of the object is imprinted on our eye, on the retina; that is to say, the retina (or the purpurine, with which, as the latest researches go to show, the retina is covered), takes on, becomes modified into, the very shape of the object seen; and the eye is, in the life of the physical plane, veritably the very ego that sees. In the moment of seeing with the physical eye, it is impossible to say: "My eye sees and not I." What is invariably said and meant is: "*I* see." The I and the organ of vision are here literally identical for all purposes. It is the same with every other sense. The immediate reason of this is that while in the converse case, the *activity* of the apparent not-self is due to its hiding a self within, in this case the *shapeability*, which is cognition, of every self is due to its hiding within a not-self, a sheath, an upâdhi. As in the one case the not-self strives to achieve infinity in pseudo-infinite reproduction, because of having become identified with a self, and therefore *the* universal Self; so, in this case, the Self becomes limited and reflective, because of having become identified with a not-self.

In order that the Self and the Not-Self, so entirely opposed to each other, should enter into dealings with each other, it is necessary that each should assume the characteristics of the other, and so, abating their opposition, come nearer to each other. The interchange of substance between nucleus and protoplasm is a good illustration.[1] In this fact we see before us

[1] Verworn. *General Physiology*. P. 518.

the principle of the genesis of upâdhis, sheaths, organisms, and organs of sense and action. The ego *becomes* (of course, illusorily and apparently, and for the time being) the organ of sense or action, in order to perceive the sensible or act upon it. "The Âtmâ who knows (*i.e.*, under the stress of the consciousness) 'may I smell this' (*becomes* or *is*) the nose (the organ of smell), for the sake of (experiencing) odour." [1]

Such is the metaphysical significance of the organs of sense and action. They are the very Jîva for the time. The Jîva is identified with them entirely while they are working. Otherwise there is no sufficient reason for a *third* something, an instrument of mediation, not only a relation but a thing, between the only two factors of the world-process, the Self, on the one side, and the Not-Self, on the other. That they are at all distinguished as instruments is only from the standpoint of the abstract Self.

The metaphysical significance of sense-media, odorous particles, saliva, air, ether, &c., is similar. The systematic and psychologically consistent names for these media, in Saṃskṛit, whatever their exact nature may be ultimately determined to be, are pṛithivî (earth) for the medium of odour, âpas or jalam (water) for taste, tejas or agni (fire) for vision, vâyu (air)

---

[1] *Chhândogya Upanishat.* VIII. xii. 4-5.

for touch, and âkâsha (ether) for sound. These media are, according to the Vedânta, the five pervading root-elements — and not the compounds we live amidst — distinguished and defined radically by their special *sensuous* and *active* qualities, which are said to go in pairs; thus, sound and speech with ear and vocal organ belonging to âkâsha; vision and figure-formation with eye and hands belonging to agni; and so forth. And their agency, to secure communion between organ and sense-object, is metaphysically necessitated in order, by the fact of pervasion and diffusion through space, to give to the sense-object the semblance of the universal Self, which reaches and includes all and is within the reach of all. This pervasion, which, metaphysically, is pseudo-infinite in extent, is actually reproduced in the fact of each brahmâṇḍa, world-system or macrocosm, being pervaded by one individuality, just as much as the piṇḍâṇḍa, the microcosm, a human organism, is pervaded by one individuality. The vast masses of the root-elements that serve as the sense-media of the organisms inhabiting our brahmâṇḍa, for instance, constitute, in their totality, the *body* of the Îshvara who *is* the brahmâṇḍa; the unity of his individuality brings together our senses and sense-bjects in these sense-media, he himself being but as an infinitesimal Jîva in a vaster brahmâṇḍa, and so on pseudo-infinitely. This is why the Îshvaras also are called विभु, vibhu, pervading. It is only the principle of overlapping individualities in another view. Later chapters may contain more on this point, *viz.*, how communion between two *separate* things, subject and object, in the way of cognition, desire, and action, is possible and takes place only because the two are also *one* as being, both of them, parts of a higher individuality, a larger subject.

The remarks made in the preceding chapter as to the pseudo-infinite series of involucra of the Jîva, one within another, should be recalled in this connection. Taking the case of vision, for instance, we find as the first step, that the act of seeing means the picturing of the object seen on the retina, which at that stage is for all purposes identical with, and is, the seer. But analysing further we find that, in the human being, the act of vision is by no means completed with this picturing on the retina. Vibrations of nerves convey the picture to a further centre in the brain—not yet definitely determined by physiological investigations. Physical research leaves the matter here for the present. But metaphysic deduces, as an inference from the inseparable conjunction of dravya, guṇa, and karma, that, whatever that brain-centre might be ultimately decided to be, it will be found that just as the vibrations and particles of the outer visible object, transmitted through the ether (or whatever other element may finally be determined to be the medium of light, and however it may be named, the Saṃskṛit name being tejas as said before), make a picture of that object on the retina, so the retinal picture, which has now in turn become 'the outer visible object' to the more-inward-receded Jîva, is transmitted in still more minute particles, by nerve-vibrations, to a corresponding subtler organ or brain-centre which is now masquerading as the seer in place of the eye, in the present condition of organisms. And further research will show the process repeated pseudo-infinitely inwards, taking the sheath into subtler and ever subtler planes of matter.

But while this series of sheaths, one within another, is theoretically pseudo - infinite, in practice and as a matter of fact—if we take any organism, in any one cycle of space and time—we shall necessarily find it consisting of only a limited and countable number of such sheaths with one unanalysable core, the very filmiest of films it may be, but unanalysable any further for the time being, which in that cycle represents, and for all purposes is, the very self of the Jîva.

From another and higher standpoint, embracing a wider cycle of space and time, that film will also be analysable, and be seen to be not the innermost core but only an outer sheath, hiding within itself another core *which* will *then* be irreducible. Evidence of this we find even physically in comparing the earliest available unicellular organisms of our terrene life and evolution with the latest most complex ones. In the human being the brain with its centres takes the place of the Self, and is the main seat of consciousness (from the standpoint of physiology), but is hedged round and overlaid with numbers of other parts of the body, nerves, ganglia, senses, etc., through which only it can be reached. In the unicellular organism the nucleus is probably the centre of consciousness,[1] and is, as it were, all the brain, the sense organs, etc., in one; in its case the Jîva has not yet learnt to make the distinction—involved in the expressions, 'my eyes' 'my ears'—between the Jîva (identified with the brain as centre of consciousness) and its sense-instruments; and hence it has got no centre of consciousness which may be separate from sense-instruments. But when the consciousness begins to make such distinction, the nucleus at once resolves into a subtler core (apparently, but not yet positively determined to be the

[1] Verworn. *General Physiology*. P. 508.

nucleolus) with different parts wrapping it round; and under the continuing stress of the individualised consciousness, there appears the progressive development and differentiation of functions and instruments which is called evolution.

It should be noted here that the expression 'my brain' has not the same significance as 'my eyes' and 'my hands.' Of course it has a certain meaning, but the consciousness of my brain being distinct and different from me is by no means so definite, full, and clear in the ordinary man as is the consciousness of the eyes and the hands being thus different and distinct. The expression gains fuller and fuller significance as the 'I' retreats further and further inwards, and is able to separate itself more and more actually from the physical body. 'My clothes' has a much fuller and clearer meaning than 'my hands and feet;' 'my hands and feet' has a much clearer and fuller meaning than 'my brain.' 'My sûkṣhma sharîra,' 'my kâraṇa sharîra,' 'my soul,' are practically (but not theoretically) meaningless in the mouths of people who have never succeeded, by means of yoga, in separating them from the outer physical body.

This development of the complex from the simple, this opening up of separated individual consciousness through layer into inner layer, this gradual growth of nerve within nerve and instrument within instrument, this definition of body within body, constitutes the evolution of the individual from the standpoint of limited cycles. To take a fanciful illustration: it is as if we should, to increase the power and range and minuteness of our vision, first put on a pair of spectacles, then add a telescope, and over that a microscope, and so on indefinitely. In this imaginary illustration the additions are outwards. In evolution, by deliberate yoga, on the nivṛitti-mârga, the re-ascent into spirit, they would be inwards, a retreating within into subtler and subtler planes of matter; on the pravṛitti-mârga, the descent into matter, they would be outwards too, each self taking on denser and denser veils of matter to enjoy the experiences of a greater and greater (seeming) definition of itself—'I (am) *this*,' 'I (am) *this*.' From the standpoint of the absolute, on the other hand, all cycles and all evolution, all functions, all instruments, and all functionings and actual workings of them on all possible planes of matter, are ever completely present in the transcendent consciousness: "I—This—Not (am)."

Thus we come back again and again to the fact of endless plane within plane of matter, all permeated and pervaded by the consciousness in its triple aspect of jñâna, ichchhâ, and kriyâ. Let us see now how these pseudo-infinite planes of matter can be co-ordinated and brought into organic unity with each other. Co-ordinated in fact they must be; for the etats—separate in their pseudo-infinity though they are by very constitution—are not and cannot be mutually entirely oblivious and independent, when the thread of the one Self runs through them all, and strings them together like beads.

Different planes of matter, though separate from, and, from one standpoint, independent of each other to such an extent that they may even seem to violate the axioms of geometry, cannot escape these axioms altogether. As usual, we have disorder as well as order, negation as well as affirmation, defiance of law and yet submission thereto, here as well as elsewhere. Consciousness *appears* to transcend mathematical laws; but it is only the universal consciousness of Pratyag-âtmâ that can at all be said to do so, and this too only when it is considered as a whole, comprehending and at the same time negating the whole of Mûla-prakṛiti. Otherwise, it itself is the source and the embodiment of the unity, the uniformity, the regularity in diversity, the fact or brief description of which is called a law, and which appears when the Self is intermingled with Mûlaprakṛiti (as it always is), under the changeless stress of the Absolute-consciousness, the Brahman. Limited individual consciousnesses are inseparably connected with limited etats, and hence can never actually transcend those laws. That they *appear* to do so from some standpoints is due to their identity with the Pratyag-âtmâ. The world of the astral plane, whose normal inhabitants are said to be yakshas, gandharvas, kinnaras, nâgas, kûṣhmâṇḍas, gnomes, undines, fairies, and such other nature-spirits, may *seem* to literally 'occupy the same space' as the physical world whose normal inhabitants are humans, animals, plants, minerals, etc. But this is not *really* so. All the facts available point to the conclusion that as soon as the human developes the body and the instruments which enable him to begin to live consciously in the astral world as he does in the physical, he sees that the two worlds, at the most, *interpenetrate*, as sand and water, or water and air, and do not actually and literally occupy the same space. In other words, planes of matter, that appear utterly disconnected from the standpoint of individual consciousnesses limited to each plane, become only *grades of density* of matter from the standpoint of a consciousness that includes all of them.

This thought may now be expanded as follows:

The simile used above, of the thread and the beads, illustrates the fact of order amidst disorder, and also covers another fact which is essential in the work of co-ordination. In the chaplet each bead touches but two others, one on each side, and not more than two; and so too we find that saṃsâra, the world-process, is triple, त्रिभुवनम्, tri-bhuvanam, त्रैलोक्यम्, trai-lokyam, whenever and wherever we take it. This fact, that it is always a triple world, whenever and wherever we take it, gives the *method* of the co-ordination, for each factor of each such triplet is also concurrently connected with two other triplets; and as this connection extends pseudo-infinitely, it results that all possible planes are ringed together always. Thus taking the three planes of our world-system, *viz.*, स्थूल, sthûla, सूक्ष्म, sûkṣhma, and कारण, kâraṇa (roughly corresponding to the physical, astral and mental of theosophical literature) and naming them F, G, and H, we should find, on research, that F is simultaneously connected with three triplets, D E F, E F G, and F G H; so G with E F G, F G H and G H I; so H with F G H, G H I and H I J; and taking any of these triplets, say H I J, the mutual relation of these three would be found to be the same as that of F G H ; that is to say, to a Jîva to whom J represented the physical, I would represent the astral and H the kâraṇa plane. And this series of triplets extends endlessly before D and after J.

Before passing on to the reason of this state of things, it may be well to note that the interpretation of tri-bhuvanam, 'the triple world,' or 'the three worlds,' advanced here, is not exactly what is commonly understood by the word, just as the inmost meaning of the sacred word, Aum, is not what is commonly given. Yet there is no conflict or inconsistency between the two interpretations. On the contrary, the other interpretations all follow necessarily from the inmost one. Students wonder now and then how it is that resemblances occur in different departments of nature; and when it is said that one and the same statement may be interpreted in many ways, each correct and each applying to one class and one department of phenomena, sober people generally suspect some sleight-of-hand. As a matter of fact, a statement of a real true principle of nature, concerning one of the ultimates, or, rather, strictly speaking, penultimates, naturally applies to all the different series of phenomena derived from and constantly embodying those penultimates ; and the wonder may as well be how there is difference between part and part of nature as how there is resemblance. Mûla-prakṛiti explains the difference; Pratyag-âtmâ the resemblance. The law of analogy, "as above so below," is capable of a far wider and truer application than is now charily given to it, and it provides the reason of the existence of allegories and parables, in which there is as much literal fact as metaphor. Because of this universal applicability of basic laws, 'tri-bhuvanam,' when it means only three different but interconnected worlds or planes of matter, according to the ordinary explanation of the word, means something which is the necessary result of the metaphysical triplicity of all the life of united Jîva and atom, *i.e.*, of the Jîva-atom. In this metaphysical triplicity, which is the inmost meaning of tri-bhuvanam, lies the reason for the state of things described in the preceding paragraph.

Everywhere we find the world and the things of the world divided into an inner and an outer, a core and a sheath, and a third something, a principle, a relation, rather than a fact or factor, binding and holding these two together. This is due to the very constitution of the Absolute as shown in the logion, *viz.*, an inner Self, an outer Not-Self, and the third something, the affirmative-negative Shakti, which ties the two together indissolubly, and yet is not a third strictly, but only a repetition of the positivity, the being, of the Self and of the negativity, the nothingness, of the Not-Self. So we find, in the department of consciousness taken by itself, an outer or real world and an inner or ideal world, and a third something, the abstract consciousness, or self-consciousness, or apperception, or pure and abstract reason, as it has been variously named, holding the two together. This pure or abstract reason is the embodiment and source, as said before, of all abstract laws and principles, which are but forms of this self-consciousness in its relations to the objects by means of which it may be realising itself at the time.

"I see this book before me"—this consciousness is a consciousness of the real, the outer world. "I remember the book, in memory; I have thoughts about it, *i.e.*, I call up mental pictures of the book in relation to other things, its author, the country, press and people in which and by whom it was printed and published and read and criticised, the other books on the same subject which have been written in other times and places, the whole history of the gradual growth of learning on the subject treated of in the book and the causes thereof, etc., etc.,"- -these are facts of the inner, the ideal world. Lastly there is the consciousness (corresponding to the Absolute) which joins together and connects, in my own self, these two sets of facts, those belonging to the 'me' and those to the 'not-me,' and weaves them into the one process of my life. That the thread of the Self through the beads of the Not-Self is, or appears as, buddhi, laws, principles, apperception, self-consciousness, &c., may become clearer if the matter is considered thus: "I know and wish and act, and *I know that* I know and wish and act"—this is self-consciousness. "I know also that I knew and wished and acted before, and shall know and wish and act afterwards, in *the same* way, when the circumstances are *the same*"—this is the same self-consciousness modified into reason, ratio-cination, rationality, the perception of the *ratio*, the relation, of sameness, of similarity, amongst not-selves, because of the *persistence and sameness*, through past, present, and future, of the Self. "Such an experience, knowledge, desire, or action, is *always* followed by such another"—this is the same self-consciousness modified into and stated as a law, a principle.

How and why does this state of things come about? Why is there an outer world and an inner world? How does this distinction between the ideal and the real, ideas and realities, arise at all and what is the distinction between them precisely?

For answer we have to refer back to the principle which is always turning up on every side under every complication of phenomena, when that complication is sifted. Pratyag-âtmâ is the unbroken continuity of the one. Mûla-prakṛiti, on the other hand, is the utterly discontinuous brokenness and separateness of the many. The two have nothing in common with each other; in fact they are ever and at every point entirely opposed to each other. And yet they are violently brought together into inviolable relation by the might of the Absolute-svabhâva, the changeless nature of the Absolute. The reconciliation of these warring principles, each equally invincible, necessitates the further principle of 'continuity in discreteness,' whereby each discrete thing is in turn a thread of continuity to even more minutely discreted things and lower sub-divisions; and, conversely, each thread of continuity is in turn a discrete and sub-divisional item in a higher thread of continuity—and this endlessly. This principle applies to the constitution of a so-called atom as also of solar systems which include smaller systems and form part of larger ones in a series that is endless either way; and it underlies the continuously overlapping series of individualities which make up the Jîva-half of the world-process.

This same principle applied to the psychic half of saṃsâra, that is to say to consciousness, and even there to the cognitional element specially (in connection with which it is most manifest), explains why there should be two worlds to consciousness, an ideal and a real, memory and sensation, and a third something holding the two together. The application may become clear if we endeavour to understand in a little more detail what is the significance of memory and the other allied psychological processes, and how and why they come into existence.

The Absolute may be correctly described as an eternal sensation in which the universal Self in one single act of consciousness senses the non-existence of the Not-Self; that is to say, of all possible pseudo-infinite not-selves in all the three divisions of time—past, present and future; of space—length, breadth and depth; of motion—approach, recess, and rhythmic vibration. Now each individual, separate, Jîva or self, out of the whole mass of pseudo-infinite Jîvas or selves, the totality of which is unified in and by the Pratyag-âtmâ, must also necessarily reproduce in itself this one single act of consciousness, this truly unique sensation, this all-embracing, all-exhausting experience, by reason of its identity with this universal Self; and yet it is impossible also for it to do so, because of its limitedness. The reconciliation of these opposed necessities gives rise to the ideal world in which we can 'look before and after' *simultaneously* (comparatively only), as distinguished from the real world in which we can have only one sensation at a time (again only comparatively), *successively*.

Thus, to begin with, the individual self requires two acts of consciousness to sense the non-existence of a single not-self. It cannot compass this in one act, like the universal Self. It must first sense the *existence*, and *then* sense the *non-existence* of that not-self. In the second place, it has to deal with pseudo-infinite not-selves; it can sense them all only in, so to say, twice pseudo-infinite acts of consciousness, which means, in other words, in endless acts of consciousness, extending through endless time, through endless space and through endless motion. Confining ourselves for the moment to the case of one self dealing with one not-self, we see that that self first senses and asserts the existence of that not-self (as identical with itself), and secondly senses and asserts the non-existence of that same not-self (as non-identical with itself). The word 'same' here embodies what we know as memory. The imposition of continuity on an ever-changing not-self by a self, in consequence and by virtue of its own continuity, is *memory* of that not-self. Putting the matter in another form, while all the possible past, present, and future of the world-process is completely and simultaneously *present* in the consciousness of the Pratyag-âtmâ, it unfolds, as a mâyâvic or illusive *appearance* of *procession*, only gradually and in succession in the actual life of the individual ; and the constant participation of the individual self in the omniscience latent and ever-present in the Pratyag-âtmâ constitutes the inner ideal world whieh is made up of memory and expectation and derivative mental processes. Consider, in this connection, the fact that, even in ordinary usage, the word present never means an imaginary point of time dividing, as with a razor, the past from the present, but always a *period*, thus, 'at the present time' 'at present,' 'in this present life,' 'the present circumstances', etc., etc.

This statement is, however, not complete by itself.

Firstly: if the separate self can freely participate in the omniscience of the Pratyag-âtmâ, how is it that our recollection and our prevision are so very limited, so very erroneous? Not one in a million can remember or forecast any facts behind and beyond this present birth; and even the facts of the present life are but very imperfectly remembered and prevised. The answer to this is that while, metaphysically, this continuity of memory and expectation in the individual self is derived from the consciousness of the Pratyag-âtmâ, practically and actually it is derived from the consciousness of the individual of the next higher order,[1] the Îshvara or Sûtrâtmâ, just as in the case of the connecting unity of sense-media; whence limitations. And as to the positive errors and forgettings within those limitations, they are due to the general causes which make knowledge and ignorance, recollection and forgetfulness, truth and error, possible, nay, necessary, in the world-process at large; these causes may be dealt with later in the chapters on cognition.

Secondly (and this is the more relevant to our present purpose), there is the difference between the *possibility* of participation and *actual* participation. As soon as there is a positive act of memory, or positive act of prevision or expectation, it becomes distinct from the *possibility* of such recollection and prevision. One piece, so to say, of the latent has become

---

[1] See Chap. xiii., *supra*, for the significance of the expression, 'the next higher individual.'

patent, and the general latency remains a latency as ever before. And all this while, from the standpoint of the Absolute, there is no difference at all between latency and patency; for, in the Absolute, all things which are limited and can be distinguished are exactly on the same level of etat, in the same way, and not one within or higher or lower than, or in any way different from another. The answer to this question, the reconciliation of these inconsistencies, can lie only in this, that what is latent to one is also patent to it in turn and simultaneously to others, while what is patent to one is also latent to it in turn and simultaneously to others; and thus the equality of all is brought about, all existing simultaneously from the stand-point of the Absolute, all serving as latent and patent, ideal and real, one within another, at the same time. The facts recorded by physical science as to the (pseudo-infinite) registration by each atom of all sights and sounds, etc., are helpful in understanding this.

We may endeavour to illustrate the fact thus. If a spectator wandered unrestingly through the halls of a vast museum, a great art-gallery, at the dead of night, with a single small lamp in one hand, each of the natural objects, the pictured scenes, the statues, the portraits, would be illumined by that lamp, in succession, for a single moment, while all the rest were in darkness, and after that single moment, would itself fall into darkness again. Let there now be not one but countless such spectators, as many in endless number as the objects of sight within the place, each spectator meandering in and out incessantly through the great crowd of all the others, each lamp bringing momentarily into light one object, and for only that spectator who holds that lamp. This immense and unmoving building is the rockbound ideation of the changeless Absolute. Each lamp-carrying spectator out of the countless crowd is one line of consciousness out of the pseudo-infinite lines of such that make up the totality of the one universal consciousness. Each coming into light of each object is its patency, is an experience of the Jîva; each falling into darkness is its lapse into the latent. From the standpoint of the objects themselves, or of the universal consciousness, there is no latency, nor patency. From that of the lines of consciousness, there is. Why there is this *appearance* of lines of consciousness should be clear from all that has gone before.

We see then that whenever and wherever we take the world-process, we shall find it to consist of an outer plane of grosser matter which corresponds to and makes up the real world, the patent, and an inner plane of subtler matter which makes up the ideal world, corresponding to the latent. At each stage, the Jîva-core consists of *matter* of the inner plane while its outer upâdhi consists of matter of the outer plane; and when a person says: "I think," "I act," it means that the matter of the inner core, which *is* the I for the time being, is actually, positively, modified by, or is itself modifying in a certain manner, the outer real world, literally in the same *kind* of though vastly subtler, way as a glass may reflect an image, or a compressed wire-spring may push back the object which compresses it. The *ideality* of the inner processes is due to the fact that the inner film of matter is *posing* and *masquerading*, for the time, as the truly *immaterial* Self.

Let us take some concrete facts to illustrate the above remarks. The lower we descend in the scale of living organisms, the less we find of that individuality, that self-consciousness, which looks 'before and after,' of memory and expectation in short. And the less we find of these, the hazier is the distinction between inner and outer, ideal and real. But as in no living organism which persists through even two moments of time can there be an utter absence of a unified consciousness, of an individuality, of the sense of 'before and after,' however vague and dim it may be, so can there not be an utter absence of inner core and outer sheath. But in the higher organisms, this distinction of a persisting core and a more or less changing sheath is much more definite. In the average man the sûkṣhma-sharîra (so named in the Vedânta system, and corresponding to the astral, or rather astro-mental, body of theosophical literature), made of a finer grade of matter than that which composes the physical plane we know of, is the inner core. This forms the individuality, the thread of continuity, the 'present,' in which the past and future, the before and after, of one physical life-period of a human being are conjoined, amidst the changes of his physical body and surroundings. The physical body itself has a certain 'form and shape' imposed upon it by this inner body, which form, roughly speaking, persists like an external thread of continuity, through the constant changes of the material of the body. This but illustrates the pseudo-infinite repetition of every principle in nature. The physical body is sheath to the astral; but in the physical body itself a still further distinction is made between a grosser and a finer, and the former, the grosser, portion becomes sheath to an inner less gross, which becomes distinguished as a लिङ्गदेह, liñga-deha, a type-body (or etheric double, in theosophical literature).

To put the matter in other words: of the pseudo-infinite variations of the logion, due to the pseudo-infinite variations of the 'this' contained in that logion, each variation may be regarded as representing one life-course, one line of consciousness. This one life-course, one line of consciousness, taking the case of the average human individual, is represented by the inner sûkṣhma-sharîra which contains latent in itself the whole of the unfoldment of the actual life of that individual, as the seed contains the tree. As one single 'present,' it includes all the time-divisions, past and future, of that life within itself. Because of this fact, the Jîva can range in memory and expectation over the whole of this one physical life; to him the whole of it is in a manner present at every moment of his life, because it is all present in the sûkṣhma-sharîra which is the ensouling core of his physical sheath and is himself. But his memory and expectation cannot go beyond the limits of the present life, because the individuality of the sûkṣhma-sharîra does not extend over other physical births. If, however, by development of mind, by persistent introspection and metaphysical or even psycho-philosophical and abstract thought, helped by yogic practices (which are only scientifically systematised processes of education of special faculties), a Jîva advances in evolution to the stage when he separates himself as much from the sûkṣhma-sharîra as from the sthûla-sharîra or physical body, then the sûkṣhma-sharîra loses, in and to him, its character of inner core, and becomes merged with the physical into the outer sheath, and another body, now called the kâraṇa-sharîra, made of a still subtler grade of matter, takes the place of the inner core. This process is repeated *ad infinitum* in the endless spirals of evolution including system within system. Such is the metaphysic of the facts stated in *The Secret Doctrine* (iii. 551 et seq.) that, to the Logos of our solar system, all the planes of that system are as the sub-planes of one plane. They would be to him, one outer real world; his own inner, ideal, world would be a grade beyond. It is like this: if there were beings who had sense-experience of only solid matter, to them liquid matter would be in the place of soul, spirit, inner or ideal substance; but if they should gradually grow very familiar with water, and begin to have some experience of gaseous matter, then solid and liquid would become ranged as *degrees* or sub-divisions of the outer plane to them, and air would take the place of soul, spirit, etc.; as air grew familiar, radiant matter, or ether, or whatever other name might be given to the next degree of matter, would take its place as principle of continuity and support and unification, in actual life and in general estimation. Witness, in illustration of one aspect of this fact, the various theories of the earlier Greek philosophers, who endeavoured to reduce the universe to one single element, earth, water, fire, air, etc., successively; and in illustration of another aspect thereof, the modern scientific theories with respect to ether. Modern scientists[1] have collected together and discussed all the attributes assigned to this hypothetical ether, and pointed out that they are in most instances exactly the opposite of those assigned to the known kinds of matter. As a matter of fact, the list of attributes thus given, *e.g.*, continuity, unlimitedness, homogeneity, non-atomicity, structurelessness, gravitationlessness, frictionlessness, etc., etc., is not a list of attributes of any kind of matter or Mûla-prakṛiti, but of Pratyag-âtmâ. But it always happens in the history of evolution, that each subtler and more pliable grade of matter, in its relation to the

---

[1] See f.i., A. E. Dolbear. *The Machinery of the Universe.* P. 93 (Romance of Science Series).

next denser and more resistent, displays the characteristics which Pratyag-âtmâ generally displays towards Mûla-prakṛiti, *viz.*, the characteristics of being a source of existence and support, and of supplying a basis of continuity, of lubrication, whereby the resistant and separate are brought into relation with each other with the least possible friction, are unified. It is worthy of remark in passing that the Saṃskṛit word स्नेह, sneha, means oil, or moisture, or water, as well as love, which is Pratyag-âtmâ in the desire-aspect, desire for unity. We may well entertain the supposition, therefore, that when modern science, becoming more and more familiar with radiant matter and protyle and ether, etc., shall have discovered their real properties, they will all fall into line with the kinds of matter now better known; and a new and hypothetical element will have to be assumed, with these same characteristics of Pratyag-âtmâ, to explain the otherwise paradoxical behaviour of the known kinds. Paurâṇic and theosophical literature speaks of two such elements, after ether or âkâsha, to be discovered within the limits of our manvantara, which have been already referred to before, *viz.*, the mahat or âdi-tattva and the buddhi or anupâdaka-tattva.

The co-ordination of these pseudo-infinite

planes of matter, then, is to be found in the fact that, whenever and wherever we take it, we find the world-process as a limited brahmâṇḍa, a world-system, small or large, which is a tri-bhuvanam, a tri-lokî, a system of three worlds or layers or planes of matter, and neither more nor less. That is to say, every Jîva, wherever and whenever he lives, lives in a world-system which to him has three factors: an outer or real world, an inner or ideal world, and the all-embracing consciousness—which connects the two, and which, being itself essentially and fully ever-present, is the basis of every 'present,' whatever stretch of time and space and motion that lower present or ideal may include. In our system, to average humanity, the outer world is the world of the physical plane and the sthûla-sharîra; the inner, of the astro-mental plane and the sûkṣhma-sharîra; the abstract consciousness (the principles or outlines on which the individual is constructed, the basic constituents of his nature, the special aspect or mode of the one consciousness which that individual is intended to manifest, anger, or love, or art, or philanthropy, etc., in pseudo-infinite variety), of the kâraṇa-sharira, the causal body, which is the *cause* of the others, in a way corresponding to that in which the Absolute-consciousness is the cause of all that occurs within it. When, by evolution and the opening up of the paths of individual consciousness through the layers of the sûkṣhma-sharîra, the latter and its material will become as much 'object' to the consciousness as the physical body and its material are now, then the kâraṇa will take the place of the sûkṣhma, and the abstract consciousness will retire to a subtler plane of matter, which has been called the buddhic, or महाकारण, mahâ-kâraṇa, or तुरीय, turîya, etc.; and then the range of memory and expectation will extend beyond the present life to past and future births, because the kâraṇa-body has a more extensive 'present,' and lasts through many physical births, even as the sûkṣhma-sharîra lasts through all the changes of the physical body in one birth. From the standpoint of the kâraṇa-body, physical births-deaths are as bright-dark fortnights, or even day-nights, of physical life would be to the sûkṣhma-sharîra.

More as to the full significance of the 'present' may appear later in the chapters dealing with cognition in a second part of this work. We may now pass on to certain inferences from the facts stated above; but before doing so it may be noted that a fact--useful to bear in mind in systematising apparently disjointed and otherwise inconsistent-seeming and confusing statements in old Saṃskṛit and theosophical literature—is that the same words are employed, and for reasons existing in the nature of things as shown above, to indicate abstract general principles and types which have a universal application, and also special facts which are peculiar only to a particular locality or system. Thus (*a*) âtmâ, (*b*) buddhi, (*c*) manas—each having one universal sense, *viz.*, (*a*) the Self, (*b*) the unifying reason, which is but the Self holding together the many and so appearing as a network of laws, and (*c*) the distinguishing and separating intelligence—are occasionally used in theosophical literature in another sense, *viz.*, the three subtlest planes of matter out of the seven of which our solar system consists. When all the seven planes are taken as sub-planes of one cosmic plane, these may be regarded as composing the inner core to the outer sheath made up of the other four; even as the three subtler sub-planes of the physical plane supply the material for the 'inner' etheric double, that pervades and holds together the outer body composed of the four grosser sub-planes of physical matter, *viz.*, solid, liquid, gaseous, and etheric.

The necessary corollary from the above statements is: that planes of matter which may be very different from each other, which may be mutually uncognisable by, and even as non-existent to, the Jîvas ordinarily inhabiting them, *i.e.*, having sheaths and bodies made of or corresponding to them, will always be seen from the standpoint of a higher Jîva, having a sufficiently extensive consciousness, to be graded or related to each other in some way or other. We can conceive of beings whose bodies are made of air, and of others made of fire-flames. These two sets of beings might even interpenetrate without being conscious of each other. But a Jîva who was familiar with both kinds of matter in all their forms would be able to distinguish between the two, and see the gradation between the atoms composing the one and the other kind of matter. A mosquito can walk upon the surface of water; for all practical purposes, the water is to it just as hard and resistant as stone. It is not so to the fish. The fish and the mosquito may not be able to understand, the one how the other lives and moves *in* water, and the other how the one can walk *upon* the the surface of it without being immersed. Man can understand both things. Pseudo-infinite necessarily are these diversities of consciousness, and each plane and each kind of matter corresponding to each variety of this diversity is again pseudo-infinite in extent of space, time, and motion, as already said. From the narrow standpoint, which knows of only one, each may seem to exclude even the possibility of others; so that if one said that there were living beings whose bodies were composed of subtler matter, that our earth was thronged with them so that our bodies and theirs were passing through each other very often and in entire unconsciousness of each other's existence, the statement would ordinarily either not be believed, as involving a breach of geometrical axioms, or if believed, would be regarded as disproving those axioms. But to a higher and broader outlook both kinds of matter and their corresponding lines of consciousness fall into their proper places, and the graded relations to each other of these planes of matter, by interpenetration, without violation of any mathematical laws, also become apparent.

And thus another connected corollary is seen to be that, by metaphysical deduction, the so-called fourth and fifth and higher dimensions of space can really not be anything differing in kind from the known three dimensions. These three dimensions themselves, length, breadth and depth, are but varieties of the *one* fact of *co-existence* which is the essential and the whole significance of space. Three straight lines intersecting each other at right angles at one central point give us these three dimensions. But a million, a billion, a pseudo-infinite number, of such triplets of lines can intersect each other at the same central point; that is to say, a pseudo-infinite number of straight lines can intersect each other at that point at angles of all possible degrees; and we can therefore justifiably speak of a pseudo-infinite number of dimensions of space. In any other sense, all so-called new dimensions resolve themselves into cases of interpenetration in various ways; and interpenetration itself, it is clear, is but the co-existence of atoms, or molecules, or component particles, in special positions towards each other. The case would be exactly similar with dimensions and divisions of time and motion.

The question of how the consciousness of a Jîva expands so as to embrace more and more planes of matter is one of general evolution, or of practical yoga when endeavoured to be accomplished deliberately.

The nature itself of the process of expansion of consciousness is nothing particularly recondite or mysterious. All education is such expansion. A Jîva takes up a new subject of study, a new line of livelihood, a new department of life and mode of existence, and forthwith a new world is opened to him, and his consciousness flows out into, and becomes co-extensive with, and assimilates, that new world. In its other aspect, of (comparatively) simultaneous communion, we find other illustrations. Take the case of an ordinary government. The consciousness of an officer in charge of the police-administration of a subdistrict is co-extensive with the police-affairs of that district; that of another in charge of its revenue-administration is similarly co-extensive with its revenue-affairs; and so with a number of other departments of administration, medical, educational, arboricultural, commercial, municipal, etc., side by side in the same sub-district. But there are larger districts made up of numbers of these sub-districts, and still larger divisions of country made up of numbers of these districts; and at each stage there are administrative officers in charge of each department, whose consciousness may be said to include the consciousnesses of their subordinates in that department, exclude those of their compeers, and be in turn included in those of their superiors. The more complicated the machinery of the government, the better the illustration will be of inclusions and exclusions and partial or complete coincidences and over-lappings and communions of consciousness. At last we come to the head of the government, whose consciousness may be said to include the consciousnesses, whose knowledge and power include the knowledges and powers, of all the public servants of the land, whose consciousness is so expanded as to enable him to be in touch with them all and feel and act through them all constantly. An officer promoted through the grades of such an administration would clearly pass through expansions of consciousness. A more common illustration, which may appear to show out the so-called immediacy of consciousness better, is that of friends and relatives. Two friends may be so intimate with each other, husband and wife, and members of a joint family, may love and be in rapport with each other so much, that they have a 'common life,' a 'common feeling,' a 'common consciousness.' But it should be borne in mind that, strictly speaking, there is no more immediacy in the one case than in the other, but only quicker cognition. Consciousness of the particular, the limited, working unavoidably through an upâdhi, necessarily deals with time as with space, and the time-element is always a definite element, however infinitesimal it may be in any given case. The word 'immediate' in such cases has only a comparative significance, as is apparent from the fact that the time of transmission of a sensation, from the end of a nerve to the seat of consciousness, has been distinctly and definitely calculated in the case of living organisms.

Such expansion of consciousness, then, is not in its nature more mysterious and recondite than any other item in the world-process, but a thing of daily and hourly occurrence. In terms of metaphysic it is the coming of an individual self into relation with a larger and larger not-self. The processes of yoga are no more and no less methods of education—using the word in its true significance of strengthening, developing, e-ducing or forth-leading of faculties already existent but weak or latent—than the processes followed in the million schools and colleges of modern life, for developing the physical and mental powers of children and youth. Every act of attention, of concentration, of regulation and balancing, of deliberately 'joining' and directing the self to an object, or to itself, of con-*jug*-ating or en-*gag*-ing it to or in anything, is an act of yoga, in the strict sense of the word, and every such act is a help to the development and expansion of the individual consciousness.

CHAPTER XVI.

SUMMATION.

All the main facts connected with Jîvas and with atoms have, it seems, been generally brought out and summed up now. Only one more point deserves a word. It concerns the distinction between the universal and the singular, and the relation between them, which was mentioned before. This triplet, belonging equally to Jîvas and to atoms, and so part of the summation of the world-process, could not well be discussed before some general notion had been gained of the distinction between the ideal world and the real world, the former being, as it were, a complete and standing picture or plan of the stream of successive events which make up the latter, and so occupying, the one to the other, the position of universal to singular.

The aphorisms of Nyâya, as we now have them, classify and describe the constituents of saṃsâra in terms of cognition, in their *subjective* aspect, as, *viz.*, the means of knowledge, the knowable, doubt, certainty, fallacy, etc., etc. On the other hand the extant aphorisms of the Vaisheṣhika school classify them as *objects* of knowledge, in their objective aspect, in terms of the cognised. Thus Kaṇâda, the author of the Vaisheṣhika aphorisms, states that there are six primary padârthas or objects, *viz.*, dravya, guṇa, karma, sâmânya, visheṣha and samavâya. The first three have been discussed before. The next three mean respectively, the 'universal or general', 'the singular or special,' and 'relation or juxtaposition'.

As has been often indicated before, the one true universal is the Pratyag-âtmâ; the many, the manifold singular, the multitude of singulars, is Mûla-prakṛiti; and the peculiar bond that exists between them is the real samavâya-sambandha, literally, the 'firm bond of juxta-position.' Beside this one universal there is, strictly speaking, no other universal, but only 'generals'. So, beside the true singulars of the Etat, there is no other real singular, but only 'specials'. The characteristic of these generals and specials is that each one of them is general to lower specials, and at the same time special to a higher general. In other words, while Pratyag-âtmâ is universal, and Mûla-prakṛiti singular, the Jîva-atom is individual or particular, combining and reconciling in itself both universal and singular.

Some difficulty in the expression of this thought is occasioned by the fact that while the meaning of universal and general and special is comparatively fixed and free from ambiguity, such is not the case with the significations of singular, individual and particular, as the words are currently used.[1] The underlying philosophical idea of their mutual relation being indeterminate, the expression is naturally doubtful also. And this very haziness of the idea is at the bottom of the long-lasting dispute between the doctrines of nominalism and realism and their various modifications. As a matter of fact, in the world around us, we actually find neither the true One, nor the true Many or Not-One, by itself. What we do find always instead is *a one* which is also *a many* at the same time. We distinguish between the two by emphasising within ourselves the Jîva-aspect, *i.e.*, the aspect of self-consciousness and Pratyag-âtmâ, and, from the standpoint thereof, beholding the Not-Self in juxtaposition to and yet in separ-

---

[1] An instance of this may be seen in the divers arrangements made of the triplets of the categories of Kant; thus at p. 221 of Schwegler's *History of Philosophy*, the triplet of 'totality, plurality and unity' is arranged in an order the reverse of that followed in the original of Kant.

ation from the Self. The facts, so viewed, are clear. The one and the many, the abstract and the concrete, the general and the special, the universal and the singular, are just as inseparable as back and front, as has been often said before. They are inseparable in fact as well as in thought (which also is a fact though manufactured in subtler material). But the phraseology requires to be settled in accordance with this fact and thought. It may be suggested here that the settlement should be thus: The word 'universal' should be confined to the true One, the Pratyag-âṭmâ, and to the modifications and manifestations of its unity, *viz.*, the laws of the pure reason, the abstract laws and principles which underlie the details of the world-process and are as it were the transformations of the Pratyag-âtmâ itself in association with the diversity of Mûla-prakṛiti. The word 'singular' should similarly be confined to the true Many, the truly separate. As the universal is the One which includes and supports all, so the singular is the exactly opposite one that would exclude all else; it indicates the pseudo-ultimate constituents of the many, which may well, for practical convenience, be technically called 'atom,' 'aṇu' or 'param-âṇu.' For that which is between these two ones, a something which is a one and a many at the same time, a whole composed of parts, the word 'particular' seems appropriate. Such a 'particular' would be 'general' (an imitation of the universal) to those it includes and supports and holds together, and 'special' (an imitation of the singular) to that by which it itself is supported along with other co-particulars; all so-called inanimate substances, all sheaths and bodies of the so-called animate, all objects of cognition or desire or action, all genera and species, types, sub-types and archetypes, would thus be 'particulars.' The word 'individual' is peculiar; it would be useful if it were confined to the Jîva-atom, which combines the true universal and the true singular, rather than only generals and specials. It is not Pratyag-âtmâ only, nor Mûla-prakṛiti only, but both; and yet, because of the unfixable, in-de-finite, pseudo-infinite nature of the atom, the Jîva-atom may be called a particular also. Whenever and wherever we may take an actual individual Jîva-atom, the atom-portion of it, its sheath, will be found to be a definite that merges on both sides into the in-de-finite; it is an infinitesimal fraction, on the one hand, of a pseudo-infinite universe, and, on the other, it is a pseudo-infinite multiple of infinitesimal fractions. "Creatures, objects, definite things, begin in the in-de-finite, and end in the in-definite; they are de-finite only midway between the two."[1]

If we were defining the main items of the world-process in terms of the Absolute, the Jîva-atom would ordinarily be called the individualised Absolute, and a world-system a particularised one; the Absolute itself being then comparatively called the universal Absolute. But in view of the statements made in the preceding paragraph, it would appear to be almost more consistent and systematic to call the Jiva-atom a singularised Absolute. Yet, though, in strictness, this would be the better description, still, for all practical purposes of metaphysical research—for the reasons for which the Jîva-atom may be regarded as a particular also—it is more useful to employ the expression 'individualised Absolute.' The 'individuality' of the Jîva in the Jîva-atom is more predominant than the 'singularity' of the atom therein for such purposes.

On the above view, recognising the nature and the necessity of the connection between the One and the Many, it becomes easy to see what the true mean of reconciliation is between

---

[1] अव्यक्तादीनि भूतानि व्यक्तमध्यानि भारत ।
अव्यक्तनिधनान्येव ... ... ॥

Bhagavad-Gîtâ. ii. 28.

nominalism and realism. Every object, being a Jîva-atom, or a conglomerate of Jîva-atoms, is general and special, abstract and concrete, at one and the same time. Therefore, when the new-born infant opens its eyes for the first time, it necessarily sees the *genus* 'woman' as well as the *special* '(individual) mother,' at one and the same time. As soon as we see any object, we see its generality as well as its speciality. Whenever we see *a one*, we see also at once the possibility, inherent in the one, of a pseudo-infinity of that one, *i.e.*, of such ones. *The* One is universal; *a* one reproduces *the* One; the universality of the true One reappears as the generality and the pseudo-infinity of the illusive one.

This fact is embodied in the grammatical affixes: 'ness,' 'ship,' 'hood' (in English), and 'tâ' or 'tva' (in Saṃskṛit), expressive of the abstract and of quality, which can be added on to any noun or adjective. It is significant that abstractness and generality should belong to, and be expressible exclusively in, terms of quality; for quality or guṇa corresponds to jñâna, which in turn corresponds specially with Pratyag-âtmâ, the one universal and abstract. Abstraction indeed means reduction into terms of Pratyag-âtmâ, making a *one* and therefore a pseudo-*uni*versal, of that which was mixed up with and part of the many. So too, the concrete is mostly expressed in terms of motion or karma, which corresponds to kriyâ, which corresponds to the Not-Self; as witness the fact that so many names or nouns *originate* in verbs. Finally, the *relation* of the two is embodied in the dravya, substance, noun or name, which combines act and fact, characteristic action and quality, in a 'thing,' and corresponds to the hidden Negation-Shakti that manifests its various forms in the declensional changes of termination of the noun (in the older languages, for the separate prepositions of modern languages are artifical separations of these terminational affixes).

From these observations it is clear that the universal [1] is one; the singular many; and genera-species pseudo-infinite; and that everywhere and always there is the possibility of distinguishing the concrete from the abstract by the mere addition of 'ness'; in other words, by concentrating the oneness and universality of the Self upon and into the concrete, and so of discovering an endless series, in an endless

[1] It may also be noted here that the Vaisheṣhika system calls the highest, or, rather, the one true universal, by the name of universal being, sattâ-sâmânya, सत्तासामान्य, which, plainly, is the objective name for the Self; and the lowest or true singular it calls aṇu or atom, which is but another name for the Etat.

gradation, of concepts, ideas, types, archetypes, etc. Plato seems to have spoken of only one archetypal world, while the legitimate inferences from the logion require a pseudo-infinity of such, higher and lower, in an endlessly ascending and descending scale. The logion itself, it should be noted, and the laws and principles that proceed from it directly, can scarcely be spoken of as types or archetypes ; for types and archetypes are comparatively definite objects, abstract-concrete (though with the aspect of abstractness or generality and commonness inclining to be predominant), while laws and principles are only relations between objects.

With these remarks we may bring to a close the observations regarding the general features of Jîvas and atoms, leaving for a second part of this work a more detailed consideration of the three aspects of the Jîva, *viz.*, jñâna, ichchhâ, and kriyâ, and bringing to a conclusion this first part with a re-statement of the summation of the world-process in consciousness.

In the preceding chapter we have seen how the endless and apparently quite disconnected diversity of atom beside atom and atom within atom, plane beside plane and plane within plane, world beside world and world within world, individuality beside individuality and individuality within individuality, collapses together into an ordered juggler's box within box under the touch of the principle of the ever-expanding individual consciousness, which, taking its source in the universal consciousness of the Pratyag-âtmâ, is incessantly threading together all the otherwise disconnected beads of Mûla-prakṛiti.

The more the nature of consciousness is pondered on, the more the nature of the Jîva will become clear. Indeed, as the most significant definition of the atom is that it is a persisting-point, *i.e.*, a line, of objectivity, of unconsciousness, in its triple aspect of cognisability, desirability, and movability, guṇa, dravya, and karma, so the most significant definition of the Jîva is that it is a persisting-point, *i.e.*, a line, of consciousness and subjectivity, in its triple aspect of cognisor, desiror, and actor. Combining these two definitions, a Jîva-atom might be defined as the individualised Absolute (thus bringing out the true significance of the current saying, that "the Jîva is verily Brahman and naught else"[1]); while a particular number of them may be said to constitute a particularised Absolute, or a world-system, a cosmos that also *appears* like the individualised Absolute to be complete in itself; and the

---

[1] जीवो ब्रह्मैव नापरः ।

totality of these individualised and particularised Absolutes to make up the universal or truly complete Absolute, the Brahman ; all this not interfering, in the slightest degree, with the fact that individual or (strictly speaking) singular, particular, and universal are not three but absolutely identical, literally one and the same.

An illustration may perhaps help to made these statements a little clearer. Suppose that life, that the world-process, consists of ten experiences: that is to say, of five sensations, each dual as pleasurable and painful, so that the two factors of each such pair, when balanced against each other, neutralise each other and leave behind a cipher, as equal credit and debit in a banker's account may do. One self, going through these experiences in one fixed order of time, space, and motion, would exhaust them all comparatively quickly, and would form one individuality, marked and defined by the ten experiences in that one order, thus making one line of consciousness. But let us now vary the order of the ten experiences ; this mere variation of order, it will be seen, implies a variation in the times, spaces, and movements connected with each item of experience. If we vary the order, then, in all possible ways, but without decreasing the number of the experiences, we have at once orders to the number of 'factorial ten,' in algebraical technicality, that is to say 3,628,800. It is clear at once that each of these millions of orders of the succession of experiences marks out and defines, and therefore amounts to, a distinct and separate individuality; for an individuality can no otherwise be described, discriminated and fixed, than by enumerating the experiences of that individuality, by narrating its biography. Yet, while each one of these orders makes a distinct individuality, it is also equally clear, at the same time, that in essence and substance and completeness all these individualities are verily and truly *one*, and that whatever difference there is between them is made up of the illusory differences of mere pure time, space and motion, all three utter emptinesses and nothings, the triple aspect of the Negation.

In place of five as the number of sensations, now substitute the number 'pseudo-infinite;' for the etats are pseudo-infinite by axiom, and each is pleasurable during the affirmation of it, and painful during the negation (as may be treated of later). The total number of our experiences then becomes $2 \times$ pseudo-infinite, and the total number of permutations of these experiences is $\underline{|2 \times \infty}$ (factorial twice pseudo-infinite). This, at first sight, should be the total number of all possible 'lines of consciousness,' or 'individualities' or 'Jîvas'. But this is so only at first sight, and we have not reached the end of our calculations even now. For we have up to now been taking the experiences all at a time. But they have to be taken in all possible combinations also, one at a time, two at a time, and three, and four, and so on, to pseudo-infinity. The result is, briefly, a pseudo-infinity of pseudo-infinities as the total number of Jîvas in the world-process, each being a distinct, immortal, ever-spirating, and ever-gyrating line of consciousness, and yet each being absolutely identical with all others, for the world-process is made up entirely and exclusively of the one universal Self, passing itself through all possible pseudo-infinite experiences, *simultaneously* from the standpoint of that universal Self, *successively* from that of the limited not-selves.

It may be asked: why this interminable variation of the order of the experiences? As usual, the answer is contained in the logion. The one-Pratyag-âtmâ is the ever-present. The many-Mûla-prakṛiti is the ever-successive, ever-past, and ever-future. The opposition between the two is utter. Yet also is there inevitable and constant juxtaposition and relation. The one is the universal, सार्विक, sârvika, or सामान्य, sâmânya; the other is the singular or individual,

विशेष, vishesha; and between them there exists unbreakable relation, समवाय, samavâya. The reconciliation of the contradiction is that the Pratyag-âtmâ becomes as multitudinous as the etats, in order to encompass them all simultaneously in the one vast present of the totality of the world-process; *and again, each single one of the multitude of the Pratyag-âtmâ (i.e., of the pseudo-infinite Jîvas) also incessantly endeavours to encompass the whole of the many in the total succession of endless time and space and motion, because each Jîva must be equal to and cannot be less than the whole of the Pratyag-âtmâ.* Take the totality of the world-process at any one point and you find all possible pseudo-infinite experiences present therein simultaneously, co-existently, side by side, in the pseudo-infinity of space—sorrows in one region, equivalent joys in another; gains here, equal losses there; life and growth in one place, a balancing death and decay in another. But, again, take any one experience, a single point or moment of consciousness, and follow it out behind and beyond, into the past and the future, along any one of the pseudo-infinite diameters that in their totality make up the solid mass of the sphere, any one of the lines of consciousness of which it is the meeting-point, the point of junction and of crossing, and along that line there will be found all possible experiences in different moments of time, in different successions.[1]

Another illustration may be attempted: Take a round ball of iron. Let this ball be composed of a number of round bullets. Let the ball have a revolutional movement of its own as a whole, on a fixed axis, so that the space occupied by it never changes. Let each of the bullets have another motion of its own, perfectly free and ever-changing in direction, but strictly confined within the periphery of the ball, and therefore necessarily so arranged that each bullet moves only by the equal displacement and movement of another. The ball now combines in itself, always and simultaneously, all the possible movements of all its constituents; and each of these constituents also passes through each one of all these possible movements, but in succession, the motion of each being so counterbalanced by that of another, from moment to moment, that the position of the ball, as a whole, in space, never changes. Finally, wherever in this illustration we have a definite limit of size or number, substitute unlimitedness. Let the whole ball be boundlessly large. Let each

---

[1] Compare the Saṃskṛit saying:

सुखस्यानंतरं दुःखं दुःखस्यानंतरं सुखं ।

"Pain (follows invariably) after pleasure, and pleasure after pain."

bullet composing it be in turn composed of smaller bullets; these of shot; these again of smaller shot; and so on pseudo-infinitely. Let these bullets and shot be of pseudo-infinite sizes; and let the peripheries of these bullets and shot be purely imaginary, so that each bullet and shot, while one such in itself, is also at the same time part of the volume inclosed by a pseudo-infinite number of peripheries of all possible sizes co-existing with and overlapping each other within the single periphery of the whole. The ball now becomes the Absolute. Its transcendent axis, of the pseudo-infinity of the numbers of which the ball is veritably composed, is the logion. Its revolution vanishes into a rock-like fixity of changelessness,[1]

---

[1] महाशिलासत्ता, Mahashilâsattâ, 'rock-like being,' frequently described in the *Yoga Vâsiṣhṭha*. This illustration is not altogether fanciful. Physical science is establishing more and more clearly every day that it is almost a literal description of what is actually taking place in all solids. And when we remember that metaphysical as well as scientific reasoning favours the belief that space is a vacuum filled full with a plenum of subtler and subtler matter; that the heavenly bodies are not moving in empty but in matter-filled space; that vast masses of subtler matter cling to and form shells for what we call these 'solid' globes, and participate in their rotatory and other motions; that the thicker the rotating shell the faster will be its movement at the surface; that the quicker the movement the greater is the resistance and the hardness, *i.e.*, solidity, etc.—if we remember these things we may see that it is possible that the illustration literally describes the actual world-process, and that we are living and

because it occupies the *whole* of space, and in the absence of a remaining and surrounding space, against which it could be seen, no revolution can be. Its universal sphericity is the Pratyag-âtmâ. Its concrete and discrete material is Mûla-prakṛiti. Its bullets within bullets, and shot within shot are the pseudo-infinite Jîva-atoms which, in their pseudo-infinitesimal sphericity of pointness, are identical with the infinite sphericity of the whole. The imaginary-ness of the periphery of each is the endlessness of the overlapping of individuality-points. The endless movement of each of these points makes a line of consciousness working out in successive time;

---

moving freely *within* masses of matter that present a surface of iron to things outside their movement. The 'discarded' old doctrines of 'cycle in epicycle, orb in orb,' of heavens one above and around another, in which the heavenly bodies were studded, as bosses in shields, etc., etc., thus seem to have a chance of being restored with a much fuller significance. This will be only in keeping with the general law of all the march of the world-process, *viz.*, that a thing passes into its opposite and then returns again to its original condition on a higher level, endlessly. Take up a newspaper, and we find illustrations of this in the most widely-separated departments of life—thus: (1) Pedlars and hawkers are replaced by great central stores, depôts, and fixed shops, and then comes the travelling salesman again; (2) duels, single combats, heroes, are replaced by massed bands, and these are superseded by bush-fighting; (3) Chinese writing is superseded by the alphabet, which again is threatened with displacement by shorthand, and so on.

while the totality of these lines of consciousness is the transcendent completeness of the Absolute.

In these illustrations we see the summation of the world-process, while also seeing how the utter emptiness which is the utter fulness of the Absolute, its changeless balance of being against nothing, is always being endeavoured to be reproduced in the individualised Absolute, the Jîva-atom. Life is balanced against death; progress against regress; anode against kathode; anabolism against katabolism; pleasure against pain; being against nothing; spirit against matter. Taking the nett result of each completed life also we see the same balancing *appear*, as has found expression, and in one sense, true expression, in words like those of Bhartṛihari, the poet-king and then the ascetic-yogî:—"What *real* difference is there between the pleasures and the pains of Indra, the high chieftain of the Gods, and those of the lowliest animal? The joys of love and of life that the one derives, under the promptings of desire, from Rambhâ and from nectar, the same are derived by the other from his lowly mate and his so-called foul and filthy food. The terrors of death again are as keen to the one as to the other. Respective karma makes a difference in their surroundings and appearances. But the nett result and the relativity of the subject and the object, enjoyer and enjoyed, sufferer and cause of suffering, are the same."[1] The equality and sameness of all Jîvas, not only in the sense of the sameness of comparative results of long periods, lifetimes, or cycles, but also at each moment of time, in the matter of pleasure and pain, may also appear further, later on, when the nature of those two all-important constituents of the life of the Self is dealt with. From the standpoint of Brahman, all is the same, all is equal; there is no difference at all, in kind as well as being; for Brahman is indeed the denial and the negation of all difference by the universal Self. Why should there be, how can there be, the reasonless horror and hideousness, the nameless heart-harrowing, of one *really* smaller, weaker, poorer, lower, humbler, more pitiable or more contemptible than another, greater, stronger, richer, higher,

---

[1] इंद्रस्याशुचिशूकरस्य च सुखे दुःखे च नास्त्यन्तरं
स्वेच्छाकल्पनया तयोः खलु सुधा विष्ठा च भोग्याशनं।
रंभा चाशुचिशूकरी च परमप्रेमास्पदं मृत्युतः
संत्रासोपि समः स्वकर्मगतिभिश्चान्योन्यभावः समः ॥

Vairágya-Shataka.

prouder, more feared or more honoured? Where would be the justification, if there were *really* such cruel injustice of difference (as the enquirer intensely felt at the beginning of his search), and not a mere *appearance* and play of sage and saint, sovereign and soldier, servant and slave, high god and lower man and lowlier worm and plant and mineral!

It has been said that the words of Bhartṛihari are true in a sense. They are true in the deepest metaphysical sense, which takes account of the *whole* of space and time and motion in their totality. But the current view of the fact of endless evolution and progress and difference is also true, in the practical sense that deals with only a *part* of space, time, and motion, instead of with the whole of them. While one Jîva cannot, in the nett result of *all* experiences, be really different from another Jîva, for both are equally Pratyag-âtmâ, yet each atom is equally necessarily different from every other atom. Hence what we have is a constant sameness underlying endless differences. If there were actual limits to time and space and motion, if the world-process did not stretch backwards and forwards pseudo-infinitely, if cycles and systems were complete in themselves instead of being parts of interminable chains in time, space and motion, if the 'all' of experiences could really be fixed in and at any point of time, space, and motion, *then* only, by striking the balance of each and every life, we should literally find a cipher as the result in each case. But there are no such actual and absolute limits. Each life-thread stretches endlessly through endless cycles and world-systems. Hence there is no real beginning and no real end to any life, but only endless apparent beginnings and apparent ends, and no *final* and complete balancing *of any*, in terms of the limited and concrete, is possible. Also, as each life, taken individually, is necessarily and actually at a *different* point of time, space, and motion from every other, therefore no *simultaneous* balancing *of all* is possible. Complete balancing and casting up of accounts is possible only from the standpoint of the *true* infinite and eternal, the Pratyag-âtmâ, wherein the *whole* of time, space, and motion, and therefore the *whole* possible life of each Jîva, is summed up. From the standpoint of the limited, the *pseudo*-infinite, on the contrary, there is an endless alternation of progress and regress, evolution and involution on an ever differing level, which is ever making a difference of goal even in endless repetition, and thus *immortally* keeping, before every Jîva-atom, an ever higher and higher 'ascent' after an ever deeper and deeper 'descent' into ever grosser and grosser planes of matter—a thought that, despite the promise of the ever-higher goals, would prove most desolately wearisome, nay, most agonisingly horrible, because of the ever deeper 'descents,' were it not that the constant summation of the whole of the pseudo-infinitely complex world-process in the utter simplicity of the Absolute, makes the endless succession of that world-process the लीला, lîlâ, the *voluntary* play, that it really is, of the Self.

Only the Self, none else, compels to anything or any mood or state or circumstance. There *is* none else so to compel.

Therefore is the process of the world a process of pseudo-infinite repetition in pseudo-infinite change, always curling back upon itself endlessly in pseudo-infinite spirals. The Jîva that, having reached the end of the pravṛitti arc of its own cycle, thus realises the utter equality, the utter sameness and identity, of all Jîvas in the supreme Self, amidst the utter diversity of the not-Self, cries out at the overpowering wonder of it: "The beholder seeth it as a marvel; the narrator speaketh it as a marvel; the listener heareth it as a marvel; and yet after the (seeing, speaking, and) hearing of it, none knoweth (the complete detail of) it!"[1] And he also cries out at the same time: "Where is there despondency, where sorrow, unto him who seeth the oneness!"[2] He sees that all Jîvas rise and fall, lower and higher, endlessly, in pseudo-infinite time and space and motion. He sees that the Jîva that is a crawling worm to-day will be the Îshvara of a great system to-morrow; and that the Jîva that is the Îshvara of a system to-day will descend into deeper densities of matter in a greater system to-morrow, to rise to the still larger Îshvara-ship of a vaster system in still another kalpa. Nay, not only *will be*, in the one sense, but also *is* in another sense. The single human being that is so weak and helpless, even as a worm, in the solar system of the Îshvara to whom he owes allegiance, is, at the same time, in turn, veritable Îshvara to the tissue-cells, leucocytes and animalcules that compose his organism, and the currents of his large life, unconsciously or consciously to himself, govern those of the minute ones. The ruler of a solar system, again would, at the same time, in turn, be an infinitesimal cell in the

---

[1] आश्चर्यवत्पश्यति कश्चिदेनमाश्चर्यवद्वदति तथैव चान्यः।
आश्चर्यवच्चैनमन्यः शृणोति श्रुत्वाप्येनं वेद न चैव कश्चित्॥

Bhagavad-Gîtâ. ii. 28.

[2] तत्र को मोहः कः शोक एकत्वमनुपश्यतः।

Isha Upaniṣhat. 7.

unimaginably vast frame of a Virât-Purusha, whose individuality includes countless billions of such systems. And throughout all this wonder the knower of Brahman also knows that there is no ruthless cruelty, no nightmare agony of helplessness in it, for, at every moment, each condition is essentially voluntary, the product of that utterly free will of the Self (and therefore of all selves), which there is none else to bend and curb in any way, the will that is truely liberated from all bondage. He knows that because all things, all Jîvas and all Îshvaras, belong to, nay, *are in* the Self already, therefore whatever a self wishes, that, with all its consequences, will surely belong to it, if it only earnestly wishes; this earnest wish itself being the essence of yoga, with its three co-equal factors of bhakti, jñâna, and karma, corresponding to ichchhâ, jñâna, and kriyâ respectively. Knowing all this, he knoweth, he *cogniseth* Brahman; and *loving* all selves as himself, desiring their welfare as his own, and *acting* for their happiness as he laboureth for his own, he *realiseth* and *is* Brahman. Such an one is truly mukta, मुक्त, free from the fearful bonds of doubt; he knows and is the Absolute, the Self *absolved* from all the limitations of the Not-Self. To him belongs the everlasting peace!

"Aum! Such is the unperishing Brahman, such is the unperishing Supreme. Knowing It, whatsoever one desireth that is his!" "The One Ruler of the many actionless, That maketh the one seed manifold! the wise that realise That One within themselves—unto them belongeth the eternal joy, unto none else, unto none else!"

---

[1] *Katha Upanishat.* [2] *Shvetâshvatara.*

ॐ

एतद्ध्येवाक्षरं ब्रह्म एतद्ध्येवाक्षरं परं ।
एतदेव विदित्वा तु यो यदिच्छति तस्य तत् ॥

एको वशी निष्क्रियाणां बहूना-
मेकं बीजं बहुधा यः करोति ।
तमात्मस्थं येऽनुपश्यंति धीरा-
स्तेषां सुखं शाश्वतं नेतरेषां ॥

ॐ

शुभमस्तु सर्वजगतां
सर्वो भद्राणि पश्यतु
लोकाः समस्ताः सुखिनो भवन्तु

ॐ

PEACE TO ALL BEINGS.

DEDICATION.

A soul all broken with its petty pains!—
The boundless glories of the Infinite!—
How may the one, unfit, feeble, slow-moving,
Harassed with all the burdens of its sins,
Tell rightly of the Other's Perfectness!
Yet, for the love of self that drave it forth,
A-searching on that ancient path of thought,
They tell is sharper than the sword-blade's edge,
In hope to find that which would bring some touch
Of solace to it in its weariness;
Because that love of self has gained its goal,
And uttermost self-seeking found the Self,
And so grown love of Self and of all selves,
It drave that soul—unworthy, full of sin,
But full of love, yea, full of agony
Amidst its new-found peace, that any self,
Thinking itself as less than the Great Self,
Should suffer pang of helpless littleness—
To cry abroad and set down what it found
In words, too poor, too weak and too confused,
That yet, eked out by the strong earnestness
Of other searching souls, may, with the blessing
Of the compassioning Guardians of our race,
Bring to these seeking souls some little peace!
    Ye that have suffered, and have passed beyond
Our human sorrowing, and yet not passed,
For Ye are suffering it of your own will,

So long as any suffer helplessly!
Ye Blessed Race of Manus, Ṛiṣhis, Buddhas,
Gods, Angels, mother-hearted Hierarchs!
Christs, Prophets, Saints! Ye Helpers of our race
Ye Holy Ones that suffer for our sake!
I lay this ill-strung wreath of bloomless words,
But with the hands of reverence, at your feet,
That, filled with freshness by their streaming life,
And consecrated by their holiness,
And cleansed of all the soiling of my sins,
They may bespread their fragrance o'er the world,
And bring Self-knowledge and Self-certainness,
And quenchless joy of all-embracing Self,
To all that suffer voiceless misery,
Or old or young, yea, even to the babe
That lieth fainting, panting for last breath,
Passing to other worlds, its pretty limbs
All writhing in the grasp of ruthless Death—
May bring it and its stricken parents peace!
    Peace unto all, sweetness, serenity,
The peace that from this doubtless knowledge flows
That there is naught beyond our very Self,
The Common Self of old and young and babe;
No Death, nor other Power out of Me,
To hurt or hinder, hearten us or help;
Knowledge that all this Process of the World,
Its laugh and smile, its groan and bitter tears,
Are all the Self's, My own, Pastime and Play;
Knowledge that all is Self, and for the Self,
And by the Self, and so Unshaken Peace!

INDEX OF SAṂSKṚIT PROPER NAMES

(The names of books being in italics).

A

Advaita-Vedânta, a system of philosophy.
Ânanda-Laharî, a hymn to Shakti, by Shañkarâchârya.

B

Bhagavad-Gîtâ.
Bhagavatî, a name of Shakti; a Goddess.
Bhava, a name of Shiva, the God of dissolution.
Bhâmatî, a commentary by Vâchaspati Mishra on the *Shârîraka-Bhâṣhya* of Shañkarâchârya.
Bhîmâchârya, an author.
Bṛihad-âraṇyaka-upaniṣhat.
Brahmâ, the God of Creation.

C

Chhândogya-upaniṣhat.

D

Devî-Bhâgavata, one of the Purâṇas.
Dvaita-Vedânta, a system of philosophy.

G

Garuḍa, the eagle-vehicle of Viṣhṇu.
Gaurî, the consort of Shiva.
Gautama, a sage, the author of the Nyâya aphorisms.
Gâyatrî, the sacred prayer; the metre of the sacred prayer; the goddess of the sacred prayer.
Gopatha-Brâhmaṇa, a part of the Vedas.

H

Hamsa, the Swan-vehicle of Brahmâ.
Hari, a name of Vishṇu.

I

Indra, the King of the gods.

K

Kaṇâda, a sage, the author of the Vaisheṣhika aphorisms
Kapila-Gîtâ.
Kaṭha-upaniṣhat.
Kâlî, an aspect of Gaurî.
Kena-upaniṣhat.

L

Lakṣhmî, the consort of Viṣhṇu.

M

Madhusûdana Sarasvatî, an author.
Mahesha, a name of Shiva.
Mahima-Stuti, a hymn to Shiva.
Mahâ-Châratа, the 'history' of the Lunar Race of divine kings, by Vyâsa.
Maitreyî, the wife of the sage Yâjñavalkya.
Mâṇḍûkya-upaniṣhat.
Manu, the law-giver.
Mukunda, a name of Viṣhṇu.

N

Nachiketâ, a sage.
Nyâya-kosha, a dictionary of the technical terms of the Nyâya philosophy.

P

Pañcha-dashî, a work on Advaita-Vedânta.
Pañchi-karaṇa-vivaraṇa, a small treatise on the doctrine of the quintuplication of the elements.

Patañjali, a sage, the author of the Yoga aphorisms.
Prajâpati, one of the Progenitors.
Prashna-upaniṣhat.
Purâṇa, a series of works, attributed to Vyâsa, on cosmogony, philosophy, and 'history' combined.
Pushpadanta, the author of the *Mahima-stuti.*

R

Rahasya-traya, a work on Tantra.
Râdhâ, a goddess.
Râma, the most famous of the Solar Race of Kings, an incarnation of Viṣhṇu.
Râmâyaṇa, the 'history' of the Solar Race of kings, and of Râma in special, by Vâlmîki, in the Saṃskṛit language; also a similar and very popular work in the Hindî language by Tulasî Dâs.
Ṛig-veda.

S

Sañkṣhepa-Shârîraka-Tîkâ, a work on Advaita-Vedânta, by Madhusûdana Sarasvatî.
Sarasvatî, the consort (or, by another tradition, the daughter) of Brahmâ.
Sâñkhya, a system of philosophy.
Shañkarâchârya, author and religious teacher and preacher of Advaita-Vedânta.
Shârîraka-Bhâṣhya, a commentary on the Brahma-sûtras or Vedânta aphorisms of Vyâsa, by Shañkarâchârya.
Shiva, the God of dissolution.
Shvetâshvatara-upaniṣhat.

T

Tantra-shâstra, a class of works, not widely known, dealing with so-called 'secret' sciences and arts.
Taittirîya-upaniṣhat.
Târa-sâra-upaniṣhat.

Tripâd-vibhûti-mahâ-nârayaṇa-upaniṣhat.
Tulasî Dâs, an author.

U

Upaniṣhat, a class of mystical and philosophical treatises forming part of the Vedas.

V

Vasiṣhṭha, a sage.
Vaisheṣhika, a system of philosophy.
Veda.
Vedânta, a system of philosophy.
Vinaya-patrika, a collection of hymns in Hindî, by Tulasî Dâs.
Viṣhṇu, the God of preservation.
Vishiṣhṭa-Advaita-Vedânta, a system of philosophy.
Vishvâmittra, a sage.

Y

Yama, the God of death.
Yâjñavalkya, a sage.
Yôga-sûtra, aphorisms of the Yoga philosophy, by Patañjali.
Yoga-Vâsiṣhṭha, a large work, in verse, ascribed to Vâlmîki, on mystical and Vedânta philosophy.

GLOSSARY OF SAṂSKṚIT WORDS.

A-chit, 'un-conscious'; inanimate; material; matter.

Âdhâra, 'that which supports.'

Âdi, 'beginning.'

Âdi-tattva, 'the first element' (of matter), next but one above âkâsha in gradation of subtlety.

Adhyâsa, 'super-imposition' or reflection of the attributes of one thing on or in another thing.

Adhyâtma-vidyâ, 'the science of the Self'; subjective science; philosophy or metaphysic.

A–dvaita, 'non-dual'; non-dualistic; monistic.

Agni, 'fire,' the root-element of matter corresponding to the organ of vision.

Aham, 'I'; Ego; Self.

Âkâsha, 'space'; 'the luminous'; the root-element or plane of matter corresponding to the organ of hearing and the quality of sound.

Â-kasmika, 'without a why,' causeless, accidental.

A-khaṇḍa, 'without parts.'

Âkuñchana, 'contraction.'

An - âdi - pravâha - sattâ, 'beginningless - flow - existence,' everlastingness.

A-mukhya-kâraṇa, 'un-principal cause'; a minor or subsidiary cause.

An-aham, 'Not-I,' Non-Ego.

Ânanda, 'bliss.'

An-âtmâ, 'Not-Self.'

An-ṛita, 'not right'; false; untrue; unlawful; unrighteous.

Ândolana, 'swinging'; revolving, weighing, pondering or balancing in the mind.

A-nirdeshya, 'not to be pointed out,' indefinable.

A-nirvachanîya, 'indescribable.'

Anta, 'end.'

Antaḥ, 'inner.'

Antaḥ-karaṇa, 'inner instrument,' the 'mind' regarded as a sense, a means of knowledge.

Antara, 'interval'; middle; interspace; difference.

Antar-yâmî, 'inner watcher or ruler'; the Self.

Aṇu, 'ion,' atom.

An-upâdaka, 'receiver-less'; the root-element of matter next above âkâsha, so-called because there is as yet no organ or 'receiver' developed by humanity for it.

Apara-pârshva, 'other side or flank.'

Apara-pakṣha, 'other side or wing.'

Aparâ-prakṛiti, 'other or un-higher, *i.e.*, lower nature.'

A-parokṣha, 'not away from the eye'; direct; immediate.

Âpas or âpaḥ, 'waters'; the root-element of matter corresponding to the organ of taste.

Apa-sarpaṇa, 'moving away.'

Ârambha, 'origin,' commencement.

Ârambha-vâda, 'the theory or doctrine of a beginning,' *i.e.*, creation of the world by a Personal God.

A-sâdhâraṇa-nimitta, 'uncommon cause or condition'; special or chief cause or condition.

A-samavâyi-kâraṇa, 'non-concomitant cause.'

Asmi, 'am.'

Atîta, 'past,' transcendent.

Âtmâ, Self (Gr: 'atmos' or 'etymon').

Atyant-âsat, 'extremely non-existent,' utterly non-existent, pure non-being.

Âvaraṇa, 'enveloping'; (power of) attraction.

Avasâna, 'end,' completion, termination.

A-vidyâ, 'non-knowledge'; nescience; ignorance; error.

A-vikârî, 'immutable.'

A-vyakta, 'unmanifested'; undefined; vague; unmanifested or root-matter; (sometimes also) unmanifested spirit.

Âyâma, 'extent,' extension, length.

Ayana, 'going,' motion.
Âyu, 'lifetime.'

Bahiḥ, 'outside'; outer, external.
Bandha or bandhana, 'bondage.'
Bhavihyat, 'that which will be'; future.
Bheda, 'dividing,' division; separateness; difference.
Bheda-mûla, 'the root or source of separateness.'
Bhûta, 'what has become'; being; creature; element.
Bindu, 'point,' drop.
Brahman, 'immensity, expansion, or extension'; the Absolute, the Supreme.
Bṛih, 'to grow or expand.'
Buddhi, 'apprehending'; consciousness; knowledge; determining intelligence; reason; the pure or determinate reason.
Buddhi-tattva, another name for the anupâdaka-tattva.

Chalana, 'going,' movement.
Chakra-vat, 'like a disc,' circular.
Chit, consciousness, 'awareness.'
Chid-ghana, 'compressed or compacted consciousness'; plenum of consciousness.

Daivî-mâyâ, 'divine illusion."
Daivî-prakṛiti, 'divine nature'; energy.
Desha, 'that which is pointed out'; direction; space; place; country.
Desh-âtîta, 'beyond space,' transcending space; spaceless.
Dharma, 'the holder,' 'the supporter'; law; duty; function; attribute.
Dravya, 'the moveable' or 'the liquifiable'; substance; thing.
Dvaita, 'duality.'
Dvan-dvam, 'two and two'; pairs; opposites; the relative; the opposed; struggle; war.

Dvandv-âtîta, 'beyond duality'; the transcendent; the Absolute.

Dvy-aṇuka, 'di-atom.'

Ekam, 'one.'

Ek-âkâram, 'one-formed'; uniform; never changing form; partless.

Etat, 'this.'

Evam, 'thus.'

Gati, 'going,' movement.

Gauṇa, 'pertaining to guṇa or quality (and not to substance)'; secondary; non-essential.

Gola, 'sphere.'

Guṇa, 'attribute, property, quality.'

Guru, 'heavy, weighty'; teacher.

Hamsa, (1) aham saḥ, 'I am that'; (2) swan.

Ichhhâ, 'desire, wish.'

Idam, 'this.'

Îshvara, 'ruler'; the Ruler of a cosmic system, or planet, or kingdom, etc.; a Jîva who has passed on to the nivṛitti-mârga, and so become a ruler of his sheaths.

Ittham, 'such.'

Jaḍa, 'inert'; unconscious; matter.

Jagat, 'that which goes or moves incessantly'; the world.

Jâgrat, 'waking.'

Jala, water, same as Âpaḥ.

Jîva or Jîv-âtmâ, 'a living being'; an individual ego; one evolving unit or line of consciousness.

Jñâna, 'cognition, knowledge.'

Jñana-ghana, 'compressed, compacted, composed of knowledge.'

Jñeya 'cognisable, knowable.'

Kâla, 'the mover'; time; death; the black.
Kâl-âtîta, 'beyond or transcending time.'
Kâl-âtîta-tâ, 'transcendence of time'; timelessness.
Kalpa, 'arrangement'; a cycle.
Karaṇa, 'means of doing'; instrument.
Kâraṇa, 'cause.'
Kâraṇa-sharîra, 'the causal body' (which is the cause or the origin of the others).
Kartâ, 'doer, actor.'
Karma, movement; action; human action regarded as meritorious or sinful and resulting in pleasure or pain to the doer.
Kârya, 'the to-be-done'; work; act.
Koṣha, 'sheath, case.'
Krama, succession.
Kriyâ, action.
Kṣhaṇa, moment.
Kṣhetra, 'field'; field of consciousness; the body wherein consciousness manifests.
Kûṭa-stha, 'rock-seated'; motionless; eternal.
Kûṭa-stha-sattâ, 'rock-seated being'; changelessness.
Kûṭa-stha-nitya, 'rock-seatedly permanent'; changelessly eternal.
Kuṭila-bhramaṇa, 'spiral motion.'

Laghu, 'light' (the opposite of heavy), small.
Lakṣhaṇa, 'sign,' mark; characteristic; attribute.
Laya, 'dissolution'; mergence.
Lîlâ, 'play,' pastime.
Liṅga-deha, 'type-body'; etheric double.
Loka, 'light' (luminous); 'visible'; world; plane.

Madhya, 'medium,' middle.
Mahâ-kalpa, 'a great cycle.'
Mahâ-kâraṇa-sharîra, 'the great causal body,' the buddhic body.

Mahâ-shilâ-sattâ, 'great rock-being'; rockboundness.

Mahâ-vidyâ, 'great knowledge'; perfect knowledge; wisdom; a name of an aspect of Shakti.

Mahat-tattva, 'the great-element'; same as the âdi-tattva, and possibly so-called because, as the primordial root, it includes in its greatness all the others.

Mâtrâ, 'matter'; measure; 'matrix'; that which measures out, *i.e.*, manifests spirit.

Mâna, 'measure'; mental measuring, weighing, inference or reasoning; thinking in high measure of oneself, pride.

Manaḥ, 'mind.'

Mândya, 'dulness, slowness.'

Mâyâ, 'that which is not'; illusion; the Energy or force of illusion, which causes the illusory appearance of a successive world-process.

Mithyâ, 'mythical'; false.

Moksha, Mukti, } 'emancipation, liberation, deliverance' (from the pains of the world-process).

Mukta, 'the freed, the liberated.'

Mukhya-kâraṇa, 'principal cause.'

Mûla-prakṛiti, 'root-nature'; primal matter.

Na, 'not'; negation.

Nânâ, the many (which are 'not').

Nimajjana, 'immersion, mergence.'

Nimitta, 'condition'; cause; instrumental cause.

Nî-rûpa, 'form-less.'

Nir-añjana, 'stainless.'

Nish-kriya, 'actionless.'

Nir-upâdhi, 'without receptacle,' without a sheath, limitation, or distinction.

Nir-vikâra, 'immutable,' changeless.

Nir-visheṣha, 'without speciality,' without distinguishing marks.

Nitya, 'permanent.'

Nitya-pralaya, 'constant dissolution.'

Nitya-sarga, 'constant creation or emanation.'

Nivṛitti, 'inversion,' 'reversion'; return; renunciation.

Nivṛitti-mârga, 'the path of renunciation.'
Nyâya, 'leading, guiding'; logic; justice.

Pada, 'position,' 'foot'; word, term; concept, notion.
Pakṣha, 'wing, side.'
Pañchî-karaṇa, 'quintuplication.'
Para-Brahman, 'supreme or absolute Brahman.'
Param, 'supreme,' highest.
Parâ-prakṛiti, 'highest or supreme nature.'
Parâ-samvit, 'supreme or absolute consciousness.'
Param-âṇu, 'extreme or smallest atom.'
Pârṣhva, 'side or flank.'
Pari-bhramaṇa, 'moving all round.'
Parimâṇa, 'measure all round,' magnitude; size.
Pariṇâma-vâda, 'the theory or doctrine of transformation,' *viz.*, of the formation of the world by gradual change and evolution (by the interaction of Puruṣha and Prakṛiti).
Pariṇâmi-nitya, 'changingly permanent,' everlasting.
Parokṣha, 'away from the eye'; indirect; mediate; hidden.
Pradhâna, 'the substrate, or reservoir'; matter, Prakṛiti; chief, main, principal.
Prakṛiti, 'nature,' 'that which is made or makes,' matter.
Prâkṛit, 'natural'; the name of a vernacular (as distinguished from Saṃskṛit, 'the perfected' language).
Prâkṛitika, 'natural.'
Pralaya, 'reabsorption,' the dissolution of a world.
Praṇava, the sacred sound or word *Aum*; (pronounced Ōṃ).
Prasâraṇa, extending, stretching out.
Prasarpaṇa, 'moving forth on all sides,' spreading.
Pratyag-âtmâ, 'the inward or abstract Self,' the universal Self or Ego.
Pravṛitti, 'pursuit,' engagement.
Pravṛitti-mârga, 'the path of pursuit.'
Prayojana, 'motive.'
Pṛithivî, 'earth'; the densest root-element of matter known to present humanity.
Puruṣha, 'the Sleeper in the body'; man; Spirit, Self.

Rajas, 'moveability,' one of the three attributes of Mûla-prakṛiti; passion; stain; blood; colour; dust, etc.
Ṛiju, 'right'; 'di-rect'; straight.

Sahakâri-kâraṇa, 'concomitant' or instrumental 'cause.'
Sah-âstitâ, 'co-existence.'
Sama, 'same'; equal; even; balanced.
Sâmya, balance, equilibrium; equality.
Sâmânya, 'sameness or equality of measure,' commonness; genus, species, generality.
Samavâya, 'juxtaposition'; intimate or inseparable relation.
Samavâyi-kâraṇa, substantial or material cause 'combined with or including which' the effect is produced.
Samaya, 'that which comes (and goes)'; time; condition.
Samhâra, 'gathering in'; re-absorption; dissolution, destruction.
Sammajjana, 'mutual mergence.'
Saṃsâra, the world-'process.'
Saṃsaraṇa, 'procession.'
Saṃskṛit, 'the perfected' language.
Saṃyoga, 'con-junction.'
Saṃ-vit, 'con-sciousness'; (vision; wit).
Sarga, 'surge'; emanation, creation.
Sarva, 'all.'
Sarva-dâ, 'always.'
Sarva-taḥ, 'from or on all sides.'
Sarva-tra, 'everywhere.'
Sarva-vyâpî, 'all-pervading.'
Sârvika, 'universal,' 'pertaining to all.'
Sat, being; existence; true, real; good.
Sad-asat, existent-and-non-existent; false; illusory.
Satyam, 'true'; having being.
Sattva, 'cognisability,' one of the attributes of Mûla-prakṛiti; being; existence; energy; goodness.
Sattâ-sâmânya, 'universal or common being.'
Shakti, 'might, ability'; power, force, Energy.
Shânta, 'peaceful.'

Shântiḥ, 'peace.'
Shûnya, 'vacuum,' emptiness; cipher, zero.
Shûnya-vâdî, 'the holder of the doctrine of emptiness,' *viz.*, that all is born from and goes back into nothing.
Sneha, 'love, affection'; oil, lubricant; water.
Soham (=Saḥ aham), 'That am I.'
Spanda, Sphuraṇa, } 'vibration.'
Sṛishti, same as Sarga.
Sthira, 'steady,' stable.
Sthiti, 'steadiness,' 'staying,' 'standing'; maintenance.
Sthûla, 'stolid'; heavy; gross; dense.
Sthûla-bhûta, 'gross (or compound) element.'
Sthûla-sharîra, 'gross body,' the physical body.
Sûkṣhma, 'subtle'; small.
Sûkṣhma-sharîra, 'the subtle body.'
Su-ṣhupti, 'good sleep,' deep and dreamless slumber.
Sva-bhâva, 'own-being'; nature; character; constitution.
Svâ-bhâvika, 'natural.'
Sva-lakṣhaṇa, 'self-marked,' thing-in-itself (?).

Tamas, 'desirability,' an attribute of Mûla-prakṛiti; inertia; substantiality; dulness; resistance; darkness.
Tan-mâtra, 'the measure of That' or 'that only'; primordial root-elements corresponding to sensations; the primal *consciousness* of sensations, which, constituting the *facts* of sound, touch, etc., gives rise, on the one hand, to the elements which serve as their substrates, and, on the other, to the sense-organs which serve as their 'receivers.'
Tattva, 'that-ness'; root-element; essence; principle.
Tejas, 'fire or light,' the root-element corresponding to vision.
Trai-lokyam or tri-lôkî, 'the three worlds.'
Trasareṇu, 'tri-atom' or 'tri-diatom.'
Tri-bhuvanam, 'the triple-world.'
Trijyâ, 'radius.'
Turîya, 'fourth.'
Tâ or tva, '-ness,' '-ship,' '-hood.'

Uddeshya, 'aim'; object.
Un-majjana, 'emergence.'
Upâdâna-kârana, 'material cause.'
Upâdhi, sheath; limitation; body; title; 'addition.'
Upa-sarpaṇa, 'approach.'

Vairâgya, 'absence of desire for, *i.e.*, attachment to the pleasures of this world or the next'; dispassion.
Vaisheṣhika, one of the systems of Indian philosophy, dealing particularly with 'species, genera,' &c.
Vakra-bhramaṇa, 'spiral motion.'
Vâk, speech, 'talk.'
Vâkya, 'speech'; sentence; proposition.
Vartamâna, 'existent'; present.
Vâyu, 'air,' the root-element corresponding to touch.
Vedânta, 'the end or crown of the Veda or all-knowledge'; the chief philosophical system of India, having many sub-divisions.
Vedântî, a holder of the Vedânta philosophy.
Vega, 'velocity.'
Vi-bhu, pervading, 'being in an especial degree, *i.e.*, everywhere.'
Vidyâ, knowledge; ('witting,' 'idea,' 'vision').
Vi-kṣhepa, 'distraction,' repulsion.
Virât-Puruṣha, 'the World-Man'; the Macrocosm.
Viṣhaya, 'object'; domain.
Vi-sheṣha, 'speciality'; characteristic; distinguishing feature.
Vishiṣhṭ-âdvaita, 'non-duality with a distinction,' a form of the Vedânta which regards consciousness, or spirit, and unconsciousness, or matter, as the two aspects of one Eternal Substance.
Viveka, 'discrimination' (between the Permanent and the Impermanent).
Vi-yoga, 'disjunction,' separation.
Vyâpta, 'pervaded or pervading.'
Vyâsa, diameter; expansion or amplification; the name of a Sage.

Vyâs-ârdha, 'the half of the diameter,' radius.
Vyâvartaka, 'distinguishing'; differentia.

Yoga, 'junction,' 'en-gage-ment,' 'con-juga-tion'; union; harmony; balance; skill; attention, *i.e.*, the union of the mind to an object; a form of practice for super-physical development.
Yuga, a 'junction' or coming together of two; a pair; a cycle.